The Design Professions and the Built Environment

First published in 1988, this book argues that discussions of urban development often neglect to consider that much of the urban environment is designed by architects and planners, and that their particular world-view is crucial to the way in which proposals are taken up, modified and carried out. The author explores this world-view, considering architects and planners approach to design and the factors which influence this — work patterns, career paths and the firms in which they operate. The author also studies their place in the political decision-making process as it affects urban questions and then explores how architects and planners roles are changing.

The Design Professions and the Built Environment

Edited by
Paul L. Knox

Routledge
Taylor & Francis Group

First published in 1988
by Croom Helm

This edition first published in 2017 by Routledge
2 Park Square, Milton Park, Abingdon, Oxon, OX14 4RN
and by Routledge
711 Third Avenue, New York, NY 10017

Routledge is an imprint of the Taylor & Francis Group, an informa business

Publisher's Note
The publisher has gone to great lengths to ensure the quality of this reprint but points
out that some imperfections in the original copies may be apparent.

Disclaimer
The publisher has made every effort to trace copyright holders and welcomes
correspondence from those they have been unable to contact.

A Library of Congress record exists under LC control number: 8724893

ISBN 13: 978-1-138-21152-0 (hbk)
ISBN 13: 978-1-315-45277-7 (ebk)
ISBN 13: 978-1-138-21154-4 (pbk)

THE DESIGN PROFESSIONS AND THE BUILT ENVIRONMENT

Edited by Paul L. Knox
Professor of Urban Affairs
Virginia Polytechnic Institute and State University

CROOM HELM
London and Sydney

NICHOLS PUBLISHING COMPANY
New York

© 1988 Paul L. Knox
Croom Helm Ltd, Provident House, Burrell Row,
Beckenham, Kent, BR3 1AT
Croom Helm Australia, 44-50 Waterloo Road,
North Ryde, 2113, New South Wales

British Library Cataloguing in Publication Data

The Design professions and the built
  environment
  1. Architectural design
  I. Knox, Paul L.
  721'.09182'1   NA200
  ISBN 0-7099-3122-0

First published in the United States of America in 1988 by Nichols
Publishing Company, Post Office Box 96, New York, NY 10024

Library of Congress Cataloging-in-Publication Data

  The Design professions and the built environment.

    1. Architecture — Environmental aspects.
  2. Architecture and society. I. Knox, Paul L.
  NA2542.35.D46   1988   720   87-24893
  ISBN 0-89397-296-7

Printed and bound in Great Britain by
Billing and Sons Limited, Worcester.

CONTENTS

Contributors

1. The Design Professions and the Built
   Environment in a Postmodern Epoch
   Paul L. Knox   1

2. Professionalization and the Social Goals of
   Architects: A History of the Federation of
   Architects, Engineers, Chemists and Technicians
   Tony Schuman   12

3. Drawing and the Social Production of
   Architecture   *Edward Robbins*   42

4. Urban Geometry in Image and Discourse
   John S. Pipkin   62

5. Issues in Architecture: Perceptions
   by the Popular and Professional Press
   Larkin Dudley and Linda Irvine   99

6. Where Architects Work: A Change Analysis
   1970-1980   *Judith R. Blau*   127

7. Myth and Paradox in the Building Enterprise
   Francis T. Ventre   147

8. Knowledge-Power and Professional Practice
Shoukry T. Roweis   175

9. Sources of Influence in Planning Practice
and their Implications for Development Negotiations
John Forester   208

10. Professional Orientations of French
Urban Planners   *Gilles Verpraet*   236

11. Making Places: Urban Design in Britain
Brian Goodey   253

12. Computer Modelling for Urban Design
John L. Brown   276

13. The Future of the Metropolis: its Urban
Design, Function and Form   *Gary Gappert*   289

Contributors

Judith R. Blau is Associate Professor of Sociology at the State University of New York at Albany and Adjunct Research Fellow at the Center for the Social Sciences at Columbia University. Her current work deals with the macro aspects of culture — at the level of cities — and the institutional aspects of culture: the internal structure of arts organizations and how arts organizations relate to their urban environments. The study reported in this volume, together with earlier investigations of scientific communities, psychiatric hospitals and architecture firms, reflects her central interest in how frames of cultural meanings and cognitive orientations interact with social structures.

John L. Brown is an Assistant Professor of Architecture at the University of Calgary. He has a Master of Architecture degree from the University of Texas (Arlington) and a Master of Science degree from Columbia University. His research interests are based in the development and application of three-dimensional computer modelling in architectural design.

Larkin Dudley is an Instructor in Urban Affairs and Planning at Virginia Polytechnic Institute and State University, where she has been teaching courses in urbanization and conducting research on the initiation of policy, management processes, and historic preservation. She is also pursuing a doctorate at VPI's Center for Public Administration with a research focus on privatization.

John Forester teaches in the Department of City and Regional Planning at Cornell University. His research explores issues of power, conflict, discretion and strategy in planning practice. His recent publications include *Confronting Values in Policy Analysis* (Sage 1987, edited with Frank Fischer) and 'Planning in the Face of Conflict', *Journal of the American Planning Association*, Summer, 1987.

Gary Gappert is Professor of Urban Studies and Director of the Institute for Futures Studies and Research at the University of Akron. He is also the co-editor of *Cities in the 21st Century* and *The Social Economy of Cities* and the author of *Post-Affluent America*. He is currently working on issues concerning the liveability of winter cities.

Brian Goodey is Reader in Urban Design and responsible for the graduate research program in the Joint Centre for Urban Design at Oxford Polytechnic. He has contributed to architectural, planning, landscape and geographical journals with an emphasis on environmental perception and on interpretive and educational techniques. He directed the *Cultural Development in European Towns* project for the Council of Europe and has since focused on the relationship between research and teaching in planning education, and on landscape change and design in urban fringe and shadow zones.

Linda Irvine is an Assistant Professor of Landscape Architecture at the University of Illinois at Urbana-Champaign. Her principal research interests relate to design theory, design communications and design education. Her current research involves the evaluation of various three-dimensional microcomputer-based modelling systems for landscape design and design communications. In addition, she is conducting a study to determine whether similarities or dissimilarities in learning styles between faculty and students affect the quality of design studio instruction in landscape architecture.

Paul Knox is Professor of Urban Affairs at Virginia Polytechnic Institute and State University. His research interests are in urban social geography. He is the author of *Social Well-Being: A Spatial Perspective*, *Urban Social Geography*, and *The Geography of Western Europe*, co-author of *Geography and Inequality*, and *The United States: An Economic and Social Geography*, and co-editor of *Public Service Provision and Urban Development*. He is currently writing *Economic Organization and Spatial Change* with John Agnew of Syracuse University.

John Pipkin is Associate Professor of Geography and Regional Planning at the State University of New York at Albany. His interests lie in urban, behavioral and quantitative geography. He has written on models of spatial choice, travel behavior and urban retail structure, and has recently become concerned with broader, structural explanations of urban processes. He authored *Urban Social Space* with Mark LaGory, and edited *Professionals and Urban Form* and *Remaking the City* with Mark LaGory and Judith Blau.

Edward Robbins is Anthropologist-in-Architecture at the Massachusetts Institute of Technology and has been interested in the relation of social and cultural production to architectural theory and ideas. He has published in *Architecture Review, Space and Society* and *Journal of Architectural Education* among others and is currently working on a monograph on an anthropological theory of architecture.

Shoukry Roweis is Associate Professor of Urban Planning at the University of Toronto (Department of Geography). His published articles discuss various aspects of urbanization and planning. His current research deals with territorial conflicts, and examines some aspects of planning in Ontario from this perspective.

Tony Schuman is an architect who teaches at the New Jersey Institute of Technology. His research on housing in the U. S., France and Nicaragua focuses on the relationship between design, public policy and community action. His writings appear in professional journals (*Journal of Architectural Education, Journal of Architectural and Planning Research, Places, Journal of Housing*), community magazines such as *City Limits*, and several books. He serves on the National Steering Committee of the Planners Network and is co-organizer of the Network/Forum series of public meetings in New York City, a successor to the Forum on Architecture, Planning and Society produced by veterans of the architects' union which is the subject of his chapter in this book.

Francis T. Ventre is Professor of Environmental Design and Director of the Environmental Systems Laboratory and of the Center for Building Economics and Industry Studies at Virginia Polytechnic Institute and State University. He has degrees from Penn State, the University of California at Berkeley, and the Massachusetts Institute of Technology. He has served as chief of the Environmental Design

Research Division for the Center for Building Technology at the U.S. National Bureau of Standards. He is a co-founder of *Environment and Behavior* and author of numerous reports and articles on building performance assessment.

Gilles Verpraet has degrees in Sociology and Urban Planning and is a Research Fellow at the National Center for Scientific Research (C.N.R.S.) in Paris. He has led a number of studies on decision processes in urban planning, on the dynamics of the planning profession, and on intercultural relations inside housing space.

Chapter 1

The Design Professions
and the Built Environment
in a Postmodern Epoch

Paul L. Knox

It has been clear for some time that both urban development and the
design professions concerned with urban development — architecture, landscape architecture, planning, and urban design — have been
responding to a new and distinctive set of social, economic, demographic, cultural and political forces. At the root of this new context
for the design professions and the built environment are structural
changes that have been developing for several decades as the dynamics of capitalism have entered a 'late' or 'advanced' stage marked
by a steady shift away from manufacturing employment towards
service employment, an increasing dominance of big conglomerate
corporations, and an internationalization of corporate activity.
Meanwhile, these same dynamics have precipitated some important
social transformations: the differentiation of the social order into
complex class fractions and the creation of a 'new' petite bourgeoisie,
for example. These social transformations, in turn, are being reproduced in space through property relations which are articulated
by the real estate sector, mediated by the design professions, and
reflected and conditioned by the built environment (Gottdiener,
1985; Lefebvre, 1974).

As these structural transformations have been gathering momentum,
other shifts — in demography, technology, and in cultural and poli-

tical life — have been taking place. These include the entry of the baby-boom generation into housing and labor markets, the changing structure and composition of private households, the development of advanced telecommunications and high-technology industries, the articulation of liberal/ecological values of the middle-class baby-boomer counterculture, the retrenchment of public expenditure with the rise of the 'new right', *and the emergence of distinctive (post-Modern) movements in the arts, literature and design.* These shifts have, collectively, contributed to what Gappert (1979) calls a 'post-affluent' condition in North American society. They are also seen by some as part of a broader sweep of change in which post-Modern movements are closely related to the structural transition to advanced capitalism:

> The economic periodization of capital into three rather than two stages (that of "late" or multinational capitalism now being added to the more traditional moments of "classical" capitalism and of the "monopoly stage" or "state imperialism") suggests the possibility of a new periodization on the level of culture as well: from this perspective, the moment of "high" modernism, of the International Style, and of the classical modern movement in all the arts . . . would "correspond" to that second stage of monopoly and imperialist capitalism that came to an end with the Second World War. Its "critique" therefore coincides with its extinction, its passing into history, as well as the emergence, in the third stage of "consumer capital", of some postmodernist practice of pastiche, of a new free play of styles and historicist allusions now willing to "learn from Las Vegas", a moment of surface rather than depth, of the "death" of the old individual subject or bourgeois ego, and of the schizophrenic celebration of the commodity fetishism of the image . . . (Jameson, 1985a, p.75).

Jurgen Habermas had already suggested that post-Modern art might represent an important, built-in channel of resistance to the instrumental rationalism of the state and the marketplace (see Bernstein, 1985); and Lyotard (1984), for all his polemic on Habermas's theory of legitimation crisis, also recognizes a 'postmodern' condition in the world's core economies, wherein the economic rationality and cultural agnosticism of industrial capitalism has been widely rejected — though not yet clearly displaced by a new aesthetics, a new economics, or a new politics.

It follows from this perspective that postmodernism is more than an artistic or literary style or an approach to design. As Dear (1986) points out:

> The hysteria surrounding the rhetoric of postmodern . . . *style* masks a more profound logic: that is, the way in which the spatial form of the built environment reflects, and in turn conditions, social relations over time and space. (p.375)

Dear helps to clarify the issue by distinguishing between postmodernism as a *style*, as a *method* and as an *epochal transition.*

In terms of style, postmodern art, literature, architecture and planning are characterized by an engagement with subjectivity and by attempts to restore meaning, rootedness, human proportions and decoration, often employing witty or ironic references to historically and/or culturally specific stylistic conventions.

In terms of method, Dear suggests, postmodernism is characterized by:

> i) the essentially hermeneutic nature of discourse, and

> ii) the importance of the 'text' (building style, in the case of architecture, for example).

At the heart of this approach is *deconstruction*: 'unpacking' the meaning of a text and its relation to author/designer and reader/viewer/user. According to Foster (1985), the purpose of deconstructing Modernism is to interrogate the 'master narratives' of the dominant ideology. This implies a *re*constructive agenda, and Foster argues that such an agenda can take two very different forms: a postmodernism of *reaction* and a postmodernism of *resistance*. This distinction, it seems to me, is crucial to an understanding of the rôles of the design professions in the social production of the built environment.

A postmodernism of reaction, according to Foster, is essentially an affective, cosmetic or therapeutic response, often involving a retreat to the lost authenticity and enchantments of traditional or vernacular themes and motifs. Most postmodern architecture can be interpreted in this way although, as Dear (1986) points out, it is potentially confusing to partition off 'postmodern architecture' or 'postmodern planning' as discrete categories. Postmodern style and method is best regarded as an ideal type, in the Weberian sense.

A postmodernism of resistance, in contrast, seeks to deconstruct Modernism in order to challenge or oppose the dominant ideas that it represents. Some of the urban planning that can be classified as 'postmodern' (mostly 'radical' planning: see below) can be interpreted in this way, though it might be possible to make an equally convincing case for 'radical' planning as a reactive phenomenon.

Allusion has already been made to the idea of postmodernism as an epochal transition: a radical break that represents the socio-cultural shifts associated with the onset of advanced capitalist commodity production. Or, as Jameson (1985b, p.113) puts it:

> A periodizing concept whose function is to correlate the emergence of new formal features in culture with the emergence of a new type of social life and a new economic order.

According to Jameson, a key feature of this transition is the replacement of old systems of organization and perception by a postmodern 'hyperspace' in which space and time are being stretched to accommodate the multinational global space of advanced capitalism (Jameson, 1984). The built environment, he goes on to suggest, provides a critical 'text' with which to decode this hyperspace.

If we can identify a 'radical break' in architecture, it is of course the trend away from the uniformity, functionalism and placelessness of the Modern Movement (or, at least, that version of the Modern Movement that had come to be adopted by centralized decisionmakers as the Esperanto of corporate power, respectability, and efficiency) towards the self-conscious and ironic use of historical and vernacular references in scenographic or decorative counterpoint to modern elements (Frampton, 1985; Portoghesi, 1982). What is less clear is whether this break also involves a widespread rejection of the social objectives and determinist claims of Modernism (Jencks, 1983, 1984), or of the symbolism intended by corporate commissioners of architecture; and whether it really amounts, as Broadbent (1980) suggests, to a Kuhnian paradigm shift within the profession as a whole.

If we can identify a 'radical break' in urban planning, it might be the shift away from the rationalist, functionalist, paternalist and evangelistic pursuit of segregated land uses and sweeping renewal schemes towards a more participatory and activist-influenced planning aimed not only at halting renewal schemes but also at preserving and enhancing the neighborhood lifeworld. This is the break associated with the 'radical critique' of the 1970s, a break that was initiated — and sustained — by the counterculture baby-boomers who grew into the new socio-cultural class of the baby-boom generation: the professionals and intellectuals in the arts and humanities, the media, education and the caring professions. As indicated above, it is a moot point as to whether this should be interpreted as a postmodernism of reaction or of resistance.

Thanks, however, to the economic recessions of the 1980s, the consequent withering of the 'urban vision' (Gold, 1984) and the emergence of public-private partnerships in the land-development process, liberalism, radicalism and resistance have in any case been largely eclipsed. Contemporary planning has come to be a pastiche of practice and theory in which both traditional elements (utopian concerns as well as rationalistic systems planning, for example) and radical elements are overshadowed by a discourse that is dominated by pragmatism. Castells has interpreted this expedience as part of the struggle to create new models of economic accumulation, social organization and political legitimation in response to the prolonged crisis (1973-1982) that stemmed from the conjunction of slowed economic growth, rising inflation, increased international monetary instability, suddenly increased energy prices, increased international competition, and intensified problems of indebtedness among less developed nations. According to this interpretation, what is happening is that new relationships between capital and labor are being forged, with capital rapidly recapturing the initiative over wages and conditions. New rôles for the public sector are also being forged, not only in reducing levels of government intervention and support but also in shifting the emphasis from collective consumption to capital accumulation and from legitimation to domination.

What is perhaps most significant for planning is that new international, regional and metropolitan divisions of labor are central to these processes: the variable geometry of capital, labor, production, markets and management will be critical in allowing new relationships to be established (Castells, 1985; Carnoy and Castells, 1984). This, after all, may be the 'radical break' that defines postmodern planning. 'Already', observes Dear (1986, p.380), 'planners are operating special areas where regular zoning restrictions have been suspended; already there are courses in "public-private" enterprise in planning schools.' The inference is that the planning that is now developng is being geared to the spatial and social logic of advanced acpitalism: to the commodification of the built environment, the recapitalization of the public realm, the legitimation of urban re-structuring, and the opening up of the hyperspace of multinational capital. If we accept that this really does add up to the 'radical break' that will define postmodern planning, it might be necessary to add a third form of reconstruction to Foster's postmodernism of reaction and postmodernism of resistance. This would be a postmodernism of *restructuring*. Given this possibility, it is worth re-examining postmodern architecture for a moment. We can see now that architecture too is being used to recapitalize, to commodify and to legitimize. Take, for example, the decollectivization/ recap-italization of housing in Britain. Symes (1985) provides the example of architects who were given the task, under an Urban Development Grant, of eradicating the public-housing image of a local authority estate, so that the apartments could be put up for sale. The result was the addition of a combination of 'private' elements (garages, entrance lobbies and driveways) and post-Modern elements (pitched, pantiled roofs, timber handrails and balconies, and landscaping) to the structurally sound but unmarketable Modern concrete-and-steel 'boxes'.

Whatever the preferred defintion or interpretation of postmodernism, it is clear enough that the design professions find themselves in a new epoch that raises a number of intriguing questions. To what extent will the new epoch be defined by the values of the baby boom generation? Will the new epoch produce some kind of 'integrating myth' to tie urban design to the social and spatial logic of advanced capitalism, or will it continue to be characterized by a pastiche that reflects the economic fragmentation and cultural pluralism of contemporary cities? Are the design professions likely to become more significant as part of the internal survival mechanisms of capitalism? More immediately, how is the interaction of changing cultural meanings, cognitive orientations, and social structures affecting the design professions and their approach to the built environment? What are the implications for education and manpower in the design professions? And what are the outcomes in terms of professional turf and the relative autonomy of the various agents within the design professions and the building enterprise?

Compared with other related fields, research on such topics is thin and fragmentary. Moreover, there has for a long time been an overwhelming emphasis on deterministic interpretations of people-environment relationships, a preoccupation with micro-scale inter-actions between the built environment and human behavior, and a tendency to treat both design and the design professions as inde-pendent variables. What are needed are approaches that encompass the reciprocal relationships between individuals, the built environ-ment, the design professions, and society at large (Knox, 1984, 1987). For these to emerge, however, it is clear that a much more intensive and purposive dialogue must take place between all those with an interest in the field: anthropologists, geographers, political scientists and sociologists as well as architects and planners.

It was in this context that the Urban Affairs Program at Virginia Polytechnic Institute (VPI) sponsored its third Policy Review Forum on the topic of "The Design Professions and the Built Environment". The Forum was held at the VPI Center for Architecture in Alexandria, Virginia, on April 25-26, 1986. Each of the chapters presented here, with the exception of Chapter 8, represents a revised version of a paper read at the Forum. It must be acknowledged at the outset that these contributions do not purport to address sys-tematically the issues attached to the question of a 'postmodern' epoch. They do, however, reflect the multi-disciplinary breadth of interest in the changing rôle and condition of the design professions. At the same time they illustrate the variety of issues that are at stake as we enter this transitional epoch: the interaction of social issues with the imperatives of professionalization, the changing relationship between the media and designers of the built environment, the changing geographical distribution of design professionals, the con-flicts and paradoxes arising from the changing position of the building and construction industry, and the shifting rôles, strategies and influence of design professionals in day-to-day situations, for example.

Within this variety, and despite a diversity of theoretical underpinnings and methodological approaches, certain themes recur. One of these concerns the imagery and symbolism surrounding the built environment and the design professions; another concerns the relative autonomy of design professionals as key actors in the social production of the built environment. Above all, however, they demonstrate the benefits of casting a multi-disciplinary net over a topic such as this. Together, they provide a wide variety of insights and issues that will demand consideration in any attempt to theorize the rôle of the design professions and the built environment in the postmodern epoch.

References

Bernstein, R. (ed.) (1985) *Habermas and Modernity*, Polity Press, Cambridge.

Broadbent, G. (1980) Architects and their Symbols, *Built Environment*, 6, 15-28.

Castells, M. (1985) High Technology, Economic Restructuring and the Urban-regional Process in the United States. In M. Castells (ed.), *High Technology, Space and Society*, Sage, Beverly Hills, 11-40.

Carnoy, M. and Castells, M. (1984) After the Crisis? *World Policy Journal*, Spring, 495-516.

Dear, M. (1986) Postmodernism and Planning, *Environment and Planning D: Society and Space*, 4, 367-384.

Foster, H. (ed.) (1985) *Postmodern Culture*, Pluto Press, London.

Frampton, K. (1985) *Modern Architecture: A Critical History*, Thames and Hudson, London.

Gappert, G. (1979) *Post-Affluent America*, New Viewpoints, New York.

Gold, J. R. (1984) The death of the urban vision? *Futures*, 16, 372-381.

Gottdiener, M. (1985) *The Social Production of Urban Space*, University of Texas Press, Austin.

Jameson, F. (1984) Postmodernism, or the cultural logic of capitalism, *New Left Review*, 146, 53-92.

Jameson, F. (1985a) Architecture and the critique of ideology, pp.51-87 in J. Ockman (ed.) *Architecture, Criticism, Ideology*, Princeton Architectural Press, Princeton, N.J.

Jameson, F. (1985b) Postmodernism and consumer society, pp.111-125 in H. Foster (ed.) *Postmodern Culture*, Pluto Press, London.

Jencks, C. (1983) Post-Modern Architecture: the true inheritor of Modernism, *RIBA Transactions*, 2, 26-41.

Jencks, C. (1984) *The Language of Post-Modern Architecture*, Rizzoli, New York.

Knox, P. L. (1984) Symbolism, Styles and Settings: the Built Environment and the Imperatives of Urbanized Capitalism, *Architecture et Comportement*, 2, 107-122.

Knox, P. L. (1987) The Social Production of the Built Environment: Architects, Architecture and the Post-Modern City, *Progress in Human Geography*, 11.

Lefebvre, H. (1974) *La Production De L'Espace*, Anthropos, Paris.

Lyotard, J. F. (1984) *The Post Modern Condition*, University of Minnesota Press, Minneapolis.

Portoghesi, P. (1982) *After Modern Architecture*, Rizzoli, New York.

Symes, M. (1985) Urban Development and the Education of Designers, *Journal of Architectural and Planning Research*, 2, 23-38.

Chapter 2

Professionalization and the Social Goals of Architects: A History of the Federation of Architects, Engineers, Chemists, and Technicians

Tony Schuman

This chapter is an account of a unique period in the annals of the architectural profession in the United States: the participation of architects in a national trade union during the Depression and war years. It attempts to explain the anomaly of a professional trade union by examining its contemporary social and political context and by locating it within the profession's own rich tradition of involvement in social issues. This history then serves as the vehicle for discussing the relationship between professional and social goals in architecture in more recent times. In each instance, the observations bear on the profession nationally but are focused on New York City, home of the most active union local in the 1930s and of the largest chapter of the profession's anti-nuclear organization in the 1980s.

Professional Values in Architecture

> The architects were a pretty good group but they were pretty badly organized, pretty badly fragmented. They were individualist. They were a good group because they had a social consciousness.[1]

12

Historically, the idea of a 'profession' represents a secularization of the religious concept of 'taking vows' where the profession of faith is replaced by one of knowledge. The movement toward 'professionalization' in fields requiring extensive training and specialized knowledge may be seen as an attempt to translate these qualifcations into social and economic rewards by claiming an exclusive right to practice (Hughes, 1967; Larson, 1977; Blau, *et al*, 1983). By successfully negotiating rigorous educational and licensing requirements, the theory goes, the professional is better able to protect and promote the value of his or her services in the private marketplace and, additionally and consequentially, to enjoy enhanced social status and self-esteem. Though a relative newcomer to the professional ranks, architecture is no exception to this model. By 1951, each state had a licensing requirement for the practice of architecture, completing a process begun in 1897 when Illinois architects led by Dankmar Adler persuaded their state legislature to set aside buildings of a certain scale and cost for design by 'real architects' as opposed to 'mere builders' (Larson, 1983).

The growth of professional education in architecture has paralleled the registration history. From a total of nine schools with three hundred sixty two students at the turn of the century, the profession counted sixty-four schools with 11,665 students by mid-century (Bannister, 1954). Educational standards are nurtured by the Association of Collegiate Schools of Architecture (ACSA), founded in 1912, and formally monitored by the National Architectural Accreditation Board (NAAB) established in 1939 by the joint action of the ACSA, the American Institute of Architects (AIA), and the National Council of Architectural Registration Boards (NCARB).

Despite these demonstrations of professional competence, however, architects have not enjoyed the material success commanded by their peers in medicine, law, or engineering. In 1984, the median annual earnings for full-time salaried workers in architecture were only $28,600, just slightly more than the average *starting* salary for engineers in private industry and less than one third the average for physicians and surgeons (U.S. Department of Labor, 1986).[2] Only 10 per cent of architects reported income of over $40,000 in 1984. In the face of these (relatively) restrained financial rewards, the countervailing attraction for prospective architects must therefore lie more in non-material benefits such as social status and self-esteem. A recent study of seventeen occupations with university-based educational systems ranked architecture third in terms of prestige but only seventh (out of ten occupations with licensing requirements) in terms of mean income (Cullen, 1983).

Sociologist Magali Sarfatti Larson (1977), in seeking to explain architecture's non-pecuniary allure, identifies an ideology of the profession based on three central ideas: a belief in the intrinsic value of work as a vocation or calling (as distinct from the entrepreneurial work ethic or as a means toward capital accumulation); the ideal of public service (emphasizing community responsibility over the impersonal goals of the marketplace); and a secular version of *noblesse oblige*. Architectural historian and critic James Marston Fitch (1967) underscores the public interest orientation of the profession by recalling that 'the tradition of the socially conscious, intellectually committed architect has a long history in the United States. One might say that the leading spokesmen of the profession in each generation were of this persuasion: Jefferson, Latrobe, Greenough; Sullivan, Wright, Neutra.'

While the critical essays and visionary sketches of this eminent cohort were infused with yearnings for a more perfect democracy and a better lot for 'the common man', the vehicle for realizing these utopian reforms generally remained unspecified, implying an underlying faith in the power of ideas and the sponsorship of enlightened leaders to transform society. This discourse within the profession, moreover, as expressed publicly through its élite spokesmen, assumed the private office and the private client as the *sine qua non* of architectural production.[3]

This profile of the socially committed architect was thrown sharply into relief by the cataclysm of the Depression, which turned conventional notions of architectural practice upside down along with the national economy: the public sector replaced the private sector as architects sought employment in government offices and the surviving private firms solicited government contracts. As Fitch observes, this switch from private to public client served to shift the architect's 'attention, if not his allegiance, toward social architecture' (Fitch, 1967, 237). The economic pressures which forced this shift toward government-sponsored social construction (housing, schools, public works) as a basis for architectural practice also prompted a reexamination of labor relations in the architectural workplace. The very real threat of unemployment and the inadequacy of of relief wages forced architects to see themselves not only as professionals but as wageworkers as well. The failing economy combined with a growing and militant national trade union movement to produce a unique episode in the history of the profession — an architects' trade union.

In August, 1933, architects joined forces with other 'technical workers' to unionize as the Federation of Architects, Engineers, Chemists, and Technicians (FAECT). The Federation survived as an independent national trade union until 1947, when it joined the Congress of Industrial Organizations (CIO) and merged with another white collar union in a jurisdictional reorganization. Although architects never accounted for more than an estimated 10-15 per cent of the overall union membership of 7,000-8,000, they played an important leadership role, furnishing National Secretaries Isaiah Ehrlich and Jules Korchien and Presidents Robert Mifflin Sentman and Lewis Allan Berne. In continuing the profession's tradition of social commitment, however, the activist leaders of the FAECT changed its form and content. By analyzing architecture as a form of production, the union identified the architectural office as a workplace where the junior architect was a worker and the partner an employer, challenging the 'happy family' image of the small, intimate office. In this endeavor, the journeymen practitioner, rather than the élite designer, emerged as a spokesman for the profession in the broader public arena; his message was not an idealistic appeal to the nation's intellects but a practical call to the country's 'technicians'.[4] This call, moreover, while based in professional concerns for design quality and workplace dignity, extended as well to broader New Deal legislation and other social issues.

If there were to be slum clearance, where would the architects
live?

As this grim humor suggests, architects were hit hard by the Depression. By the union's estimate, unemployment among architects
reached 90 per cent during the depths of the crisis in the early
1930's. The AIA acknowledged the closing of half of the nation's
architecture firms. Yet despite this situation architects remained, for
the most part, unorganized. A few had been members of the Union
of Technical Men, Local 37 of the International Federation of
Technical Engineers, Architects, and Draftsmen's Union, American
Federation of Labor (IFTEAUD-AFL), founded in New York City
in 1929, but this local was expelled by the International for 'excessive
radicalism'. In the summer of 1933, while there were several technical employee organizations in New York City, most of the members were civil service engineers, and the groups were only loosely
joined as the United Committee of Architects, Engineers, and
Chemists. The obstacle to greater effectiveness lay in the anti-union
attitudes of most technical professional workers. In the union's estimation, they were 'almost totally without economic organization,
full of illusions as to their role in industry, with strong prejudices
against unions or contact with the organized labor movement'
(FAECT, 1937a, p.10).

In these circumstances, it is perhaps not surprising that the
galvanizing incident which launched the union was an act by the
professional societies taken as a slap in the face — the publication
of wage and work rules by the American Institute of Architects and
by the Engineering Societies as part of the National Recovery Act.
The codes were published on the morning of August 12, 1933, stipulating, among other provisions, a wage rate of fifty cents an hour
for architectural draftsmen and forty cents for their counterparts in
engineering. A meeting called for that evening by the United Committee, which generally drew only ten to twelve diehards, was attended by some two hundred angry draftsmen. A follow-up meeting
on August 23 was attended by more than five hundred technical
workers, and resulted in the formation of a union to be called the
Federation of Architects, Engineers, Chemists, and Technicians
(FAECT). A delegation was hastily assembled to go to Washington

Federation of Architects, Engineers, Chemists, and Technicians (FAECT). A delegation was hastily assembled to go to Washington to testify at the code hearings and was instrumental in the codes being withdrawn for revision (see Appendix 1). Locals were formed within the next six months in Philadelphia and Chicago, and when the fledgling union held its first national convention in Chicago in December, 1934, participants represented additional locals in Washington D.C., Pittsburgh, Youngstown, Detroit, New Jersey, Buffalo, Boston, Denver, San Francisco, Baltimore, Florida, Maine, Seattle, North Carolina, and the Tennessee Valley. Over fifteen locals had been organized in the first year, averaging several hundred members each. At its peak, the union claimed a dues-paying membership of over 7,000 members.

Given the impact of the Depression on private architectural practice, the cutbacks and short hours in the civil service sector, and the number of architects drawing relief wages, the Federation was preoccupied during the 1930s with issues of national policy. The Resolutions passed by the first National Convention of the FAECT reflect this orientation. They called for the formation of an independent organization for 'advancing and protecting the economic interests of the technical man' with the following specific objectives: 1) to formulate FAECT standards on wage and working conditions to replace the proposed professional codes; 2) to protect the hours and wages of civil service workers and to oppose their replacement by technicians paid the lower relief scale [$27/week in New York City in 1934]; 3) to support the proposed Workers Unemployment and Social Insurance Bills; 4) to support the public works construction program; 5) to campaign for a National Housing Program (FAECT, 1934). In the issue of the FAECT *National Bulletin* celebrating their fourth anniversary in 1937, the union identified the successful establishment of prevailing wages on WPA projects as 'the single greatest struggle' of the Federation's campaigns.

While the major issues were national in scope, the Federation engaged a series of more traditional trade union struggles on the local level. In New York City, these included successful organizing campaigns at such disparate loci as the American Museum of Natural History, R. H. Macy & Company, and architectural firms including

Gibbs and Hill and Percival Goodman. At the same time, the Federation sought to protect wage levels in the public sector, a stance which on at least one occasion caused it to challenge a program which it strongly advocated — public housing. In December, 1934, correspondence from Elroy Webber, Chairman of the Architects' Section of the FAECT, to Langdon W. Post, Chairman of the pioneering New York City Housing Authority, expressed both the Federation's support of the nation's first public housing program and its fear that the program's economies would rest, in part, on relief labor rates for qualified architects and draftsmen.

Professional Concerns in the Union

This concern for the twin potential of the incipient public housing program as promoting a social benefit but also as exerting a downward pressure on architectural wages reflects well the internal dynamic of a professional trade union. If one wing of the membership was primarily concerned with traditional trade union issues, another was focused more on professional concerns in architecture and city planning. The Federation counted among its membership many of the progressive thinkers in these fields, among them Frederick L. Ackerman, first Technical Director of the NYC Housing Authority; Sam Ratensky, first Director of Design at the NYCHA; architects Simon Breines, Percival Goodman, Henry Churchill, James Marston Fitch, Norman Rice, and Tom Creighton (Editor of *Progressive Architecture*). Federation members were active in the Housing Study Guild, a seminal force for housing reform led by Lewis Mumford, Catherine Bauer, Clarence Stein, Albert Mayer, Ackerman, and Churchill. The pages of the FAECT *Bulletin* carried a variety of articles on housing legislation, design, and construction. Henry Churchill's column 'Housing in Review' in January, 1936, reviewed the Carl Mackley Houses designed by Oscar Stonorov and Alfred Kastner for the American Federation of Hosiery Workers; Frederick Ackerman reported in January, 1937, on a symposium on the construction industry sponsored by the Washington, D.C., chapter; Simon Breines analyzed the Wagner-Steagall Housing Bill in the February, 1937 issue.[5]

collection of the Avery Library at Columbia University, became an integral part of the FAECT School, founded by the New York chapter in the Spring of 1936 to prepare technical employees for the professional licensing examinations in architecture and engineering. The school quickly added courses to prepare technical workers in the public sector (in various Works Progress Administration offices) for their eventual re-entry into private industry work with advanced instruction in engineering and chemistry, as well as industrial design and two Architecture Workshops — a traditional Beaux-Arts atelier and a new 'Creative' Workshop to incorporate the thinking of the Modern Movement. While recognizing that many students in the school were not necessarily interested in the question of trade unionism, the Federation School made every effort to encourage the linking of technical studies with social and economic factors. In the early years, the School offered a group of Trade Union courses 'planned especially for technicians' including Organizational Methods and Problems, History of American Labor, and Public Speaking. With the addition of the Henry Wright Library, a Housing and Town Planning sector was also organized.

Enrollment in the school grew rapidly from a registration of 25 in the initial spring semester of 1936 to a cohort of over 600 by the fall of 1937 (FAECT, 1937b, p.12). In that year the school sponsored a sketch competition for a Labor Exhibit for the 1939 New York World's Fair which was to be 'the first Union Financed, Union Designed, and Union Built structure in the U.S.' (see Appendix 2).

In contrast to the union's whole-hearted embrace of public construction programs and public sector architectural services, the AIA fought to protect and expand the proportion of federally financed work farmed out to private offices, even when this put them in conflict with broader national social goals. A case in point was their opposition to an Order by the Procurement Division of the Treasury Department in June, 1934, stipulating that work on more than 300 new post offices would be done by in-house government architects. The AIA, citing the decimation of the profession by the Depression, expressed the fear that the Treasury Department's action would imply that architects were not 'worthy or competent to participate in the Post Office Building Program' and might lead to 'a loss of public

expressed the fear that the Treasury Department's action would imply that architects were not 'worthy or competent to participate in the Post Office Building Program' and might lead to 'a loss of public confidence in the architect' (Baldwin, 1934). The Director of Procurement responded that 42 per cent of the dollar value of the Federal Building Program was already on contract to the private sector and that most of the post office buildings represented small projects covered by standard designs which could expedite construction: 'The main objective of the plan is to place buildings under contract and put men to work in the construction industry in the shortest possible time, thus accomplishing the greatest good for the greatest number.' The AIA turned for support to the construction and business communities. The General Chairman of the Construction League argued, 'The progressive development of artistic and economical design is due to the individual freedom of action of the architect or engineer operating in his own office, knowing that future commissions depended upon the success of his personal efforts.' The Chamber of Commerce was more blunt in stressing the ideological basis of their support: 'On principle, the Chamber believes there is good reason why the Government's employment of personnel for functions not directly governmental should be limited to persons technically qualified in private practice.' When these arguments failed to sway the Treasury Department, the AIA beat a tactical retreat, concluding in a confidential internal memorandum that a fresh approach was needed with regard to public works construction, 'from a viewpoint completely divorced from every implication of selfish personal interest on the part of the architect . . . or of any plea for consideration based wholly on the architect's necessities.'

Union Politics

> New York was considered the key city of the world in terms
> of liberality, in terms of radical movements, in terms of almost
> anything that was in my estimation a bright light.

It was no secret that a number of the leaders of the FAECT held leftist political views, although by no means were they all secret members of the Communist Party, as the Dies Committee charges; nor did the Party control the daily actions of the rank and file union members who were communists.[6] The intrigue of FAECT politics therefore lay not in the paranoia of Rep. Dies, who saw in the union 'A story of communist infiltration into the foundations of the national defense program', but in the interaction between social ideology and trade unionism. This interplay, in turn, was acted out in three arenas: the relationship between the union leaders and its rank-and-file; the relationship between the FAECT and other white collar technical unions; and the attacks on progressive unions during the Cold War period.

In the view of engineer Martin Cooper, an organizer and Vice-President of the FAECT, a significant social fact of the 1930s was 'how the white collar movement became a highly radicalized movement . . . radicalized in the sense of becoming unionists, not necessarily socialists or communists.' If the union leadership in New York City was dominated by organizers with, in Cooper's works, 'political know-how' — meaning they had a class consciousness drawn from personal or family experience in Europe — the general membership was wary even of the idea of a trade union. The leadership, for its part, was always conscious of this gap in perspective. In the Resolution of Educational Work submitted by the New York Chapter and passed unanimously by the First National Convention, the framers reasoned 'it is necessary to take into consideration the nature of our organization and our objectives, the background of our members with respect to their relation to the social and economic structure as a group...' (FAECT, 1934). To this end, the Federation did not define itself as a genuine trade union but rather as 'an economic organization, functioning in much the same manner as a labor union.' Within the union, the emphasis was primarily on day-to-day economic issues. It was this commitment to improving the lot of lower paid technical employees that gained for the union the allegiance of conservatives such as Vito P. Battista, whose ideological disagreements with the left leadership extended even to their advocacy of public housing. Although Battista regarded them as naïve idealists in this regard, he respected their work on behalf of 'the little guy'.[7]

That the union's basic thrust was traditional trade unionism did not preclude efforts to politicize the membership in directions which

were often in harmony with objectives associated with the Communist Party and their front organizations. At the First National
Convention, for example, a resolution was proposed on 'War and
Fascism.' Against the arguments of some members that fascism was
not only antisemitic but also anti-trade union came an outpouring
of candid opinion, starting with the Detroit delegate who said, 'I will
fight if you mention fascism without mentioning communism'
(FAECT, 1934). It was clearly a loaded resolution which put
squarely on the table the issue of communist influence within the
union. The Buffalo delegate, for example, who asserted his agreement with the 'economic viewpoint' of communism while opposing
its 'social viewpoint,' gave the following report:

> For us to gain the name of being a communistic organization
> would mean that the Buffalo membership will pass out of the
> picture entirely. I was instructed to find out if the national
> office is controlled by communists.

A delegate from Youngstown argued that 'communism and fascism
should be separate from the organization. Although we may have
leanings toward communism, etc., that is not our business now. Our
aim is to better our economic condition.' The motion on War and
Fascism was tabled and sent to local chapters, where it apparently
rested.

That same convention also took up the issue of racial discrimination,
being forced to address the question when the Allerton Hotel, site
of the meeting, refused to allow an invited black guest the use of the
passenger elevator. The confrontation prompted a 'Special Session
on the Question of the Admission of an Invited Negro Speaker.'
Although some delegates insisted that support for the Negro guest
would cost the union support south of the Mason-Dixon line, and
the Buffalo delegate cautioned that a stand on racial discrimination
would be equated with left-wing politics, the Federation stood firm,
threatening to move the Convention from the hotel if the guest, an
electrical engineer, was not treated with respect. Here, the progressives prevailed on both the Convention and the hotel management.

Union politics were also at the root of the Federation's relations with the American Federation of Labor (AFL). The predecessor Union of Technical Men had been thrown out of the AFL for 'wrecking' Local 37 of IFTEADU through their 'subversive connections' (FAECT, 1973c). IFTEADU President C.L. Rosenmund was especially upset by the militant tactics favored by the Local, particularly an unsuccessful strike in 1929 against the Board of Transportation when several hundred men were fired over a wage increase protest.

Despite this early antagonism, the desire of the FAECT to enter the mainstream of organized labor obliged them to negotiate with the IFTEADU in order to join the AFL, in 1935 the only existing national labor organization. The FAECT Bulletins of 1935-1937 carried regular reports on activities of the AFL and on efforts to link forces with the IFTEADU headed by Rosenmund. Although the FAECT was wary of conservative tendencies within the AFL, notably their eagerness in 1935 to join the American Legion in an anti-communist crusade and their emphasis on craft as opposed to industrial unionism, they also saw certain advantages to affiliation — connections with the building trades who were already members and, if the Federation entered *en masse*, a reduction by half of the *per capita* membership fee. For two years the Federation and the Union traded proposals and charges. Rosenmund kept up his campaign to purge 'subversive elements' from the FAECT, and the Federation in turn belittled IFTEADU's national membership as being only 1,500 workers employed principally in government navy shipbuilding yards, while the FAECT claimed membership of 6,500. Each accused the other of being more interested in signing up members than in promoting their welfare. A third party to many of these discussions was the Architects Guild of America, organized in 1934 for architects and architectural draftsmen with only two chapters, a national headquarters in New York City and a branch in Washington, D.C. This Guild had joined with FAECT members in picketing Commissioner Post at the NYCHA in protest of relief wages for architects and draftsmen working on public housing. But when the FAECT proposed a merger, the Guild demurred, insisting on separate status for themselves as an architectural local which would maintain a craft lien basis for the organization.

Although the national convention of the IFTEADU held in 1936 in Newport, Rhode Island, voted for blanket admission of the FAECT into the Intenational, this entry was effectively blocked by Rosenmund, who stipulated that the Federation would not be allowed to maintain its integrity as an independent local with the International; the FAECT members would have to join the IFTEADU as individuals. The issue became moot in 1937 with the founding by John L. Lewis of the Committee for Industrial Organizations (predecessor of the *Congress* of Industrial Organizations). That same year the FAECT joined the CIO as a charter union, with the President of the Federation serving as a Vice President of the CIO. As part of a jurisdictional reshuffling, the civil service members of the FAECT switched membership to the American Federation of State, County, and Munucipal Employees (AFSCME) CIO. Despite the transfer of this contingent to a fraternal union, the FAECT continued to take an interest in and express opinions on civil service matters, notably in defense of public sector professional services. In 1941, for example, the Federation chapter in New York City spoke out in an FAECT issue of the *CIO News* against the 'farming out' of work on municipal construction projects to private sector firms, defending in-house architectural services on the basis of speed and lower cost (*Tech Talk*, 1941). Similarly, at a New York City Board of Estimate hearing in March of 1944 on a 'Post-War Public Works Program', the Federation argued that in the past two years the civil service staff in school design had completed eighteen projects, with another five on the boards, while none had been completed in the private sector.

Despite this continued interest in civil service matters, however, the principal thrust of the Federation's activities shifted in 1937 to organizing in the private sector. Over the next ten years, the union became an important presence in the engineering field, waging successful organizing drives at industrial giants like General Electric, RCA, ITT affiliates, and Shell Oil. During the War, the union's presence in these key defense industries as well as government installations like Lawrence laboratories in California (both Oppenheimer brothers were FAECT members) drew the attention and spleen of Rep. Dies, whose Committee on un-American Activities held hearings on the FAECT in 1941, accusing the Federation of being 'under the complete control of the Communist party' (Dies, 1941).

With the War's end, the FAECT was buffeted, along with other left trade unions, by attacks from federal legislators backed by a conservative CIO leadership who shared the mission of ridding the labor movement of communist influence. The Taft-Hartley Act, passed by Congress in June, 1947, required loyalty oaths for trade union officials, outlawed mass picketing, and authorized injunctions, 'cooling-off' periods, and 'right-to-work' provisions. Under the brunt of these pressures, and anticipating the impact of the Taft-Hartley bill then under discussion, the FAECT relinquished its independent status in March, 1946, and became Local 231 of the Union of Office and Professional Workers of America (UOPWA). This union, in turn, was expelled from the CIO in 1948 and effectively destroyed. In 1950, the remnants of the UOPWA affiliated with District 65 of the Distributive, Processing, and Office Workers of America (DPO), which served as a collecting center for members of radical unions in the 1948-1950 period. District 65 eventually affiliated with the United Automobile Workers (UAW) in 1980.

The Union Legacy

Although the union activity of the FAECT members came to a halt after the War, their social activism did not. In New York City, FAECT veterans brought their concerns into the professional mainstream by pursuing different issues through the local chapter of the AIA. Starting in the late 1940s, progressives in the profession took note of the absence of black architects. FAECT architects Isaiah Ehrlich, Henry Wright, Tom Creighton, and Richard Stein, in conjunction with the Deans of local schools of Architecture, undertook a survey of well-known offices around 1950 which revealed that less than 1 per cent of the architects and draftsmen were black, and there were no Negro students. These findings prompted the formation of the Committee for the Advancement of the Negro in Architecture, which in 1956 organized and exhibit of the work of black architects co-sponsored by the New York Chapter of the AIA, the New York Society of Architects, and the Architectural League. The groups shared expenses and produced an exhibition at the Architectural

League which served two goals: making the profession conscious of the need for integration efforts; and encouraging blacks to study architecture. The Committee continued its efforts within the structure of the New York chapter of the AIA as the Equal Opportunity Committee.

In the 1960s, former FAECT members were active in mobilizing opposition to the Vietnam War among architects, playing an important role in organizing the Architects and Engineers Against the War. These efforts eventually bore fruit on a national scale when the AIA National Convention in 1969 passed a resolution condemning the war and published a full-page ad in the *New York Times* (see Appendix 3). In terms of education, the FAECT contingent produced for many years a public lecture series called the Forum on Architecture, Planning, and Society. Held at the New York AIA headquarters then in the Willkie Building on West 40th Street, these meetings, held four or five times a year, presented speakers whose viewpoint linked physical design to social concerns on issues such as transportation, housing, and regional planning. The Network/Forum series of public meetings on issues in planning and design, now held at the City University of New York Graduate Center, is a direct successor to this Forum. Similarly, the Institute of Design and Construction operated by Vito P. Battista in downtown Brooklyn, is a direct descendant of the FAECT School, offering technical programs and licensing exam review courses.

Social Concerns in the Profession

Private Sector Unionism

> The employers were very small in size and maintained a close personal relationship with their employees. They didn't know who to fight against.

If the collapse of the Federation after the War may be seen as part of a broader attack on political trade unionism, its future would have been problematic in any event because of its inability to organize in the private sector. During the depths of the Depression, when widespread unemployment made draftsmen aware of their vulner-

Ralph Pomerance survived the Depression in part through Mayor LaGuardia's 'shelf of public works' (designs for public buildings to be built after the crisis) and who was an active supporter of the Federation, recalls that the union was able to sign up only three of the eight or nine employees his firm had at the time.[8] The blurring of employer/employee distinctions in the small offices contributed to this lack of enthusiasm for the union, as did the general expectation of junior architects that they would one day have their own firms. On this interpretation, the union and the AIA were in agreement, as indicated by this commentary from the AIA report on *The Architect in Mid-Century* (Bannister, 1954, p.52):

> Paralleling the expansion of labor unions during the 1930s sporadic efforts were made to organize architectural employees. The movement made little headway. This was probably due to the preponderance of small firms, which foster close relations between employer and employee, and the independent spirit and mobility of status characteristic of these employees. There are few vocations in which creative talent and capacity are so promptly recognized. Then, too, the freedom which draftsmen enjoy to become independent practitioners tends to dissipate the clash of interests often prevalent in business and industrial organizations.

The intimacy of the small office, with its implicit career trajectory for the promising junior architect or draftsman was reinforced by a socialization process which offered self-esteem in place of economic status (Larson, 1977, p.227). This professional profile may be traced to the wellsprings of professional practice in the United States in the period surrounding the Civil War when Richard Morris Hunt and Henry Hobson Richardson returned from their classical studies in Paris to establish office-ateliers. A contemporary account by an architect in Richardson's office described the psychological dynamic as follows (Van Rensselaer, 1888, p.123):

> [Richardson's office] was filled with a score of workers ranging in age and grade from the boyish novice up to the capable, experienced artist, all fraternally bound together and loyally

devoted to their chief, all laboring together on work which had
a single inspiration and a common accent, and each feeling a
personal pride in results which the world knows as the master's
only.

This romantic evocation of the camaraderie of the small office,
however, fails to explain the absence of trade union activity in the
present era of the large firm. While the typical pre-Depression office
was indeed small — in 1926 only 2.7 per cent of architectural firms
had twenty or more employees (Bannister, 1954) — by 1980 one
fourth of all architects worked in firms of twenty-six or more employees; and although only 1.1 per cent of all firms in 1980 employed
over seventy-five professional staff members, these large offices accounted for 10 per cent of all practising architects (ACSA, 1982).[9]
With a large number of low-paid draftspersons and designers employed in larger and generally more impersonal firms, why wouldn't
this labor force be ripe for organizing?

A thorough analysis of this question lies beyond the scope of the
present essay, and includes numerous factors exogenous to the profession. Nonetheless, some significant changes may be cited within
the structure of the profession which may help explain the resistance
to unionization. The most evident of these is the rapid expansion
of professional education in architecture coupled with the gradual
elimination of the pure apprenticeship route to licensing currently
underway. As recently as 1950, only slightly more than half of all
registered architects in the United States (56 per cent) held at least
a first professional degree, and 23 per cent had their entire professional training in offices (Bannister, 1954, p.110). There are at
present fourteen state boards which require an NAAB-accredited
degree or acceptable equivalent for examination or reciprocal registration. Since July, 1984, the umbrella registration organization, the
NCARB, has required an NAAB-accredited degree of candidates for
certification (NCARB, 1986).

This increased premium placed on university-based professional education responds to and encourages the proliferation of academic
programs — in the number of schools, the number of students, and
the variety of degree programs. By 1979, there were a hundred

This increased premium placed on university-based professional education responds to and encourages the proliferation of academic programs — in the number of schools, the number of students, and the variety of degree programs. By 1979, there were a hundred schools of architecture in North America with 19,000 students in accredited degree programs and an additional 17,000 students in non-professional curricula (ACSA, 1982). Although the schools differ in their emphasis on pragmatic versus theoretical concerns and vary in student body profile from low-tuition undergraduate state schools to expensive private graduate schools, all contribute to the increasing professionalization of architecture — that is, the movement for enhanced social and economic status based on education and tested ability. In this context, trade unionism represents a *loss* of social status because it is the historical vehicle for the empowerment of those lacking access to higher education — the working class. One need not subscribe to the Althusserian concept of the school as the 'dominant apparatus of the state' (Larson, 1977, 239) to imagine that students pursuing professional degree programs in architecture anticipate upward career mobility and managerial or proprietary status in their eventual work.

In recent years, the class identification of architects has become even more closely associated with wealth and status through the promotion of architectural drawings as commodities and architects as celebrities (Vogel, 1986). In design terms this orientation is reflected in both the schools and professional offices by a withdrawal from social concerns into a preoccupation with formal and esthetic issues. In the political arena, this mood is linked to the withdrawal of federal support for public housing and community development projects. In the public eye this elevation of the architect to stardom has been accomplished through a proliferation of books, journals, magazines, feature stories, film and stage treatments, and, ultimately, a television series. In the process, however, despite a welcome renewal of attention to figurative and urban design, we are witnessing a paradoxical increase in the public presence of architecture (as media event) accompanied by a decline in its public purpose, where bad urban planning is presumed to be justified by good architectural design. [10]

Architects for Social Responsibility

> Even to this day among architects you can have a committee
> for social responsibility that's willing to fight for a peace ef-
> fort.

In the present political environment, with its emphasis on
entrepreneurial professionalism and the privatization of public services, it is perhaps less remarkable that the forum for expression of
social concerns in architecture has changed than that the tradition
still maintains a public presence at all.   Nonetheless, if the
'committee' referred to above — Architects/Designers/Planners for
Social Responsibility (ADPSR) — may be seen as carrying into the
1980s the mantle of social commitment represented in the 1930s by
the union, it is worth examining some fundamental ways in which
the present effort differs from its predecessor in the profession.
Where the FAECT was concerned with both workplace issues and a
range of broader concerns including housing, public works, racism,
militarism, and technical education, ADPSR has a single goal: to
raise awareness and mobilize opinion within the design and planning
professions against the build-up of nuclear armaments and the threat
of nuclear war. [11] Where the FAECT made common cause with
engineers and other 'technical men', ADPSR (in New York, at least)
has been slow to incorporate members of other professions in their
work. Where the leadership of the FAECT consisted of journeymen
practitioners, the Board of Advisors of ADPSR in New York represents the professional élite: of twenty seven members, twenty four
are Fellows of the AIA. Where the FAECT depended on monthly
dues for sustenance, ADPSR, in addition to paid membership categories, benefits from auctions of original drawings by well-known
architects at prestigious art galleries.

ADPSR represents a curious hybrid of two distinct strains with the
history of social activism in architecture. In its deference to acknowledge leaders of the profession it follows the tradition of the
élite, individual spokesperson; in its structure as a membership organization it recalls the organizing strategy of the union. The synthesis of the two might be described as the professionalization of
social concerns in architecture. The merit of the approach is that it

invites the allegiance of the professional élite — those architects through whom the profession is known and respected in the public arean — in a matter of pressing social import. At the same time, however, the organization lacks the clarity of purpose and structure of the union.

Clearly the moment of the FAECT was in another era. As Martin Cooper observes, the union was a product of 'the history of the times — the unemployment, the Depression, the callousness of the Hoover administration.' It took not only an economic crisis but a climate favorable to trade union activity and social idealism in general to overcome the disinclination of architects to see themselves as workers as well as professionals — a sort of *duresse oblige*. This very conflict in identity gave the union its particular character, obliging it to address the concerns of the membership for professional development as well as for protection at the workplace. In the process, the FAECT undertook a series of initiatives which expand the repertory of professional activity in support of social goals. While the form of socially conscious contemporary practice will not follow the lines of 1930s trade unionism, the architectural profession in the United States can read in this brief episode a call to conscience.

Notes

1. Martin Cooper, former Vice-President of FAECT, taped interview, December 30, 1985; Robert F. Wagner Labor Archives, Tamiment Institute Library, New York University. All the quotations at each sub-section head are from this interview, as are quotations from Cooper in the text. In addition, the author conducted interviews with the following union members and officers: VIto P. Battista (March 4, 1986); Simon Breines (March 20, 1986); Lewis Allan Berne (March 19, 1986); Isaiah Ehrlich (March 17, 1986); and Maxfield Vogel (November 23, 1985).

2. There are several inherent difficulties in using data from the Bureau of Labor Statistics of the U.S. Department of Labor to assess the economic aspects of the architectural profession. The *Occupational Outlook Handbook* cited here is not consistent in

therefore understates median earnings by not including proprietorships and partnerships where incomes are not wage-based; the category of 'architect' is based on occupational identification for the U.S. Census Bureau and not on registration through licensing. In 1979 there were 55,200 licensed architects in the United States; the 1980 Census recorded 107,693 architects. Further, the Standard Industrial Classification system used by the BLS to analyze employment and wages in the United States aggregates data for architects and engineers.

Although the figures cited here may therefore exaggerate slightly the penury of architects relative to other professions, the basic proposition still holds. A Reader Poll on Compensation reported by *Progressive Architecture* magazine in October, 1986 (Dixon, 1986) based on 1,000 responses (60 per cent of them from registered architects, and 40 per cent from owners or principals of firms) showed that while the median income for the responding group was between $30,000 and $40,000, 65 per cent were dissatisfied with their compensation and 95 per cent agreed that compared to other professions architectural practice does not receive adequate compensation.

3. This is certainly the case of Frank Lloyd Wright's efforts to locate utopia in the well-designed single family home — 'the Usonian on his own acreage' (Wright, 1958). In petitioning for government sponsorship of his 'search for democratic form' Wright sought support not from the public at large but from eminent professionals and 'capitalists', despite the wide public exposure his Broadacre City proposal had received through radio broadcasts, feature stories, and a model exhibited at Radio City Music Hall and taken on national tour (Sergeant, 1984).

4. The male gender specificity used in this paper to refer to the architectural profession in the 1930s reflects both the mode of expression and gender composition in the profession during that period. A reminder that class and racial sensitivity preceded (and perhaps necessitated) the women's movement may be seen in the union's reference to the 'charming ladies' of the Women's Auxiliary.

5. These issues of the *National Bulletin FAECT* may all be found at Avery Library, Columbia University, whose collection includes Volume 2, No. 1 (January, 1935) through Volume IV, No. 7 (October, 1937).

6. According to Isaiah Ehrlich, a founder of the FAECT who served as the first National Secretary prior to the Chicago convention in 1934 and who was an open member of the Communist Party USA, the Party did not intervene in the operation of the union, although union activists who were members of the Party did on occasion raise union issues at Party meetings. While conservative union members were quick to brand all union progressives as Party hacks, the leftists within the union were split among communists, socialists, Trotskyists, and social democrats.

7. Interview with Vito P. Battista, March 4, 1986. Despite ideological disagreements, Battista respected the work of the union organizers: 'They stuck to their guns, which was all right; it was their point of view. They raised standards of draftsmen who were left high and dry.'

8. Interview with Simon Breines, March 20, 1986. While Breines estimates that 60 per cent of his firm's work has been done for government agencies (schools, housing, medical facilities) his decision to remain in private practice reflects his view that after the War only architects with 'limited expectations or weak skills' remained in the municipal sector.

9. While this tendency toward bigness has its roots early in this century — McKim, Mead, & White employed a professional staff of eighty-nine at the time of McKim's death in 1909, and Daniel Burnham's Chicago headquarters had 180 employees in 1912 with branches in New York and San Francisco — these first steps toward growth were dwarfed by the post World War II expansion of large offices such as Skidmore, Owings, and Merrill. Founded in 1936, SOM by 1958 was a national operation with fourteen general partners, fifteen associate partners, thirty-nine participating associates, and over a thousand employees (Boyle, 1977).

10. This comment is occasioned by the frequency with which architects and architectural critics acknowledge environmental defi-
ciencies of proposed architectural projects (notably the
overbuilding of Manhattan facilitated by air rights transfers) but
bury their misgivings in appreciation of the designs' aesthetic
merits.

11. While ADPSR chapters in some cities have set a broader agenda,
the single issue approach characterizes the most numerous and
most active chapter — New York City. Roughly 500 of the national membership of 2,000 belong to the New York chapter.

References

ACSA (1982) *Member School Survey*, ACSA, Washington, D.C.

Baldwin, F.C. (1934) *Employment of Private Architects by the Treasury Department: The Public Works Program of the AIA*, AIA
Executive Committee, Washington, D.C.

Bannister, T.C.,(ed.) (1954) *The Architect at Mid-Century: Evolution
and Achievement*, Reinhold Publishing Co., New York.

Blau, J.R.; La Gory, M.E.; Pipkin, J.S.; (eds.) (1983) *Professionals
and Urban Form*, SUNY Press, Albany, N.Y.

Boyle, B.M. (1977) Architectural Practice in America, 1865-1965:
Ideal and Reality, in S. Kostof (ed.) *The Architect: Chapters in
the History of the Profession*, Oxford University Press, New York.

Cullen, J. (1983) Structural Aspects of the Architectural Profession,
in Blau *et al.* (eds.) *Professionals and Urban Form*, SUNY Press,
Albany, N.Y.

Dies, M. (1941) The Federation of Architects, Engineers, Chemists,
and Technicians - A Story of Communist Infiltration into the
Foundations of the National-Defense Program, in *Congressional
Record*, Washington, D.C.

Dixon, J.M. (1986) Reader Poll: Compensation, *Progressive Architecture*, October, 1986, pp.15-16.

FAECT (1934) Minutes of First FAECT National Convention, Chicago, Illinois, December, 1934, Wagner Archives, Tamiment Library, New York University, N.Y.

FAECT (1937a) FAECT Four Years Old!, *National Bulletin*, Vol. IV, No. 6, Sept., 1937, 10.

FAECT (1937b) Chapter School Grows in Influence, *National Bulletin*, Vol. IV, No. 6, Sept., 1937, pp.12-13.

FAECT (1937c) *National Bulletin*, Vol. III, No. 2, Feb., 1937.

FAECT (1941) *Tech Talk*, Vol. IX, No. 4. Wagner Archives.

Fitch, J.M. (1967) The Profession of Architecture, pp. 231-241 in K.S. Lynn (ed.) *The Professions in America*, Beacon Press, Boston.

Hughes, E.C. (1967) Professions, in K.S. Lynn (ed.) *The Professions in America*, Beacon Press, Boston.

Kostof, S. (ed.) *The Architect: Chapters in the History of the Profession*, Oxford University Press, N.Y.

Larson, M.S. (1977) *The Rise of Professionalism*, University of California Press, Berkeley, CA.

Larson, M.S. (1983) Emblem and Exception: The Historical Definition of the Architect's Professional Role, in J.R. Blau *et al.* (eds.), *Professionals and Urban Form*, SUNY Press, Albany, N.Y.

NCARB (1986) Member Board Requirements, Washington, D.C.

Sergeant, J. (1984) *Frank Lloyd Wright's Usonian Houses*, Whitney Library of Design, N.Y.

NCARB (1986) Member Board Requirements, Washington, D.C.

Sergeant, J. (1984) *Frank Lloyd Wright's Usonian Houses*, Whitney Library of Design, N.Y.

U.S. Department of Labor (1986) *Occupational Outlook Handbook*, Bureau of Labor Statistics, Washington, D.C.

Van Rensselaer, M.G. (1888) *Henry Hobson Richardson and His Works*, Boston; cited by Boyle (1977).

Vogel, C. (1986) The Celebrity Cult, in *The New York Times Magazine*, December 7, 1986, 114-115.

Wright, F.L. (1958) *The Living City*, New American Library, N.Y.

Appendix 1 Bulletin No. 1, Federation of Architects, Engineers, Chemists and Technicians. New York, N.Y., Fall, 1933.

Bulletin No. 1

The Federation of Architects, Engineers, Chemists and Technicians is a NATIONAL organization of the EMPLOYEE members of these professions, from the lowest to the highest grades who find themselves compelled to organize for the *protection* of their *economic interests* and for the improvement of their economic standing and professional standing.

Unfortunately it required a depression of major proportions to clearly show to all of us the great need of an organization that could speak and act for the technical employees at all times. Statistics show that 98 per cent of Architects, 83 per cent of engineers and comparably high percentages of Chemists and former Civil Service Technicians have been laid off and are unable to find work in their professions. During the boom years we never received sa.aries, commensurate with the responsibilities involved or even approaching the compensation paid other professional people having the same amount of training. Now, many of our colleagues, after years of unemployment have been compelled to accept relief work at menial tasks, and in the rare cases where professional work could be secured, rates as low as forty cents an hour are offered. In many cases Technicians were forced to seek charity. Certain corporations led their technicians to believe that by working for pay lower than prevailing in good times they could expect steady employment during hard times but these people too were laid off by the thousands although full dividends were always maintained.

The condition of those still employed is well known: in general the technical men and women have been the first to receive wage slashes (up to 50 and 60 per cent), and they have been unable to successfully object because they can speak only as individuals, which is ineffectual.

A code for the construction industry was proposed by the A.J.A., which specified 50 cents per hour minimum for Architectural Draftsmen; another code was presented by the old line Engineering Societies whereby engineers could be paid as little as 40 cents per hour. It is obvious that the entire membership of these organizations, which consists largely of employees, were never consulted about this matter so vital to their economic welfare. It is highly significant that the *only organization in the United States* that opposed these codes at the hearings in Washington was the Federation of Architects, Engineers, Chemists and Technicians which is *composed exclusively of employees.*

It is well known that employers consult each other regarding wages and hours for employees, including technicians, and sometimes maintain organizations for this specific purpose, and we as employees must do the same.

The character of our professions make it necessary for about 95 per cent of technical people to work as employees, so that the contention made in past years that we are part of the management is absurd. We have been treated exactly as all other unorganized employees.

There is obviously a great need for an organization composed exclusively of technical employees. We see that under the N.R.A. only the well organized and determined groups of employees in various industries are able to put across a "collective bargaining" that really protects the individual employee. The employers as a whole have endeavored to nullify the real meaning of "collective bargaining" by writing into the codes the right for the employers to make individual contracts with the employee and insisting on the right to hire and fire employees on the basis of merit. This clause, the engineering groups have also written into their codes and we can only defeat this move by a powerful organization of the technical employees. The Federation of Architects, Engineers, Chemists and Technicians is organized to meet this need; it is national in scope, it is formed on a broad democratic basis and its by-laws are still tentative and will be subject to the will of all new members. Every technician whether unemployed, or employed by private concerns or Civil Service, is eligible for enrollment as a member. All our membership lists are kept strictly confidential.

The following are some of the activities of this organization to date:

It has opposed unfair codes in Washington as stated above, including the Chemical Code, and as a result all these codes were withdrawn for revision, and it continues such work.

It has presented and is working for the adoption of a national code for all technicians, which provides fair wages and will really increase jobs, and also maintain proper standards. Our code would benefit those thousands of technicians who are or were associated with industries for which codes were passed or are pending, giving no benefit whatsoever to the technicians, or specifically exempting them as the steel code did. Our standard wage and working conditions proposals would automatically eliminate many evils arising from contracts under-bidding such as unfair wages, etc.

It is meanwhile striving to have many codes revised, such as the Steel Code, Coal Code, etc., to obtain fair consideration for the technicians involved, pending adoption of our national code. It sends representatives to government and private authorities to oppose wage cuts and lay-offs.

Works for the elevation of wage scales to proper levels, particularly where there have been wage cuts, and the return of laid off technicians to their former positions.

It is striving to get work started immediately on all public works and favors the extention of the Public Works Program to create more jobs. Our committees have discussed this matter at various times with government authorities, stressing the need for such action.

Our Relief Committee speaks and acts for those technicians in need, but who are not heeded when speaking alone.

There are chapters operating or forming in over seventy cities including Philadelphia, Chicago, Newark, Pittsburgh, etc.

Every architect, engineer, chemist and associated technician in the United States *is invited to join and help organize all fellow technicians for our economic welfare and professional betterment, not only in the near future but for all times.*

The constructive influence of such an organization consisting of thousands of members on the outcome of various measures affecting ourselves needs no explanation. We are determined to bring about a "new deal" for all technical employees. Other organizations take no heed of your economic plight. Unless you organize *now*, you can expect no help from any quarter.

The Federation of Architects, Engineers, Chemists and Technicians

NATIONAL HEADQUARTERS

232—7th Avenue, at 23rd Street, New York City, N. Y. 209

Appendix 2   Sketch Competition for a Preliminary Design for a Labor Exhibit, FAECT, April 6, 1937.

For Release April 6, 1937

Federation of Architects, Engineers, Chemists and Technicians
New York Chapter   114 East 16th Street, New York City

Sketch Competition for a Preliminary Design for a Labor Exhibit

Under the Auspices of the F.A.E.C.T. School

It is the hope and belief of the sponsors of this competition that a labor exhibit will be built at the 1939 New York World's Fair, which will be the first Union Financed, Union Designed and Union Built Structure in the U.S.

Purpose of Competition

To develop a Labor Exhibit for the New York World's Fair, 1939. The exhibit is to be a dramatic and educational presentation of the history, aims and activities of the Trade Union movement in the United States.

Since a comprehensive exhibit such as that contemplated has never been attempted in the United States, no finished program can be written at this time. It is the intention of this competition, therefor, to evolve a theme, the development of which will determine the preliminary design.

Those competitors submitting designs that meet with the approval of the jury shall be eligible to become members of the World's Fair Trade Union Design Group. This group will then develop the preliminary design and prepare whatever drawings, models, posters and descriptive material may be required to adequately present the proposal to all labor unions and other sympathetic bodies. The purpose of this presentation shall be to stimulate interest and gain the financial and moral support necessary to obtain our objective.

In the event that the exhibit is financed, the aforementioned group will constitute a cooperative designing staff to carry out the ultimate designs and working drawings for the project. The members of this group will be rated as senior draftsmen and remuneration will be based on ability and responsibility, - subject to FAECT wage scale requirements.

Eligibility

Competitors must be members of a bona fide trade union, or, if an employer, must have a union office. An individual or group may submit one or more designs.

Requirements

The competitor has complete freedom in his design and conception subject to the conditions and restrictions as outlined hereafter.

1. **Site** - The plot is 300 x 300 feet with a major avenue on the south. Streets on the other three sides are limited to pedestrian use.
2. **Exhibits** - The designer may use such methods of display as he sees fit. He may have part of the exhibits out of doors. He may use motion pictures, paintings, sculpture, dioramas, charts, lettering or any other method for dramatically telling the story.
   a) **General Exhibits** - Such exhibits will deal with the history, aims and activities of the labor movement as a whole and will be the dominant feature.
   b) **Individual Exhibits** - These will provide for the displays of individual trade unions.

Labor Exhibit Program, Page 2.

Note: It is suggested that this portion of the labor exhibit
be so designed as to easily permit additions or extensions, -
to accomodate unions that decide to participate at the 11th
hour.

3. Area of Structure - The total area of the structure or structures must
   not exceed 40,060 sq. ft. The height of structures is optional.
   Although designers may use different levels or mezzanines, the
   building should be preferably one story in height.
4. Other Considerations - The designer may use his own discretion with
   reference to entrance and exit facilities, but it should be borne
   in mind that the buildings must handle large crowds. The exhibit
   is to be open in the summer only. The construction is temporary.

In addition to the aforementioned requirements, the designer may provide
gardens, places for refreshments, rest and relaxation, entertainment, etc.

Presentation
Plans, Sections and any other drawings necessary to explain the scheme are
to be presented at a scale of 1/16" = 1'-0", # A model may be substituted
for the perspective or isometric. Any medium may be used. Drawings should
be on opaque paper 27" x 40" in size, - if drawings are on tracing paper,
they should be mounted to facilitate handling.
  Note: In addition to these drawings the competitor may submit a written
  statement explaining the general principles or any feature or features
  of his presentation. This statement should not exceed 300 words.

Delivery of Drawings
All material being presented in this competition must be delivered to the
Secretary of the FAECT School, 114 East 16th Street, New York City, on or
before Monday, April 26th. Those outside the New York Area must have
shipped the material not later than April 26th.

Identification of Drawings
All drawings must be signed with a nom de plume. This mark shall be placed
on a sealed envelope containing the name and address of the competitor.

Responsibility
The FAECT School will take every precaution but the competitor must assume
responsibility in the event of loss or damage to his or her drawings, etc.
The FAECT School retains the right to use any or all material submitted
for exhibition purposes or for use in connection with further developments
of the project. All material will be available to competitors after six
months.

Judgement and Exhibition
Drawings will be judged within one week after April 26th. Dates for an
exhibition and review of the judgement will be announced to all competitors.

Jury of Award
The jury shall consist of officers of the New York Chapter, FAECT; officers
of cooperating trade unions; a representative of the Board of Design of the
World's Fair. The jury will be assisted, in an advisory capacity, by the
Technical and Organizational Committees responsible for the initiation of
this project.

a perspective or isometric at 1/8" scale.

Appendix 3   Resolution of the American Institute of Architects, *New York Times*, July 8, 1969.

It has become clear in both moral and economic terms that our nation can no longer afford or pretend to intervene in the political and military affairs of nations throughout the world, maintain a military and weapons establishment of unlimited size, explore the moon and, at the same time, rebuild our decaying cities, provide an adequate supply of housing, and finance domestic programs needed to solve pressing social problems.

THEREFORE, BE IT RESOLVED BY THE ARCHITECTS OF AMERICA THAT:

One. We call upon the President and the Congress to assume responsibility for a comprehensive reexamination and reordering of our national priorities, recognizing that we have neither unlimited wealth nor wisdom, and that we cannot sensibly hope to instruct other nations in the paths they should follow when we are increasingly   able to demonstrate that we know how to maintain a viable society at home.

Two. We call upon our leaders, at all levels of government, to recognize that an efficient and humane environment is basic to the maintenance of a harmonious and prosperous society and that the skills to produce it are well within our grasp. At the same time, we wish to remind our representatives that neither hope, time, nor technology will solve the problems that presently make urban life a dirty, difficult and dangerous experience. Only a wholehearted commitment of will and money will enable us to apply the skills r. eded to erase the shame of urban America.

Approved and adopted by The American Institute of Architects at its annual convention in Chicago, Illinois, June 26th, 1969.

The American Institute of Architects
1735 New York Avenue, N.W., Washington, D.C. 20006

Chapter 3

Drawing and the Social Production of Architecture

Edward Robbins

Visual representations have come to play an increasingly important rôle in architecture, at least since the late Middle Ages in Europe. Discussions of visual representation in architecture for the most part have emphasized drawings as evidence of the elaboration of various ideas, as formal logics or as autonomous representations of architecture as creative art (Graves, 1977; Lotz, 1977; Porter, 1979; Silvetti, 1982). The relation of visual representation to social practice and the question of what types and rôles of visual representation are associated with what forms of practice and what architectural actors has received considerably less attention (Silvetti, 1982).

Whatever else they might be, visual representations are the material embodiment of both design logics and ideas as well as a social division of labor in the production of architecture. Visual representations are also — and most critically in more recent architectural practice — *the means by which architects direct and control the production of architecture*. It is to the problem of how one might examine visual representation, drawing in our specific case, as evidence of architectural practice that our discussion is directed. What follows is a preliminary and only suggestive argument about how drawings might broaden our knowledge of architecture.

Drawings have come to form a significant part of the architectural design experience since at least the 15th century (Toker, 1985). Vis-

42

ual media have been utilized in a variety of ways and for different reasons since the Greeks and Egyptians (Coulton, 1977) if not before. Graphics as a device with which to explore, present and communicate came into their own with the development of scale and knowledge of calibration (either geometric or numerical), linear perspective and the emergence of architecture as a profession in the 18th century (Porter, 1979; Kristoff, 1977). Drawing, in some quarters, is thought to be what is special about architectural design and the genius and contribution of architectural practice and knowledge.

In architecture, drawings have been and can be used in a number of ways. They may be used by designers to help them think about and test design ideas and focus on design problems (Schon, 1981; Sekler, 1978). From Michelangelo's sketches of the image of a head transforming itself into the Porta Pia (Chimacoff, 1982) to the endless sketches of Le Corbusier for all his projects (Le Corbusier, 1981), thinking by drawing has played an essential rôle in architectural design.

Drawings have also been one important instrument for communicating design ideas by and to a whole variety of actors. From medieval drawings of buildings presented to patrons to the rendering of buildings for contemporary architectural journals, drawing has been an essential voice, to mix a metaphor, in the development of an architectural language (at least for those who believe architecture to be a language). Drawings from the very abstract to the precisely calibrated and annotated have been used to communicate designs to architectural colleagues, consultants and construction workers. From the templates of ancient times, to the contemporary pattern book, from the sketchbooks of the medieval masons to the myriad of drawings in contemporary practice, drawings have been a central means to communicate design ideas so that they might be realized in building.

Also, drawing has played a critical rôle in the development of architectural memory. From early illustrations of building to Gothic design manuals, from the lodgebooks of the medieval masons (Bucher, 1979) to the development of four color polychrome reproductions of architectural drawings, drawing has been one chief means through which architects could save their ideas for posterity. It is through the analyses of drawing that we derive so much of our understanding of earlier architectural epochs and of what it was that architects saw and wanted us to know about what they saw.

Drawing has played so central a rôle in architectural history that for us in our contemporary situation, to paraphrase one architect who has so aptly put it, drawing has come to 'invent itself' (Silvetti, 1982). That is to say, a design can become a thing-in-itself with qualities and life believed to be entirely autonomous. As its own raison d'être, drawing is seen to stand on its own right as art to be viewed in museums and galleries rather than as only a part of architectural practice.

Drawings also represent a whole series of complex viewpoints about space and its relation to architecture. Axonometrics emphasize relations and penetrate volumes. On the one hand, they may be viewed as implying a cubist sensibility and a godlike eye (Porter, 1979) and on the other hand, they may allow us to better picture the urban fabric of which most buildings are a part and imply a more democratic architectural possibility (Silvetti, 1982). A plan offers instead a view of horizontal organization. We address the design as if we lived above and parallel to it. Elevations give us façades and flatten the architectural world. Perspective allows us to move through a design but suggests that, as in the song, 'We are the world' and that the world we are is ours alone. Whatever any form of visualization does, it is certainly not neutral nor without implications for what design should be (Fig. 3.1).

What kind, where, why and by whom drawings are used and the great number of possible answers we can give to such questions suggests that drawings are about more than design ideas and values. Rather the variation we see in the production and utilization of drawings in architecture leads us to posit that drawings embody within themselves a whole series of external social and cultural relations. These relations can both be derived from architectural drawings and found within architectural drawings because they are a crucial means by which architectural design ties the world *it* is making to the world *of* its making.

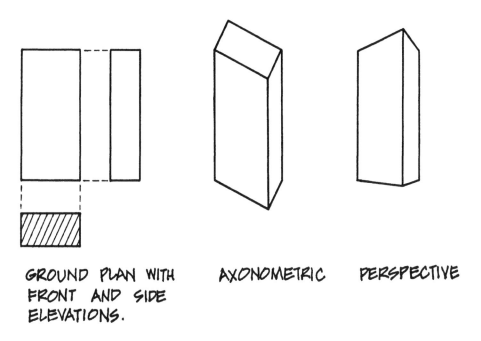

GROUND PLAN WITH   AXONOMETRIC   PERSPECTIVE
FRONT AND SIDE
ELEVATIONS.

Fig. 3.1: Drawing by R. Fischler

Drawing in architecture is shaped by the knowledge, virtues and viewpoints we associate with building and the knowledge we have about how to visualize and share what it is we want to realize. Equally though, architectural drawing is about what architects are expected to do in relation to others in the architectural process, and the nature of control over that process.

Two examples of drawing and their relation to architectural practice will be offered in order to see what we can learn about the association of drawing with issues of control and the division of the labor process in architecture. One will be based on the work of Franklin Toker and his discovery of the Sansedoni elevation of 1340. The other will be based on an interview about the architect in practice that I conducted with John Myer of Arrowstreet about his winning design for the Massachusetts State Archive.

Drawing and Medieval Practice

Franklin Toker's [1] discovery of the Sansedoni contract with its associated drawing of an elevation (Fig. 3.2), he argues, bears all the
hallmarks of the modern blueprint. It is orthogonal, is drawn to

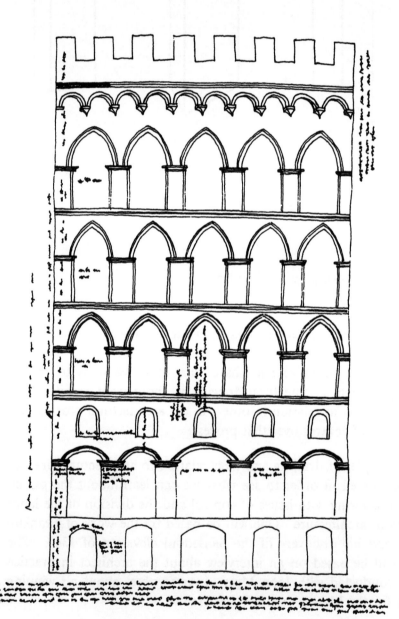

Fig. 3.2:   Drawing of Sansedoni elevation (from Toker)

scale, provides dimensional measurements and is accompanied by written annotations.

Closer examination reveals some substantial differences. For one thing, the drawing is not so sufficiently detailed and elaborated to actually guide and control the production of the building as we know modern blueprints do today. More about what is to be put in the building and more of the patron's wishes about the building is located in the written contract.

Moreover, the nature and substance of the relation of the elevation to the actual construction of the Palazzo Sansedoni is considerably different from the use and importance of drawing in our own time. The degree of variation built into the terms of agreement between patron and builder allowed for a greater freedom and on-site flexibility. Many decisions were left unstated and outside the domain of architectural possibility the elevation illustrated. The bend on the building necessitated by the street on which the Palazzo sits appears in no part of the elevation. Shifts in dimension, and the properties of important architectural elements like doors and windows, are left relatively unspecified. No reference is made on the elevation to how such decisions will be made.

Clearly the elevation was a working drawing of some order appearing as it does on a contract and not as an autonomous drawing. However, the drawing represented more of an idea than an actual working guide to construction. Decisions about construction were left to those on-site, the various masons and other masters and to a trust in conventional understandings of architectural form, structure and expression. Masons, on site, shifted the building and decided on other structural and associated issues. What the architect appeared to want to define in his drawing was the nature of the underlying geometrics and ideals surrounding and embedded in the Palazzo.

Thus, the Sansedoni elevation represented a shift and a new way of thinking about design within what had been a particular social division of labor in the design and construction of buildings in the Middle Ages. Until evidence of drawings of the type represented by the Sansedoni elevation, the production of building was an entirely on-site endeavor. Master masons or architects designed, guided and built on-site. With the evidence of the Sansedoni elevation a new relationship between architect as designer and the production of building appeared to be developing. The elevation was the effort of one individual defining a special status as idealizer of the building and general intellectual overseer of the design and its mathematical domains.

The new form of intellectual practice was authorized in the written contract and buttressed by the organization of architectural practice for the design and realization of the Palazzo Sansedoni. Involved in the project were four architects. One drew the elevation, one co-ordinated the work, and two were on-site coordinators; one for the patron and the other for the architects. The combination of drawing and written contract allowed the architects to frame a new relation to the project. Institution of a second-in-command, the *appareilleur* of the later thirteenth century, gave leave to the chief architect to work away from the site and to guide more than one project at the same time.

To work away from the site, the architect needed a means to communicate not the structural specificities of the site nor the conventional elements of architectural expression. Rather, the architect needed to communicate and control the central ideas which would guide the project. The development of scaled drawing, and mathematical models for design made such control possible. The ability of the on-site craftsmen to work from a drawing and to assure the realization of the design idea within the constraints of the site and the specific changes these made necessary provided the basis for a new architectural actor, i.e. the conceptual designer and a new architectural act, i.e. what Toker (1985) calls 'design by remote control'.

The Sansedoni elevation is one of the actual drawings which bear witness to the beginnings of a new architectural division of labor and control of design but it is not the only evidence (Harvey, 1971). The Sansedoni elevation, though, illustrates an early and primitive attempt at architectural control. Its sparse information bears witness to a world in which the designer of a building worked within a narrowly and conventionally constrained set of possibilities; a world within which most architectural realization was controlled by local craftsmen and local architectural tradition. The Sansedoni elevation also bears witness, and makes possible, the first attempts by architects to escape such limitations. As Toker argues,

> The relatively primitive working drawings used by Gothic masters encouraged professional specialization but (it) prevented a fixed split between architects and builders. That split would come only with the perfection of the working drawing after the mid-sixteenth century (1985, p.87).

Other factors than drawing, of course, would be crucial to the development of the social division of labor between mental work and hand work, design and building, in architecture. Drawing, though, would be a critical instrument through which the split would be accomplished.

As a new and apparently autonomous instrument in the process of architectural design, drawing took on a new importance. The separation of conception from realization and the separation of the actors associated with each from each other necessitated a proliferation of drawing types, e.g. conceptual drawings, working drawings, design specification, design rendering among others. The new drawing created whole new architectural logics based on design without necessary realization, e.g., formalism, and further enabled the architect to move away from the conventional to the more idiosyncratic in design. The ability to conceive of and specify a building through drawing alone offered architects new opportunities; building ideas could be developed without their realization through actual construction. Drawing made possible a whole new architectural discourse in which drawing defined the essence of architectural design.

This, in turn (or at the same time), further separated the architect designer from others in the social division of labor in architecture. This social division of labor became as a result even more elaborated as the architectural profession itself would divide between thinkers and doers, visionaries and practitioners.

The resulting shift from a conventionally constrained and relatively non-hierarchical and unelaborated social division of labor in architecture to an idiosyncratic and hierarchical design practice created a need for even more elaborated and precise visual representations with which to control the conception and design of buildings.

Contemporary Practice

A recent project by John Myer [2] of Arrowstreet will serve as an example of more recent developments in the relation between architectural drawing and architectural practice. What we will look at will be only a very small selection of all the drawings that went into the conception, development and realization of the Massachusetts Archive. This in itself is a powerful comparison with the Sansedoni elevation where only one drawing sufficed. What we will look at, though only suggestively, is the variation in drawing types, drawing functions, and the forms of control and relation to the social division of labor each drawing illustrates.

The drawings we will look at range from a series of personal studies to extremely precise and heavily annotated design specifications for building construction. Three general stages in architectural practice are represented in the drawings; they are design conception, design development and design specification, the latter otherwise known as working drawings. The range of drawings though is limited to those of the architect except for one working drawing and thus do not fully represent the complexity and elaboration represented in drawing. Drawings of other architects on the project, engineers, consultants and contractors have been left out of our discussion. Nonetheless, for our purposes the point we wish to make will be served and the place of the designer as conceptualizer of the design idea and the use of drawing as a mechanism of control within a complex division of labor will hopefully be illustrated.

The drawings, and other visuals, although selected by myself, are presented in the order they were shown and discussed by John Myer during an interview he gave me as part of a larger project on the problem of an anthropology of architecture (Robbins, 1984).

Figure 3.3 was produced as part of a series of studies for the early stages of the competition for the Archive. It was an attempt to control the building's relationship to the site and to study issues of massing. Initially meant for the architect and his colleagues, it was thought clear and informative enough to be included in the final program package meant for the competition jury.

Fig. 3.3:   Drawing by John Myer

The drawing illustrates several important issues. First, it reveals a shift from the Sansedoni elevation where decisions about site and massing were defined by conventionally understood notions of site. Second, and more important, the sketch represents an attempt by the architect designer to get conceptual control of the siting of the building; it was a personal reference. Nonetheless, the drawing was felt to be what the architect wanted the architectural jury to know about his ideas for the Archive and was used as a form of communication and visual argument for Arrowstreet's proposal.

The drawing is neither a template for design nor an abstract statement of a general architectural idea. Rather, it is an instrument of dialogue between the architect and his design problem, the architect and his colleagues and the architect and the kient (or the jury). Two points are significant. One is that the drawing is a representation of a social process of design in which there is little understood conventionality either within the design community or the community at large.   Second, the dialogue is hierarchical and architectocentric, to use a neologism. All the referencing is around and through the architect designer with other actors being given access to the drawing and its ideas by the architect alone. The drawing represents various levels of control from the personal to the hierarchic and social. The drawing's use in the architectural process revolves around the judgement of a single individual first and then becomes a social mode of discourse only secondarily. Thus what the drawing is and how it enters the architectural process is based on the acceptance of a hierarchical division of architectural decisionmaking. How it is eventually used is based on a social division of labor within the firm and the larger social order, the jury, which will decide whose building will be built. A dialogue is made necessary within the social division of labor but it is the architect who, in this case, sets the terms of reference.

Figure 3.4 was also used in the competition package to give in the architect's words, 'a sense of a low-lying fortress associated with land and seascape. . .' What is visualized is an idea sketched according to the architect as part of a twenty-four hour charette in which a conceptual center for the project was the goal.   Other drawings and references were also used.   A Japanese print of a whale, and photograph of a sea cave both served as critical visual associations for the architect.   As Myer stated, the print of the whale 'explained (my) feeling for the site; half under water and half above...'. The sea cave represented for Myer a memory which was intensified in the imaging of the Archive.

The three representations just described were all attempts by the architect to derive a conceptual metaphor for the project.   With no conventional images, and the rôle of the architect framed, in our architectural culture, by his/her ability to bring new and interesting ideas to the problem, drawing can be and is used to get control of concepts, memory and metaphor in order to derive a design.   This is not a natural consequence of architecture but of a particular moment in architectural practice which separates concept from convention and intellectualization from realization.

What is of note for us is that the process by which the designer derives his/her design is generally kept away from the client even though a visual record of the search is available. While Fig. 3.4 was eventually used in the presentation to the jury, other drawings and images were not. Some might be shared with other designers and researchers like myself but they were felt to be too revealing to be shown to a general public. As Myer argued, 'I would show these (the charette sketches) to other designers to see how I think but never to a client. . . I don't want to reveal myself in thought (my design self). I only want to reveal myself in control when I deal with a client.'

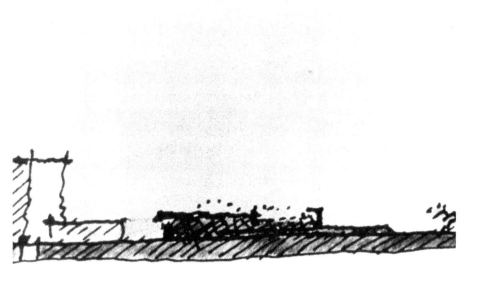

Fig. 3.4: Drawing by John Myer

Figure 3.4 was shown to the client because Myer felt it to be complete enough to represent a finished idea. The selection of drawings though represents more than a problem with architectural ideas. They represent a way of maintaining an intellectual and social division between conceptualization and concept and between designing and design. The separation is maintained, I submit, to reinforce the special place and special area of control and expertise the architect claims within our society's social division of labor. What is shared is never the searching self but the already-formed self and it is the architect who gets to choose how this is defined. Who sees what, an assumption about visual privilege, is a statement about who can understand what aspects of architectural conceptualization and in what ways. It is something the architect can control by means of claiming exclusive knowledge of the design process and insight into design as a creative and associative process. Thus the selective use and disclosure of architectural sketches.

As an aside, the central rôle of architects in the world of conceiving and realizing building can be confirmed by my particular interest in architectural drawing. If I were to present sketches done by construction workers, or shop foremen, these would be of substantially less interest to most of us in the general public. Our social division between conceptual and practical work leads one set of drawings to be hidden because they might reveal too much and another set of drawings to be hidden because no one is interested. If we go back to the Sansedoni elevation and the Middle Ages, the recognition of the rôle of masons in architecture as illustrated by their templates and lodgebooks are of critical scholarly interest as are the marks they made on the stones they crafted (James, 1979, 1982).

Figure 3.5 represents another facet of the social division of labor. It is a drawing orienting a previous drawing. 'I did this for myself and my associates so that they would understand its logic." Unlike the Sansedoni elevation there is no sharing of responsibility between architect and workers. The architect, to control the process, must even annotate his ideas for his own staff of architects. The designer must not only control his sense of his initial design but must also control how and in what direction the design will be developed. Unlike the Sansedoni elevation, nothing is left to chance nor to convention. Here the interior logic of the designer is to be made explicit and drawing is the instrument of control. A hierarchy of control is clearly represented.

Figure 3.6 further illustrates the relationship of designer to the control of design. It is the drawing of the possible piles that might be used to support the archive. The information would come from engineers not the architect. Yet the architect has appropriated the engineers world and made of that world an image which to the designer suggests a 'jelly-fish'. Why such a drawing would be produced is partly so that the architect might relate engineering problems to the building design. Partly though, it is an appropriation and a way of taking possession of work done by others, work over which the architect really has no technical control, and defining it as an image over which the architect does have intellectual control. Thus drawing can be used ideologically to reaffirm control even where little practical control exists initially. What the engineer knows is made secondary to what the architect images in his/her drawing. So much so that the engineering is now not clearly present.

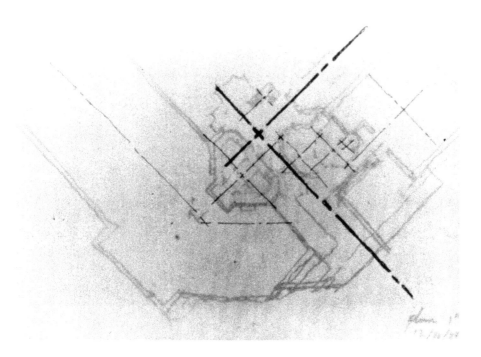

Fig. 3.5:   Drawing by John Myer

What the architect has done in Fig. 3.6 is to reinstate the importance of concept over development, and the world of the architect over the world of the engineer. It is a drawing as much about professional division of labor and the competition it defines, as it is a study of possible piles.   Why else all the artifice and why not merely the engineers drawing? The drawing reports no real technical information, it images parts of a building we will never see and it offers more information than the architect needs for the decision for which he/she is technically responsible. The drawing is a far cry from the Sansedoni elevation where architect and mason are not yet in competition for total ascendancy in design.

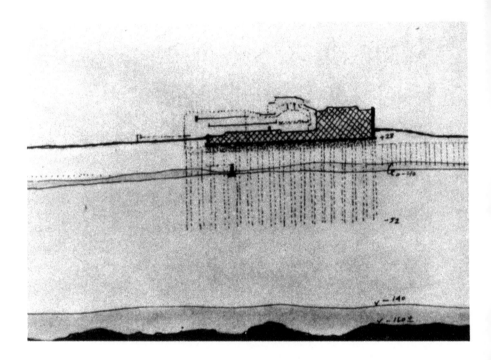

Fig. 3.6:   Drawing by John Myer

We could go on and talk about working drawings with their precise and elaborate annotations of what is to be realized (Figure 3.7). We could discuss the historically increasing elaboration of design specifications and the social division of labor within the architecture and construction industries, the problems of labor fragmentation and legal liability and the social distance between mental worker and hand worker in design conception and realization and the lack of mutual respect and understanding each has of the other. And I think we could demonstrate how this appears in working drawings. This would take though a thorough historical analysis of working drawings and modes of design specification; a paper we hope to do at another time.

What a brief comparison between modern working drawings and the Sansedoni elevation reveals is how few, if any, decisions are given to modern construction workers compared to medieval masons. Whether this is a function of the complexity of modern design and buildings or the result of conflicts for status, reward and control within contemporary social divisions of labor we will not address here. However, that differences in social relations are illustrated and paralleled by differences in the mode of drawing should not be ignored.

Looking at drawings from one period to another not only reveals the changes in architectural ideas, it offers an opportunity to learn about the rôle of convention and creativity, about sources of architectural imagination as well as the social relations of production which underlay the design and eventual realization of an architectural idea. To take advantage of the opportunity architectural drawings provide, we need to look at them in new ways. As we noted at the beginning of our paper, drawings represent a whole variety of ideas and attitudes about architecture and the means to use drawings as evidence in these ways is well developed. If we look at drawing as evidence of social processes we need to ask different questions.

We need to ask about who is given the right, the capacity and the responsibility to produce any particular kind of drawing and who is expected or allowed to see and engage the drawing. How drawings are privileged and given social status, who is thought to understand a given drawing type and how drawings are distributed through architectural practice can tell us a great deal about architectural status, architectural culture and the social relations of architecture as intellectual production. Analysis of the range and variety of drawing types and the stages at which they are employed (e.g. at design conception, development or specification, by whom and for what purpose) will flesh out the bare bones of the structure of architecture as a social practice. It will tell us what the structure means architecturally as well as what it is institutionally or organizationally. For example, we will know more about what professionalization means as a function of architectural imagination and expression.

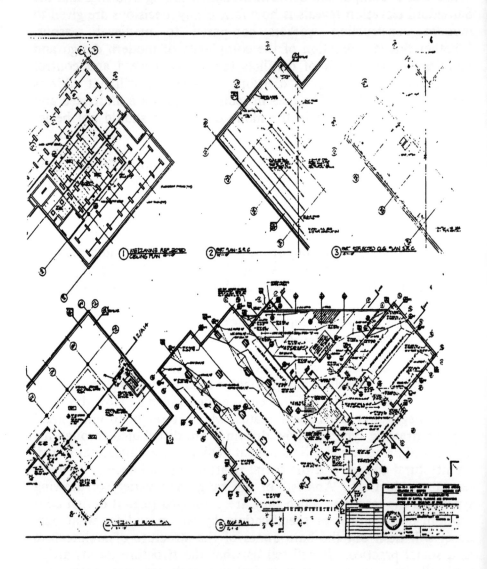

Fig. 3.7:   Arrowstreet working drawing

How precise and elaborate drawings are and who defines their precision and elaboration might give us a greater insight into issues of architecture as a form of intellectual and social control. It might also tell us more about problems of architectural rights and responsibilities. What this implies for building in a world where an architect can design in New York for a project in Khartoum, might be better understood if we first understand how particular notions about drawing limit possibilities of social interchange and also architectural flexibility.

Finally, looking at drawing will tell us about architectural status and privilege. Moreover, it will tell us precisely what status and privilege imply as a social, cultural and intellectual practice and cultural content. Drawing, viewed in historical and comparative framework, will provide the researcher with an opportunity to place the image and content of architectural practice (Saint, 1983) within the structure of that practice (Blau, 1984). With that the false separation made between social understanding and intellectual understanding and between production and idea may well be overcome.

Notes

1. I would like to thank Franklin Toker for generously allowing me to draw on his important work on the Sansedoni elevation.

2. I would also like to thank John Myer of Arrowstreet for a most generous and open interview and for his willingness to offer his drawings for social analysis over which he had no control.

References

Blau, Judith (1984) *Architects and Firms: A Sociological Perspective on Architecture*, MIT Press, Cambridge.

Bucher, François (1979) *Architector: The Lodge Books and Sketchbooks of Medieval Architects*, Abaris Books, New York.

Chimacoff, Alan (1982) Figure, System and Memory: The Process of Design, pp. 139-158 in Akin, O. and Weinel, E. (eds.) *Representation and Architecture*, Information Dynamics, Maryland.

Coulton, J. J. (1977) *Ancient Greek Architects at Work*, Cornell University Press, Ithaca.

Graves, Michael (1977) The Necessity for Drawing: Tangible Speculation, *Architectural Design* 6/77: pp.384-393.

Harvey, John (1971) *The Master Builders: Architecture in the Middle Ages*, Thames & Hudson, London.

James, John (1979, 1981) (vol. 1, vol. 2) *The Contractors of Chartres*, limited edition.

Kristoff, Spiro (ed.) (1977) *The Architect: Chapters in the History of a Profession*, Oxford University Press, New York.

Le Corbusier (1981) *Sketch Books*, Architectural History Foundation/MIT Press, Cambridge.

Lotz, Wolfgang (1977) *Studies in Italian Renaissance Architecture*, MIT Press, Cambridge.

Porter, Tom (1979) *How Architects Visualize*, Van Nostrand, New York.

Robbins, Edward (1984) Architecture and Culture: A Research Strategy, *Design Studies*, 5, pp.175-178.

Saint, Andrew (1983) *The Image of the Architect*, Yale University Press, New Haven.

Schon, Donald (1981) *The Reflective Practitioner: How Professionals Think in Action*, Basic Books, New York.

Sekler, Edward (1978) *Le Corbusier at Work: The Genesis of the Carpenter Center for the Visual Arts*, Harvard University Press, Cambridge.

Silvetti, Jorge (1982) Representation and Activity in Architecture: The Pregnant Moment, pp. 159-184 in Akin, O. and Weinel, E. (eds) *Representation and Architecture*, Information Dynamics, Maryland.

Toker, Franklin (1985) Gothic architecture by Remote Control: an Illustrated Building Contract of 1340, *Art Bulletin*, LXVII, 65-95.

Chapter 4

Urban Geometry in Image and Discourse

John S. Pipkin

However far away from the design studio planners and architects may be drawn by other imperatives of their practice, the geometry of settlement space — its topological and metric structure in the large and the small — remains central to thought on urban design. Distinctive spatial skills and esthetic criteria; the media of map, model and plan; the sociospatial reasoning of a Frank Lloyd Wright or a Le Corbusier; the micro-territorial phrasing of codes and regulations: all these have reproduced a space-centered tradition of planning and design that is relatively isolated from the mainstream of socioeconomic theory on the city. Geographers, environmental psychologists and some urban sociologists have shared a similar theoretical isolation.

For example, we know that 'space speaks' in the sense of microgeographic and proxemics research. Management of personal space and privacy is tied up with task performance (as in behavioral interference theories of crowding), with nonverbal social communication (á la Hall and Goffman). We know that surveillance and perceived control are crucial to well-being in a set of bounded spaces extending from the room, through the neighborhood, to the nation. Knowledge and control of space, familiarity and surveillance, are deeply tied to psychological security and to social solidarity. We know that cognitive images of space mold, and are formed by, repetitive travel in cities. We know that attachments to place may have deep evolutionary roots but that 'territoriality' may be sublimated or transferred to abstract conceptual realms (e.g. professional turfs in career structures). We know that tolerance for social diversity and needs for homogeneity vary inversely with perceived distance. The hidden effects — both permissive and coercive — of design geometry have also become clearer and clearer from the layout of furniture in rooms, through all scales of public and private space, to the metropolitan region. But the various subdisciplines which emphasize space as a medium of knowledge (environmental psychology, proxemics, microgeography, 'human ethology', behavioral geography and ecological psychology) and *practice* (architecture and urban design) are not well connected with the classical social science theories of class, knowledge, ideology and power. As Giddens has variously pointed out, there is a lack of concepts which would build space (or space-time) explicitly into social theory (Giddens, 1981, 1984). This observation has become a commonplace in the new, synthetic 'socio-structuralist' view of social geography, of which the collection by Gregory and Urry (1985) provides an inventory.

By and large the new emphases are consistent with a shift of interest in urban social science away from the workplace (the heartland of production) and government (the heartland of Weber's bureaucracy) toward the sphere of collective consumption and the 'margins of everyday life': the home, the street, the school, the prison and the hospital, into the concrete flow of everyday conduct, and toward 'consciousness' rather than 'material relations'. Within geography, I think, there remains a noticeable contrast between the concerns of this 'socio-structural' view and that of more economically-oriented theorists such as Harvey and Scott. Scott (1986) has recently reasserted the theoretical and material primacy of production relations in the urban process.

Several concerns are typical of the social structural approach. Space-time arrangements are seen as fundamentally implicated in all urban processes, but not as a distinct set of 'dependent' or 'independent' variables. The poles of structure and action — of structural determination and individual autonomy — are subsumed in a view which sees structures of legitimation, domination and signification as simultaneously the medium and the outcome of *so-*

cial action (Giddens, 1984). Geometry is as fundamentally implicated in economic processes (Urry, 1985). Indeed the socio-structural approach is strongly holistic in its formulation of the social, the political and the economic.

Two theoretical strands dominate the social structural approach: the structuration theory of Giddens (1984) and the time-geography of Hagerstrand (e.g. 1975). Each view has strong proponents within geography (e.g. Thrift and Pred, respectively), but each perspective has a genuinely synthetic and 'interdisciplinary' stance.

Structuration theory emphasizes the duality of social structures as enabling and constraining on action, and problematizes the legitimation of action (Moos and Dear, 1986). Time-geography proposes a dual analysis of the detailed fabric of everyday life which is seen as a constrained, continuous, physical path that can be represented as a space-time manifold, and as a nested series of intentional projects, defined by personal and institutional goals, constrained in various ways by power, custom, law, by the physical properties of space and time, and by a contingent technology of movement.

In this developing theoretical consensus, power in its broadest senses of domination and legitimation is placed at the center of social theory. Power is expressed in many ways but Pred and others identify three critical levels: i) power as a person's ability to perform specified practices; ii) power as a social relation; and iii) power as embodied much more subtly in the legitimizations underlying discourse, for example in constituting a 'natural' or unexamined realm of objects (Pred, 1981).

It would be rash to dogmatize about the limitations of these new and apparently converging theoretical perspectives. But I want to argue here that they do not adequately problematize the cognitive structure of spatial knowledge and its relations to language at various levels of discourse. Both time-geography and structuration theory are primarily action oriented. Specifically, they do not find a place for the complex of visually-, geometrically-oriented representations associated with space cognition. I mean by this all perceptual and cognitive representations of space in holistic, visually oriented modes: primarily the visual elements, surface images and parallel processes that make up 'mental maps' of cities, but also other such images implicated in urban design, proxemics research and so on, ranging from a child's 'image' of where the 'neighborhood' ends, to the three dimensional, explicitly visual images evoked in experimental settings (e.g. Foley and Cohen, 1984).

I want to identify the interplay of these modes with *language* as a crucial problem in connecting work on urban cognition with social theory. For me this need came home after a careful reading, from the viewpoint of 'behavioral geography,' of Studs Terkel's four volumes of interviews: *Division Street America, Hard Times, Working* and *American Dreams: Lost and Found.* Certainly these irregularly obtained and selectively edited interviews have many failings of method, rigor and consistency from the point of view of formal discourse analysis. Nevertheless as ordinary urbanites speak in an unconstrained way about their own lives and their recollections of change, the time-space structure of cities pervades almost every statement. I should emphasize that I am not referring to explicit statements about urban structure and planning of cities, although there are many of these, particularly in *Division Street.* I refer to the complex and multilevelled way in which cognitive geometry and expectations (schemata) about urban space are implicated in thoughts and words about virtually everything: from politics and race relations to working and unemployment. Among these rich materials two things were particularly striking. One was the central role of continuous switching between 'here and there' and 'them and us', the social construction of a hierarchy of bounded spaces, each with its interplay of contact and privacy: the room, the house, the street, the neighborhood, the community, and Greater Chicago. Second was the rôle of 'intrusions' into private discourse from the public domain of government, politics, the professions, new media and advertising: for example in the changing vocabulary of ethnicity as 'Negro' in *Division Street* becomes 'Black' in *American Dreams,* absorption of the public, media-borne consensus on urban renewal, architectural styles, the neighborhood as an evocative but abstracted token in advertising, urban homesteading, reversing evaluations of downtown, and so on.

To look at how urban geometry enters into discourse via *cognitive* and *communicative* processes is not a common procedure in social geography, or for that matter in environmental psychology or urban design. Data would ideally comprise protocols, transcripts, texts and records of formal and informal utterances. An integrative under-standing of such materials must take in issues of cognition and communication, and must address informal, formal, and media dis-courses which implicate urban geometry. A fundamental theoretical tension arises between the individualistic, psychologically-oriented perspective on imagery, and the social-constructivist view, which privileges language in the extended context of discourse, as the principal or indeed the unique medium of the 'social construction of reality', although image-like representations are a major medium through which people think about urban space, and in which urban geometry is implicated in thought and speech on many levels. I want to point out several of these levels, to identify some of the ways in which urban images enter into discourse, and to identify some issues that arise where social and cognitive theory meet and apparently conflict.

Geometry in Knowledge

Social-structural accounts of urbanism have implicitly adopted a model that emphasizes the social rather than the developmental and cognitive construction of knowledge. A central distinction in this view is that between the communal, formal, public and scrutinized aspects of knowledge which are uniquely embodied in language, and the inarticulate, unexamined, non-discursive and informal knowledge tied up in action, practice and in the continuous flow of conduct in the ordinary settings of life. For example, in one of the most explicit accounts of geographical knowledge, Thrift (1985) distinguishes four levels or types of social 'stocks of knowledge'. At the lowest level is the unconscious, not in a Freudian sense, but denoting 'forgotten practices still implicit in action'. Next, practical knowledge, which is not transmitted linguistically but is acquired by watching, imitat-ing and doing. At the next level, empirical knowledge, linguistic transmission, rationalization and institutionalization of knowledge begins, as in the educational process, culminating in the unified and coordinated bodies of knowledge that Thrift terms 'natural philosophy'.

Thrift's interest in this schema of knowledge lies in the insight it gives into the 'geography of knowledge': the differential availability of types of knowing over space and time. His approach, like Berger and Luckmann's, fails, I feel, adequately to problematize the *cognitive structure* of knowledge itself, as I attempt to show below. It fails, specifically, to find a role for *conscious* knowledge, which is discursively available to consciousness, but which is in intrinsically non-linguistic form, such as quasi-pictorial surface images.

Freud tells us: 'thinking in pictures is, therefore, only a very incomplete form of becoming conscious. In some ways, too, it stands nearer to unconscious processes than does thinking in words, and it is unquestionably older than the latter both ontogenetically and phylogenetically' (1921, p. 21). The phylogenetic priority of vision as the principal sensory system for primates — in binocular vision, enlarged visual cortex and behavioral correlates — is emphasized in Lachman and Lachman (1979). The ontogenic primacy of the visual system has been well confirmed in developmental research. A distinctive role for the visual system in memory and thought has been amply confirmed in cognitive research, though there is considerable debate about the implications of experimental evidence for the psychological and physiological structure of memory (e.g. Richardson, 1980, Morris and Hampson, 1983). Lachman and Lachman even suggest that the conceptual and lexical systems may have developed parasitically on vision (1979).

While auditory, tactile and olfactory systems have their own implications for memory and cognition, and despite claims that they are significant in urban imagery (e.g. Porteous, 1985), visual images are plainly the most important to a consideration of urban geometry. Indeed by geometry we essentially mean those aspects of holistic, metric and topological structure captured and represented by the visual system. In a subtle philosophical analysis of memory Smith (1966) inquires how claims made by and about memory can be justified. He is particularly concerned with the distinction between remembering 'how' (practical consciousness) and remembering 'that'.

He finds a central and distinctive role for imagery as the most fundamental kind of remembering. In attempting to secure memory claims, he maintains, we always come back to memory images, which represent the 'terminal point of checking' (p. 103) and ' . . . the memory of presented appearances . . . at the introspective level . . . is the court of final appeal for all our memory claims.' (p. 176). Smith implicates memory in all kinds of effective performance that are not strictly 'motor response,' extending the domain of recall — and of imagery — far into the sphere of practiced action and into the arena of the social structural theorists' practical consciousness.

The most uncontroversial finding has been that imagery has a quasipictorial, percept-like quality that can be evoked at will in consciousness, and that such images posses emergent properties that cannot be reduced simply or exhaustively to lexical form. The use of such imagery may correlate with spatial skills, 'important intellectual capacities that cannot be measured verbally' (Rhoades, 1981, p. 247), though Richardson, for example, in a comprehensive survey, reports a failure to connect imagery ability with various measures of mental performance (1980, p. 141). There is evidence that people exhibit coding preferences, which may or may not be related to coding abilities, between imaging and verbal modes. There is also evidence that different types of material display different levels if 'imageability' related to concreteness.

Matters become less clear when imagery is pursued into long-term memory, into the physiological structure of the brain, and into processes of comprehension. Consider memory. There are many models of memory, some stressing the structure of representation, and some processing or computational aspects. Models of representations include associative, lexical, propositional, pictorial, categorical, episodic and schema memories. Each is conceptually distinct. For example it is a very different thing to remember the abstract content of a proposition than to recall the exact words in which it was expressed. In all cases the three domains of model, psychology and physiology are distinct and only tenuously connected by experimental evidence. Moreover, the various theories of memory apply at different levels. It is by no means clear which of the lower levels are implicated at higher levels of processing. For example, according to Rumelhart and Norman (1985), many of the concepts of propositional memory (e.g. semantic network representations) are applicable only at the most basic, elementary level, namely that of the single sentence or proposition. Models of episodic and schema memory address an altogether higher level of knowledge and processing. At the lowest level of representations, debate has centered on alternative dual and common coding theories of memory.

Bower (1972) posited a common generative grammar ultimately responsible for the production of pictorial and propositional forms that 'come to the attention' of consciousness. Pylyshyn (1973) argues similarly in a critique of imaging, while Kosslyn sees images as taking on their emergent properties only as they are generated from more fundamental long-term representations. In Kosslyn and Schwartz's theory of imagery (1978) *surface representations* (with spatial structure and visual properties) are generated from deeper representations, which include both propositional elements, but also *literal* components (e.g. aspects of coordinate systems) which are invoked to create the surface images. In Johnson-Laird's theory of mental models surface images are the consciously perceivable aspects of mental models. Such models function to resolve ambiguities in (less determinate) long term propositional representations (Johnson-Laird, 1981: Morris and Hampson, 1983, p. 141). An influential advocate of dual coding theories has been Paivio (1971), who maintains that images and verbal processes employ distinct coding systems at deeper levels of consciousness than short-term memory. Episodic memory was defined by Tulving (1972), in contradistinction to semantic memory, as the repository of personal experiences. Atkinson and Schiffrin (1968) proposed that episodic memory operates at three distinct levels: the sensory register, the short-term store and long-term memory. It is possible that each level can process semantic and visual information, though this is not clear for abstract 'impersonal' semantic memory (Lachman, Lachman and Butterfield, 1979). Others feel that the notion of structural levels of representation is misguided. Craik and Lockhart (1972) emphasize levels of processing, seeing memory as a by-product of the different kinds of processes that operate on stimuli. 'Properties of the memory trace are therefore a consequence of the type of processing executed' (McDaniel, Friedman and Bourne, 1978, p.156).

Physiological evidence, from brain injuries, for example, has been taken to support the dual coding theories. In most people the right hemisphere deals mainly with nonverbal material, with pictorial long-term memory in the right temporal lobe: The left hemisphere processes words. Each hemisphere in turn is specialized, the posterior dealing with the 'reception, elaboration and storage of information' while the anterior parts regulate action (Richardson, 1980, p. 134).

One distinctive role of imagery may be in schemata memory. In these theories it is assumed that memory and attention are guided by generalized schemata of expectations or events and objects (e.g. Bobrow and Norman, 1975). Schemata, for example are 'data structures for representing the generic concepts stored in memory' (p.35) They contain variables, with default values. They can embed within one another, and they can represent knowledge at all levels of abstraction. The essence of schemata as opposed to categorical model of memory is that schemata are more concrete and are temporally or spatially structured, while categorical memory is abstract, possessing a hierarchical structure of superordinate, subordinate and coordinate classes.

Mandler (1979) suggests that traditional experimental work on memory, for example, memorization of word lists, is strongly biased toward categorical/semantic models of memory. She claims that taxonomic knowledge may well be only a 'secondary kind of organization that has been built onto a basically schematically organized memory system.' The activity of schemata may be revealed in the interplay of 'gist' and 'details' in recall and recognition. For example, schemata-relevant (expected) information may be more accurately remembered, while opposed or unexpected information is more poorly recalled when a particular schema is active. Brewer and Treyens (1981), in investigating memory for places, found that memory scores for objects were positively correlated with schema expectancy and saliency ratings. They identify five ways in which schemata could be implicated in memory performance in: determining which objects are encoded (remembered), acting as framework for new information, integrating episodic information, guiding the retrieval process, and determining what information is expressed verbally in communicating about scenes. In each of these stages spatial/imaginal features are irreducibly involved. In the realm of comprehension similar debates have occurred over the kinds of processes and representations required to understand sentences and connected discourses. Early (surface) processes such as speech perception, and later (deeper) processes such as parsing and extraction of semantic context combine to produce the *synthesized code*, which is more abstract than the surface structures from which it is derived, and which arguably has both semantic and image components (Lachman, Lachman and Butterfield, 1979).

These findings indicate that geometry is involved in knowing in a fundamental way. Spatial patterns in the environment are not merely one object of knowing. On the contrary, through the medium of visual perception and its associated cognitive process, imagery arises, possessing emergent geometric structure, as a fundamental type of representation (non-propositional in form), dealt with by non-semantic, parallel processes. This is indisputably true for surface representations in thought and short-term memory, and may possibly be true at deeper levels of the mind. Thus:

• Imagery possesses emergent properties that are accessible to consciousness and which are routinely used to perform complex judgments and tasks. In fact, as Gilmartin and Patton (1984) show in scrutinizing the idea of sex-based differences in map-use, many distinct kinds of judgments are evoked in judging distances in urban space.

• Yet imagery is absolutely private, in a stronger sense than implied by the trivial observation that all mental experience is ultimately private. For, as Smith (1966) points out, it is impossible in principle to describe 'how an image look'. One can only state 'what it looks like' — a philosophically crucial distinction. If — to take an extreme position on cognitive representations — all cognitive representations were semantic, private knowledge would be materially more public (i.e. common and/or communicable without residue) than is in fact the case.

- Imagery is intrinsically intentional (Richardson, 1980). The structure of image reflects not only the objective properties of the system imaged, but also the purpose and context in which it is elicited, which will always be implicated in some specific cognitive task or judgment.

- Imagery systems, though they may be distinct, do not function independently of verbal production. Two crucial processes are *image mediation* of tasks (e.g. recall), particularly concrete ones; and the use of *schemata*. A spatial schema may guide both memory and performance. Specifically, it may govern verbal performance. Brewer and Treyens (1981) studied data on written recall on the setting of a room. There was a powerful effect of schemata on response. Subjects tended to make assumptions about what their audience knew, not noting down explicitly unnecessary information. For example, they would use the definite article 'to introduce objects they feel are given by the room schema' (p. 228).

Although there are sometimes striking discrepancies in the terminologies of environmental and experimental cognitive psychology, the role of imagery is well known in research on the cognitive structure of urban space (e.g. Downs and Stea, 1977; Moore 1976, 1979). Quasi-visual surface images are used in performing various judgment tasks (e.g. the "working representations of Foley and Cohen, 1984). While imagery is central to people's acquisition and use of cognitive maps, imagery of cities is by no means reducible to cognitive maps in the usual sense of a relatively holistic, metric and abstract representation, whether experienced in consciousness, or revealed by a subject in making consistent metric judgments. Such a consistent, projective, holistic representation seems to be the last stage in an evolution of image elements through egocentric and partially coordinated stages (Moore, 1976). Others have seen comprehensive survey knowledge as a successor to piecemeal route-learning. It is clear that cognitive maps in this special sense are only one of the kinds of imaginal representations of space available to consciousness. Foley and Cohen (1984) examine others, including visual/motor images of walking through sites, three-dimensional and pictorial images of scenes. Generally the more abstract representations reflect greater knowledge and experience with places and a greater sensitivity to distance relationships. It is by no means clear that a typical cognitive schema of urban space need satisfy the formal requirements of a metric space. It is a nice question, for example, whether we can visualize a space in which distances are not symmetrical. It seems likely that cities are imaged piecemeal in portions and that only as these images coalesce do they form a full metric space in the strict sense. This coalescence can be measured experimentally using the principle of projective convergence (Kirasic, Allen and Siegel, 1984).

Finally, although images are more concrete and perceptually and intentionally bound than other types of mental representation they need not have been constructed by direct interaction with the sites themselves. As suggested by the schemata theories, people can infer a good deal about the geometry of buildings, places, and even whole cities given appropriate (typically graphic) media (e.g. Hunt, 1984).

Spatial knowledge, then, and specifically cognitive maps and other mental constructs of urban space, falls rather awkwardly between the social-theoretical concepts of discursive and practical consciousness. Images associated with this knowledge are emphatically available to consciousness, in the form of surface images. In both real and experimental settings people can make complex and explicitly conscious judgments from them, such as distance or proximity judgments. Yet the knowledge is in an intrinsically and irreducibly non-linguistic form: certainly in surface images, and, if the dual coding theories obtain, at deeper levels too. Giddens defines discursive consciousness as 'those forms of recall which the actor is able to express verbally' (1984, p. 49). Moos and Dear concur: 'Discursive consciousness refers to that which the agent can verbalize' (1986, p. 235). Elsewhere, Giddens defines discursive consciousness as 'something [which] can be brought to or held in consciousness' (1979, p. 25). And again practical knowledge is embodied in what actors know how to do as distinguished from what they are able to talk about (Giddens, 1979, p. 73). One might facetiously say that surface images are *not* discursive, because they cannot in principle be verbalized in all their emergent properties, yet they *are* discursive, because they can be brought to and held in consciousness in the form of quasi-pictorial surface images.

The crucial fact is that image-knowledge is generated by processes and representations which are not accessible to (discursive) consciousness, but it manifests itself in surface images which are fully conscious, but which cannot *exhaustively* enter into verbal discourse, for they are in a different and richer modality than language. Consciousness — thought, attention and the 'mind's eye' — are not, then, coterminous with language, propositional representation and the reach of verbal expression. Images of urban space are not unique in this regard. On the contrary, on Smith's account *all* subjectively verifiable knowledge leads ultimately to images. But visual recall of two- or three dimensional extended figures entails holistic, parallel-processed, visually oriented elements and properties that are at the very heart of what we mean by spatial. If we wish to assert the primacy of language in social construction, and simultaneously maintain the centrality of space for social theory, we must examine the interplay between these two intrinsically, psychologically, and (perhaps) physiologically distinct modes of knowing.

Already, at the level of the knowing subject, we are confronted with two sets of transformations. One set constructs surface images from inaccessible deep structures, thereby endowing (in common code theories) or recovering (in the dual code theories) the emergent properties of space. The other set, to which we will turn next, relates space in consciousness to space in speech and discourse.

Language and Social Reality

An immense literature places language at the center of the processes of objectification, internalization and transmission that form social reality. The original ideas in the sociology of knowledge (e.g. Mannheim, 1952) were reformulated by Schutz (1971) and Berger and Luckmann (1967) in a form that uniquely privileges language. In everyday life the 'accumulation' and the 'consistency' of the world are maintained by ordinary speech. Speech objectifies thought and makes it concrete. Even our own opinions may remain amorphous until we utter them when, perhaps, they surprise us. Beyond the intimate settings of everyday life language provides the 'massive edifice' of the conceptual world that is 'objectivated' and passed between generations (Berger and Luckmann, 1967).

More recently, Urry notes, the linguistic turn in social theory continues: in the extreme view all kinds of social practice are cast as linguistic, in a broad sense, as systems of meaning and signification (1985, p. 23). In the context of urban and architectural symbolism the urban fabric has itself been likened to a language. Research in semiotics shows the manifold ways in which architectural and structural elements of urban form encode messages: indeed modern urban form is multicoded in an overdeterminate way with many layers of messages about consumerism, functions, power and social priorities (Gottdiener, 1984). But as Lagopoulos (1984) and others argue, it is seriously misleading to attempt to reduce the semiotics of cities, buildings or settlement space to a linguistic code. Lagopoulos gives many strong reasons for maintaining a distinction. For example urban form is primarily a system of use and only secondarily a code. The message does not have an identifiable sender and receiver, and the interpretive encounter between two conscious subjects — the essence of the hermeneutic view of communication — is missing. Moreover the message is structured spatially and not temporally as in IndoEuropean languages.

Even within a broader context of theoretical semiotics natural languages are accorded a special significance because of their unique role in translation (from one natural language to another) and transposition between media (e.g. from book to film) (Greimas, 1983). It seems, therefore, that to connect urban images with social theory we need not only a semiotic perspective, but also insight into how urban symbolism is 'transcoded' (Lagopoulos) into ordinary discourse. For our purposes it is necessary to distinguish two levels of analysis and two views of the role of subjects. Linguistic analysis tends to focus on the semantics, syntax and pragmatics of the sentences. Discourse analysis, by contrast, is concerned with extended utterances in speech and writing (Grimes, 1975; Kreckel, 1981).

The usual *subject-based* view of discourse emphasizes the role of subjective construction and interpretations in face-to-face encounters. For example Berger and Bradac (1982) provide a theoretical account that place language and tactics in the use of language at the center of interpersonal communication. Exchange of messages not only initiates and shapes relationships; in a fundamental sense the exchanges *constitute* the relationship (Berger and Bradac 1982, p. 112). They see the reduction of uncertainty, for example in behavioral expectations, as a principal goal of communication. In face-to-face contacts speech conveys social messages in many ways: semantically, in its tone, pitch and fluency: in syntactic choices, in volume, speed, accent, intensity, register and vocabulary. Such communications not only 'maintain reality' in Berger and Luckmann's sense, they also serve the two social roles of i) maintaining equilibrium and cohesion in relations; and ii) exerting domination through persuasion, justification of coercion. Away from direct interpersonal contact other sign systems such as expression, gesture and proxemic body language are no longer available, and language bears the burden of communication exclusively. Only language in writing and the media transcends the bounds of face-to-face interaction in this way.

Beyond these bounds we encounter a profoundly divergent, non-hermeneutic view of discourse: discourses as *subjectless practices*. Foucault developed this view mainly with reference to the realm of written and public discourses, for example as maintained in academic disciplines and professional practices. He systematically downplays the role of communicating and interpreting subjects, and strongly emphasizes the connections between discourses and power (e.g. Foucault, 1974, 1980). His view is hard to translate into concrete assertions due to his aversion to explicit 'totalizing theoretical statements'. His style is 'fragmentary, digressive, abounding in hypotheses and sparing in conclusions' (Gordon in Foucault 1980, p. ix). Foucault stresses discourse as a complex, differentiated practice, governed by rules that are not all given in consciousness ('the analysis of statements without reference to a cogito'). He claims that discourses comprise a distinct level of analysis, possessing their own relations, distinct from their linguistic structure and the external relation they describe. Foucault was not directly concerned with the speaker/writer's intentions, nor with the listener's response, but with the discourse itself, as an object of analysis not reducible to the thought of individual agents. Nor was he in the least concerned with the logical cohesion and implicit regularities of discourse. Indeed, in Foucault's view, discourses are profoundly fragmentary and discontinuous. Their internal structure — complex and multi-layered — is to be uncovered by *archaeology*. Their antecedents — with which they are profoundly discontinuous — are to be discovered by *genealogy* which aims to undermine the naturalness of the present order by juxtaposing it with alien but consistent worlds of the past. The crucial operation in the analysis of discourses is the description of their rules of formation: accounting for the utterances generated, why they are possible and why they and no others are produced (Gordon, in Foucault, 1980, p. 244).

The central underlying social process is the creation of 'effective instruments for the formation and accumulation of knowledge'; for knowledge is power in the specific sense that relations of power cannot be established, consolidated or implemented without the production, accumulation, circulation and functioning of a discourse' (1980, p. 93). Power inheres in discourses at many levels: from their basic constitution of a domain of objects to the surface exhortations, imperatives, qualifications, persuasions or legitimations they may imply, directly or indirectly. Ultimately discourses focus in a 'grid of technologies' which act on the body. (In a series of books Foucault developed this idea in analyses of prisons, barracks, clinics; and of law criminology, psychotherapy and psychiatry as disciplines and practices.) This is an ostensibly unlikely or at least oblique view of power by the lights of conventional theory. For example in the standard Marxist view the labor process is the primary focus of power relations between classes, and physical domination and expropriation are its model in the mode of production, while 'post-Marxists' emphasize practical incorporation. On the other hand sympathetic commentators such as Gordon and Poster (1984) see Foucault's view of power in discourse as uniquely appropriate to the information age. An excellent example of structuralist discourse analysis is provided in Burton and Carlen's study of official discourse in British investigatory commissions (Burton and Carlen, 1979).

In one of his more explicit and prescriptive statements, Foucault stipulated several methodological precautions which reveal relatively clearly his intentions for discourse analysis (1980). First, we should not be primarily concerned with the central, regulated and legitimate forms of power. We 'should be concerned with power in its ultimate destinations' where it becomes 'capillary': that is in the real contexts and settings of everyday life. Secondly, we should not be concerned with intentional or decision-oriented aspects of power, but should rather look for the point at which intention gets 'completely invested in practices.' Thirdly, Foucault emphasizes the volatile and diffuse nature of power in practice settings. It is something which circulates. It is 'never in anybody's hands'; it is employed and exercised through a 'net-like organization'. Finally, Foucault argues for an ascending analysis of power, because power is invested and annexed by global structures, rather than emanating from central institutions in a consistent way. He argues strongly that 'top-down' analysis is erroneous and misleading. Although Foucault is at pains to develop an inclusive view of discourses, taking in all manifestations of language in print, everyday speech and electronic media, he tends to focus on large corpuses of archival or other written materials, as typified by existing or emerging academic disciplines and professional practices. He could not be said to have provided explicit tools for analysis of everyday discourses.

The separation of discourse from subject is taken still farther by another 'post-structuralist', Jean Baudrillard, who is violently critical of Foucault. To some extent Baudrillard severs the signs in discourse not only from their subjects, but from their objects (referents) too. Like Foucault, Baudrillard sees the realm of symbolism as central to modern society. In the most radical terms Baudrillard argues that modes of domination associated with the labor process and physical production have been superseded by a 'political economy of the sign', a general code of rational abstraction, 'the domestication of language in the case of signification, the domestication of all social and symbolic relations into the schema of representation are not only contemporary with political economy, they are its very process' (Baudrillard, 1975, p. 130).

According to Baudrillard a critical semiotic event has been the separation of sign from signifier and referent. There is a radical change
in the functioning of the sign. 'In the mode of signification signified
and referent are abolished to the sole profit of the play of the
signifiers, in a generalized formalization in which the code no longer
refers back to any subjective of objective reality, but to its own logic'
(p. 127). Thus emancipated from objects, he claims, signs may be
used in arbitrary combinations, 'floating' in the space of social
practices, to be combined with referents and signifieds at will. He
illustrates with example from advertising, where we routinely see
links created between drinks and community, deodorants and self-
confidence, and Wheaties with female pride. Like Foucault,
Baudrillard resolutely downplays those aspects of the mode of
signification that are associated with consciousness, intentionality
and choice. 'The form sign applies to the whole social process and
is largely unconscious . . . one must not confuse it with the conscious
psychology of prestige and differentiation' (1975, p. 122).

Geometry in Language

Findings on imagery in thought clearly pose a challenge to the
supra-individual, linguistic account of knowledge. Language is, indeed, the principal medium of social construction, being uniquely
privileged by its power of objectifying and transmitting information
outside of person-to-person interactions. Yet in the mind, as we
have seen, imagery may be dominant in many kinds of tasks involving movement around cities, and in thinking about 'urban issues'.
Spatially structured imagery seems to be unavoidably involved in the
kinds of *overt* behaviors (e.g. navigation in new or familiar places)
and *laboratory* exercises (e.g. distance judgments) that behavioral
geographers and environmental psychologists have dealt with.

Because of the primacy of visual/spatial organization for humans it
is well known that all languages have rich semantic and grammatical
resources for dealing with spatial relationships. Miller and
Johnson-Laird (1976) provide a detailed survey of these resources
which include: enormous vocabularies for expressing location; special treatment of verbs of motion (e.g. German prepositions, Slavic
verbs of motion); and prepositions serving complex locative func-

1976, p. 376). Apparently some languages have far richer resources than English for dealing with space. The Brazilian language of Maxakali, for example, 'goes heavy on describing spatial reference. Up to one half of each paragraph may be taken up with describing exactly where the action took place' (Grimes, 1975, p. 52).

In the context of the discussion above we need to know how gestalt, spatial properties are translated into language, and the social implications that this loss of information entails. This issue is not independent of some of the open questions on cognitive representations and processes. For example, within the framework of propositional models of the deep structure of memory: are spatial (and/or) temporal predicates coded *within* the propositions they refer to, or as separate ancillary propositions? Some theories of propositional memory assume the former (e.g. Kintsch, 1974; Anderson, 1976) and some the latter (e.g. Anderson and Bower, 1974). The question has various implications for recall (e.g. Peleg, 1982). Two key facts about the translation of spatial imaging into language are the following:

1. The nature of language requires specification of a reference system. Space perception starts as fundamentally egocentric. To interpret a spatial expression requires that the hearer or reader be oriented in a certain sense to the speaker's (writer's) intention. There are two fundamental frames of reference available: *deictic* and *intrinsic* (Miller and Johnson-Laird, 1976, p. 394). An intrinsic reference contains all the information required to specify relative locations. Deictic references require interpretation (using cues not present in the utterance) to interpret them. Such cues include 'pointing words' such as 'here', 'there', 'in front of' and 'behind.' Deictic words tie the message to the cognitive state and present position of the speaker. The hearer must share certain suppositions, or seek clarification to understand the message. 'In the deictic system spatial terms are interpreted relative to intrinsic parts of ego, whereas in the intrinsic system they are interpreted relative to the intrinsic parts of something else' (Miller and Johnson-Laird, 1976, p.396). The confusions that sometimes arise over left and right typify the problem: do you mean my right or yours?

Johnson-Laird, 1976, 396). The confusions that sometimes arise over left and right typify the problem: do you mean my right or yours?

2. The fundamental process of translating metricized, determinate geometric images into speech seems to me to involve translating a metric space into two other kinds of structures. Given a suitably defined set of objects speech expresses (i) relations — primarily binary ones — e.f. 'is nearer than'; and (ii) a partial or complete topology of sets: e.g. 'A is near home.' 'B is close by.' Since relations are always reducible to sets (indeed, a binary relation on a set is a subset of the cartesian products of the set with itself), I would argue that set structures of containment and intersection, as in the formal definition of a topological space, are the fundamental structures implied in speech on spatial relations. Notice that in generating such statements the *metric* structure of the image — its relations of distance and absolute direction — is largely suppressed. Any metric information can be supplied in principle, in an arbitrarily long series of relational statements, or by directly stating an arbitrarily precise metric proposition ('A is 2.7314 miles from B'). But in practice, we don't speak or write like this, and metric information is ordinarily suppressed in producing sentences that either directly describe or indirectly invoke spatial structures.

Geometry in Discourse

Modern discourse analysis is an interdisciplinary affair synthesizing, or at least juxtaposing, perspectives from linguistics, sociology, anthropology and psychology. Its methodology is correspondingly heterodox, combining element of rhetoric, exegesis, semiology, literary criticism and structuralism. Two principal concerns are: extension of the study of language beyond the bounds of the sentence into the semantics, grammar and pragmatics of larger discourses and, in the realm of pragmatics, the scrutiny of the cognitive and social contexts of language use as a situated practice. The latter entails analysis of the knowledge, intentions, behavioral expectations and interpretive procedures of the participants .

Grimes (1975) identifies two elements of a widely accepted approach, which he terms generative semantics. These two elements are closely analogous to Foucault's rules of formation, though in Grimes' exposition they are more subject-bound than in Foucault's. The first concern is with the intentional context of what is said (the underlying structure); the second is with the mechanics and patterns of communication which transform the underlying structure into what is actually said.

Grimes is far more explicit than Foucault in proposing a method for analysis of the contents and context of discourse. Regarding content, he dissects texts into events, participants, and 'non-events', including setting, background evaluations and collateral (contextual information on what 'might have been' in events described). In its full elaboration this method is appropriate for edited texts, such as oral or written narratives. Thurman, in an unpublished piece, proposed a method of graphically representing the content of a discourse using what Grimes terms a Thurman chart (Grimes, 1975, p. 83)

To understand how implicit geometric structure underpins discourse I want to focus on two questions. First, how can we reconstruct the underlying spatial arrangements of settings? Secondly, do the emergent image-like properties of spatial schemata pose any distinctive problems for the analysis of the social pragmatics of discourse? As suggested above, most collections of statements, for example narratives, induce or imply a partial topological structure on space. This structure takes the form of a collection of image-like surface structures (mental models of the 'synthesized code') to monitor the spatial structure implicit in a series of statements (Johnson-Laird, 1981, p. 118).

I want to propose a treatment of space in discourse analogous to Litteral's treatment of the temporal structure of events. The essence of Litteral's idea is that the bounds (rather than the metric duration) of events is the principal concern in discourse; what is needed is a method of exhibiting the complex systems of overlaps, precedence and simultaneity, implied by the temporal event markers in the text/speech, such as verb tenses, 'meanwhiles,', 'thens', 'befores' and 'afters,' in extended discourse. He proposes to specify events as open sets of a one-dimensional complete set (the time line). The finite intersection of these sets are the base of a topology expressing the linguistic structure of time (Grimes, 1975 , p. 38). Litteral proposes a subtle indexing system that enables us to distinguish disjoint, simultaneous and partially simultaneous events. This topological specification 'is precise, but with a precision that is something other than the precision of a stopwatch ... It is rather the kind of precision that is appropriate to the linguistic system itself,' (Grimes, 1975, p. 39). It is clear that, mutatis mutandis, a similar system can be used to infer the spatial structure implicit in a discourse. The principal 'mutation' required is to take account of the fact that space possesses a two-dimensional structure and lacks the coercive unidimensional quality of time. I am trying to work this out with texts from the Terkel volumes. A small sample is given as an Appendix. Such a model would provide a starting point for reconstructing the implicit geometric structure underlying a particular set of utterances by *one* speaker, as in one narrative or a single text.

But the interpretive perspective of discourse analysis looks at the *reciprocity* of knowledge in face-to-face exchanges or in more extended spans of discourse involving more than one speaker. The main conceptual problem here is to account for the effects of shared perspectives on knowledge, and for the residue of uncommunicated or incommunicable information (Kreckel, 1981; Thrift, 1985). A speaker or writer elaborates only until it can be assumed that the hearer or reader knows what is necessary to understand the statement. Grimes uses the linguistic concept of referential index, which measures the degree to which 'two parts of sentence refer to the same thing . . . the assumption on the part of the speaker that the hearer has in mind referential picture equivalent to his (sic) own as a result of what he has said is at the root of the speaker's decision to elaborate no further. If we symbolize the semantic development by a tree of propositions, the end of each branch of the tree is either a predicate or a referential index' (Grimes, 1975, p. 184).

Kreckel and Thrift emphasize a trichotomy of information that is i) intrinsically private ('experience'); or ii) is the product of past interaction and mutual experience ('shared knowledge'); or iii) is

is much more shaky. As indicated above, it appears possible to map the implicit spatial structure of a single text or utterance into a topology of containments or a relational algebra of proximities (i.e. into a set of unary or binary predicates that assert set membership of proximity relations). It is harder to see how to represent the interplay and the convergence or divergence of individual perspectives in a extended dialog. Two effects would need to be considered. First, in all extended dialogs feedback and resonance occur, tending to *overdetermine* the information by implying, inferring or stating it in various ways (Kreckel, 1981). The second effect is peculiar to the geometry underlying discourse (Pipkin, 1985): the *metric* structure of space tends to be grossly *underdetermined* in the transformation to language.

Beyond the realm of intersubjective interpretation, according to Foucault, discourses become *subjectless*, and entrain with power in the media, the professions and in academic disciplines. Here we need to know how debate that effects the built urban form invokes perceived spatial arrangements (in the territorial bases of neighborhood organizations, project boosterism, perceived ranges of externality effects, differential participation in public hearings, and so on). Also we need to explore how concepts injected into discourses in the media and other public forums from professional and academic sources resonate with the 'inarticulate' place images of people. On one hand, everyday experience (and sources such as the Terkel interviews) suggests that the vocabulary of professional debate does filter down into everyday discourse. On the other hand, as Foucault insists, the 'power' of discourses not only emanates from the center, but also it appropriates marginal and 'capillary' discourses into its own structure. Foucault provides only the vaguest prescriptions on the details of the methods required to uncover these processes. Nor are his own voluminous researches on clinics, psychiatry and criminology particularly illuminating on how 'grids of technology' affect not bodies but constructed spaces.

At still another stage of abstraction Baudrillard indicates how, under the mode of information, the signifiers of discourses become separated from their referents, recombining in what might be called *objectless* discourses. Under this heading may come the free and arbitrary use of the notions of neighborhood, proximity and turf in advertising, boosterism, urban politics and, by metaphorical extension, in domains other than real urban space. Again it is hard to make explicit prescriptions on method.

Concluding Remarks

The spaces we live in are built as surely by words as by labor. Language is the primary matrix through which social reality is formed and transmitted between individuals and generations. As electronic media and other remote communications pervade life, the primacy of language may well be reinforced, the visual impact of television notwithstanding. Yet we know from behavioral geography and from cognitive and environmental psychology, to say nothing of the design disciplines, that a quite different and intrinsically non-linguistic mode of knowing, spatial imagery, is fundamental. A wide array of research suggests that cognitive space is central to both the behavior and thought of urbanites. Its significance goes far beyond thought and speech specifically *about* urban settings. Common experience and materials such as the Terkel collections show that geometrical arrangements are implicated directly and metaphorically in thought and speech on all kinds of urban issues. Indeed any sufficiently elaborate discourse *imposes* an implicit geometry on its objects, because spatial structure is deeply ingrained in the syntax and grammar of all language. Yet in the transformation from image-knowledge to linguistic knowledge something is lost. I have tried to point to some theoretical issues that arise in attempting to reconcile the cognitive and social (linguistic construction) views of knowledge.

There are objections to treating knowledge as a determinate object that is passively 'processed' between cognitive levels and 'transmitted' between agents. For example, as indicated above, some cognitive theories emphasize that knowing *is* a process as much as a set of representations. However, we can claim, with more than just metaphorical force, that spatial knowledge undergoes a series of transformations as it moves from the intrinsically private, mainly visual experience of people to, let us say, public/professional discourse in a planning hearing on neighborhood revitalization. Con-

metaphorical force, that spatial knowledge undergoes a series of transformations as it moves from the intrinsically private, mainly visual experience of people to, let us say, public/professional discourse in a planning hearing on neighborhood revitalization. Considering the materials above, we can hypothesize the following series of transformations between levels. Some of these are extremely well confirmed in experimental cognitive research. Others, notably the French structuralist perspectives of Foucault and Baudrillard, are intrinsically complex, cryptic, and difficult to unfold in operational terms. They are also intellectually and politically controversial in English language social science.

• Internal transformations occur between visual and non-visual modes, at deep and surface (conscious) levels, in a fashion which problematizes the conventional distinction between discursive and practical consciousness. Introspective imagery is the 'court of last appeal'. While arbitrarily precise metric statements can be made, normally the transformation to language grossly favors relational and topological structure over metrics, abetted by the syntax and grammar of natural language.

• Geometry in the extended discourse of one subject. Beyond the sentence or proposition, in extended discourse such as a narrative, coherence (unity) of the discourse is maintained by co-reference between elements. Johnson-Laird proposes a specific criterion of coherence: a discourse is coherent if it is possible to construct a single mental model from it (Johnson-Laird, 1983, p. 370). I have proposed, and illustrate briefly in an Appendix, how one may infer the topological structure explicit in a text or statement.

• Geometry in the language of intersubjective encounters. In extended discourse between two or more subjects the implicit geometry of here/there, far/near, next to/away from, is elaborated only until there is mutual consent to elaborate no further. The resulting explicit geometry may or may not be complete and consistent. More crucial is the question of 'slippage' between the intrinsic geometries the subjects have in mind; whether they are

hermeneutic encounters between subjects work toward coherence and consistency of the implicit and explicit geometries in discourse. The contrast between the realm of intersubjectively corroborated geometry and that of 'subjectless' discourses is captured in Foucault's distinction between the interiority and exteriority of discourse. When the spatial terminology of here/there, them/us, near/far, spatial distance/social distance, inside/outside goes out to live a life of its own in public, professional and media discourse, the cognitive and intersubjective guarantees of geometric consistency (e.g. implied distance and set relations in Euclidean space) are lost. We need to know how such discourses become decentered sources of power over the urban space, and how such discourse shapes its subject. This subject-turned-object is not the body itself, as in Foucault's studies of sexuality and punishment, but the built urban form. A 'genealogy' and 'archaeology' of the neighborhood concept in American and British planning might illustrate the point, and through analyzing interview materials such as the Terkel collections, one might also hope to show how professional discourse, as refracted in the media, shapes the intersubjective 'interiors' of discourse.

• Loss of the object. Finally, à la Baudrillard, it may be that spatially resonant vocabulary becomes entirely divorced from spatial referents, to combine and recombine in other worlds of discourse and power. Here not subjective, nor intersubjective, nor even objective correspondence rules constrain the uses and abuses to which evocative and erstwhile spatial words ('nearby', 'neighborhood', 'community') can be put.

The central methodological problem for the approach advocated here — reconstruction of the geometry explicit in the syntax and vocabulary of texts using relational and set-theoretical structures — is to connect this topology with the implicit, metric, survey knowledge in people's minds: the cognitive maps of a single speaker/writer, or the intersecting maps of speakers in a dialog. The case of the single speaker/writer is by far the easier to address.

Two more general features are obvious in this series of transformations. Firstly they operate to suppress the gestalt and metric
properties of spatial imagery (underdetermination). The
'disassembly' of the holistic, emergent properties of images as they
pass through these transformations seems to mirror in reverse, rather
accurately, the stages in an individual's construction of urban space
from the egocentric, deictic and ordinal stage of route learning,
through projective, abstractly coordinated spaces. Crude topological
structure is the most robust. Because of the nature of language, this
is the *only* structure that can ordinarily be inferred *directly* from the
surface of texts (e.g. from syntax, locatives, verbs of motion etc.)
without probing the interpretive (geometric, metric) understandings
of speakers and audiences. To the extent that discourses on public
space become subjectless and discontinuous à la Foucault. So the
metric implications of the text become underdetermined.

Secondly, cognitive and intersubjective guarantees of validity (over-
determination) become less tenable as we move farther from the
clasical hermeneutic case of extended 'sincere' person to person dialog. Presumably the slippages and unconformities could be appropriated within the discourse (rhetorically: 'come on, it's not that far,
it's quite near', or ideologically: 'the problem won't extend as far
as *our* neighborhood'), as has been argued in more detail elsewhere
(Pipkin, 1985). Here, surely, is an important and distinctively
'spatial' locus in the exercise of power (e.g. in legitimation).
Understanding of these transformations and their implications seems
essential to connect cognitive and social theories of urban space.

Appendix

This small sample is an attempt to reconstruct the spatial
(topological) structure implicit in a statement in Terkel's *Division
Street* (pp. 319-324). The speaker is a one-time architect-designer who
moved, with his wife, to live a work in the Ecumenical Institute in
the West Side black ghetto of Chicago. The 'Deerfield incident' was
a proposed integrated housing complex stopped by a town referen-
dum. Elements of the text which indicate location or direction are
inferred and marked (o = situated object or event; s = reference to

situated subject, pronoun, possessive etc.; R = region; v = verb of
motion; p = preposition, locative, adverbial phrase, etc.)

1 *I* seriously doubt that *we* could ever *move back* to   s   s   v
2 *Northbrook.* It's not that *we* don't love *everybody*   R   s   s
3 who's *there.* It's not that *we* don't appreciate   p   s
4 what *we* had *there.* It's just that *there's a job*   s   p   p   o
5 to be done *down here* and *there are* not enough   p   p
6 *hands* to do it. . . .   o

7 *We* were becoming more deeply involved in *church* work.   s   o
8 *I* was putting in an eighty-hour week, forty *at* the   s   p
9 *job* and forty *at the church.* *I* dissociated a   o   p   o   s
10 Christian life from a man's vocation. *I* saw a   s
11 Christian life in which a man would think of the
12 church as a building and not really relate faith
13 with being involved with people.
14 About a year ago, *we* canceled a *bridge engagement.*   s   o
15 and a *party* and spent a weekend *at the Ecumenical*   o   p   o
16 *Institute.* It changed *our* lives. It opened up to   s
17 *us* the thing that *we* both wanted. Only *we* couldn't   s   s   s
18 put *our* hands on it, a way in which you could give   s
19 your total self. *You* didn't have to go *Downtown*   s   v   R
20 and work *your* forty hours a week and *come back* and   s   v
21 try to figure some way to make *your* life more   s
22 meaningful. *We* found a *renter* for *our house* and   s   s   o
23 *came here.*
24 When *we* first told *our friends* about the move, it   s   s
25 was met with: "My word, *you guys* are nuts."   s
26 (Laughs.) *I* guess everyone's image of a teacher or   s
27 a church worker is one in which *you* live *out here*   s   p
28 and *you commute out there.* This is a horrible   s   v   p
29 thing. You've got to live with people to
30 understand what their problems are. Some of *them*   s
31 were quite shocked. A lot of *our friends* thought,   s
32 "Maybe, but *I* doubt it." Once *we made the move,*   s   s   v
33 *we ourselves* realized *we* were no longer in doubt.   s   s

34 You see, *we moved* into *Northbook* just months   s   v   R
35 after the *Deerfield incident. We're just south* of   o   s   p
36 *Deerfield.* There was much talk and concern   R
37 naturally. *There* are only *eleven Negroes* living   p   s
38 *in Northbook,* and all of *them live in the homes*   R   s   p
39 *where they work.* The majority of *people* claim   p   s
40 there is no problem. The reason is *they've* never   s
41 confronted *themselves* with what *they* would do if   s   s
42 something like *Deerfield* happened. Most of *our*   o
43 *friends* are *church-affiliated.* But when it   s   p
44 connects with life it becomes uncomfortable.
45 *I* don't think *they* really believe that the   s   s
46 *situations we* talk about exist. *They* don't want   o   s   s
47 to believe it. There's some fear that *we* might   s
48 influence *them,* of *coming down to visit,* of   s   v
49 showing *them* what life is really like *in* the *inner*   s   R
50 *city.*

An incomplete topology of the surface structure of the text may be
inferred by noting situated objects and subjects, locatives, verbs of
motion and other semantic and syntactic features.   By 'surface
structure' I mean the *explicit* structure of the text, considered in
isolation, without probing the subject's implicit meanings in some
extra-textual manner.   This approach is obligatory unless the
speaker/writer is available for interview. The objective is to establish
the topological structure of elements and regions that represents a
consistent and coherent model (in the sense of Johnson-Laird) of the
space implied in the discourse.   The approach is intended to be
analogous to Litteral's treatment of time.

In attempting this kind of analysis a threefold division of the text
referents becomes necessary. Firstly, elements can be classified as
situated or *unsituated* with respect to the frame of the narrative. For
example it is clear that the 'you' and 'their' of lines 29 and 30 refer
to unsituated subjects — the statement is intended abstractly. But
then, at the end of line 30, 'them' becomes situated again; it refers
to friends in Northbrook. Among the *situated* elements of the text
it is necessary to draw another distinction between elements or subjects whose location is specified by the text, and those which remain

unspecified. Thus the 'eleven Negroes' in line 37 are situated in Northbrook, while it is never made clear where the 'church' is located (line 9), and whether, in fact, it is near the Ecumenical Institute. Notice that of the five 'regions' specified (Northbrook, the inner city, Deerfield, the neighborhood of the Ecumenical Institute and Downtown) containment or exclusion relationships are only sometimes made clear. For example it is evident that Northbrook and the neighborhood of the Ecumenical Institute are disjoint, but what about Downtown and the inner city? Note also the ambiguity of 'just south of' in line 35. A reasonable inference is that this refers to the Ecumenical Institute (on the West Side), but this is not unequivocally specified by the text. Elements and subjects, then, may be classed as *unsituated, situated and specified* and *situated and unspecified*. The specified situated elements may be put into element/set relationships that satisfy the formal criterion of a topology and the interpretative criterion of a *consistent* mental model. This approach is at best a crude starting point for uncovering the structure of space in ordinary discourse. It does bring forcibly home how much geometric and specifically *metric* structure is suppressed in the surface structures of ordinary speech.

References

Anderson, J.R. (1976) *Language, Memory and Thought*, Erlbaum, Hillsdale, N.J.

Anderson, J.R. and G.H. Bower (1974) *Human Associative Memory*, Winston, Washington D.C.

Atkinson, R.C. and R.M. Schiffrin (1968) Human memory: a proposed system and its control processes, in K.W. Spence and J.T. Spence (eds.), *Advances in the Psychology of Learning and Motivation Research and Theory*, Vol. 2, Academic Press, N.Y.

Baudrillard, J. (1975) *The Mirror of Production*, (tr. M. Poster), Telos Press, St. Louis.

Anderson, J.R. and G.H. Bower (1974) *Human Associative Memory*, Winston, Washington D.C.

Atkinson, R.C. and R.M. Schiffrin (1968) Human memory: a proposed system and its control processes, in K.W. Spence and J.T. Spence (eds.), *Advances in the Psychology of Learning and Motivation Research and Theory, Vol. 2*, Academic Press, New York.

Baudrillard, J. (1975) *The Mirror of Production*, (tr. M. Poster), Telos Press, St. Louis.

Bennett, D.C. (1975) *Spatial and Temporal Uses of English Prepositions: An Essay in Stratificational Semantics*, Longman, London.

Berger, C.R. and J.J. Bradac (1982) *Language and Knowledge: Uncertainty in Interpersonal Relations*, Arnold, London.

Berger, P. and T. Luckmann (1967) *The Social Construction of Reality*, Lane, London.

Bobrow, D.G. and D.A. Norman (1975) Some principles of memory schemata, in D.G. Bobrow and D.A. Norman (eds.), *Representation and Understanding: Studies in Cognitive Science*, Academic Press, New York.

Bower, G. H. (1972) Mental imagery and associative learning, in L. W. Gregg (ed.) *Cognition in Learning and Memory*, Wiley, New York

Brewer, W. F. and Treyens, J. C. (1981) Rôle of Schemata in memory for places, *Cognitive Psychology*, 13, 207-230.

Burton, F. and P. Carlen (1979) *Official Discourse: On Discourse Analysis, Government Publications, Ideology and the State*, Routledge and Kegan Paul, London.

Foos, P.W. (1983) Using sentences to convey spatial information, *Journal of Psycholinguistic Research*, 12, 223-234.

Foley, J.E. and Cohen, A. L. (1984) Working mental representation of the environment, *Environment and Behavior*, 16, 713-729.

Foucault, M. (1974) *The Archaeology of Knowledge*, (tr. A. Sheridan Smith), Tavistock, London.

Foucault, M. (1980) Two lectures pp. 78-108 in M. Foucault (M. Gordon, ed.) *Power and Knowledge: Selected Interviews and other Writing*, Pantheon, N.Y.

Friendly, M. (1979) Methods for finding graphic representations of associative memory structure, pp. 85-129 in C.R. Puff (ed.) *Memory Organization and Structure*, Academic Press, NY.

Freud, S. (1921) *Complete Psychological Works Vol. XIX*, (tr. J. Strachey), Hogarth Press, London.

Gale, N. and R.G. Golledge (1982) On the subjective partitioning of space, *Annals, Association of American Geographers*, 72, 60-67.

Giddens, A. (1979) *Central Problems in Social Theory*, Macmillan, London.

Giddens, A. (1981) *A Contemporary Critique of Historical Materialism*, University of California Press, Berkeley.

Giddens, A. (1984) *The Constitution of Society*, University of California Press, Berkeley.

Giddens, A. (1985) Time, space and regionalisation, pp. 265-285 in D. Gregory and J. Urry (eds.), *Social Relations and Spatial Structures*, Macmillan, London.

Gilmartin, P.P. and J.C. Patton (1984) Comparing the sexes on spatial abilities: map-use skills, *Annals, Association of American Geographers*, 74, 605-619.

Gottdiener, M. (1984) The semiotics of urban culture, MS, University of California, Riverside.

Gregory, D. and J. Urry (eds.) (1985) *Social Relations and Spatial Structures*, Macmillan, London.

Greimas, A.J. (1983) *Structural Semantics*, (tr. D. McDowell, R. Schleiffer and A. Velie), University of Nebraska Press, Lincoln.

Grimes, J.E. (1975) *The Thread of Discourse*, Mouton, The Hague.

Hagerstrand, T. (1975) Time, space and human conditions, in A. Karlqvist, L. Lundquist and F. Snickars (eds.), *Dynamic Allocation of Urban Space*, Lexington Books, Lexington, MA.

Hunt, M.E. (1984) Environmental learning without being there, *Environment and Behavior*, 16, 307-334.

Johnson-Laird, P.N. (1981) Mental models of meaning, pp. 106-126 in A.K. Joshi, B.L. Webber and I.A. Sag (eds.), *Elements of Discourse Understanding*, Cambridge University Press, Cambridge.

Johnson-Laird, P.N. (1983) *Mental Models*, Cambridge University Press, Cambridge.

Kelter, S., H. Grotzbach, R. Freiheit, B. Hohle, S. Wutzig and E. Diesch (1984) Object identification: the mental representation of physical and conceptual attributes, *Memory and Cognition*, 12, 123-133.

Kintsch, W. (1974) *The Representation of Meaning in Memory*, Erlbaum, Hillsdale, N. J.

Kirasic, K.C., G.L. Allen and A.W. Siegel (1984) Expression of configurational knowledge of large-scale environments, *Environment and Behavior*, 16, 687-712.

Kosslyn, S.M. and S.P. Schwartz (1978) Visual images as spatial representations in active memory, in E.M. Riseman and A.R. Hanson (eds.), *Computer Vision Systems*, Academic Press, NY.

Kreckel, M. (1981) *Communicative Acts and Shared Knowledge in Natural Discourse*, Academic Press, NY.

Lachman, R., J. Lachman and E. Butterfield (1979) *Cognitive Psychology and Information Processing*, Erlbaum, Hillsdale, N. J.

Lachman, J. and R. Lachman (1979) Theories of memory organization and human evolution, pp. 133-193 in C.R. Puff (ed.) *Memory Organization and Structure*, Academic Press, NY.

Lagopoulos, A. (Forthcoming) The semiotics of settlement space, in T. Sebeok (ed.), *Encylopedic Dictionary of Semiotics*, Mouton. In MS 1984.

Litteral, R. (1972) Rhetorical predicates and the time topology of Angkor, *Foundations of Language*, 8, 391-410.

Mandler, J.M. (1979) Categorical and schematic organization in memory, pp. 259-299 in C.R. Puff (ed.), *Memory Organization and Structure*, Academic Press, NY.

Mannheim, K. (1952) *Essays on the Sociology of Knowledge*, Routledge and Kegan Paul, London.

McDaniel, M., A. Friedman and L. Bourne (1978) Remembering the level of information in words, *Memory and Cognition*, 6, 156-164.

Miller, G.A. and P.N. Johnson-Laird (1976) *Language and Perception*, Bellnap, Harvard University Press, Cambridge, MA.

Mandler, J.M. (1979) Categorical and schematic organization in memory, pp. 259-299 in C.R. Puff (ed.), *Memory Organization and Structure*, Academic Press, NY.

Mannheim, K. (1952) *Essays on the Sociology of Knowledge*, Routledge and Kegan Paul, London.

McDaniel, M., A. Friedman and L. Bourne (1978) Remembering the level of information in words, *Memory and Cognition*, 6, 156-164.

Miller, G.A. and P.N. Johnson-Laird (1976) *Language and Perception*, Bellnap, Harvard University Press, Cambridge, MA.

Moore, G.T., (1973) Developmental differences in environmental cognition, in W. Preisser (ed.), *Environmental Design Research*, Dowden, Hutchinson and Ross, Stroudsburg, PA

Moore, G.T. (1976) Theory and research on the development of environmental cognition in G.T. Moore and R.G. Golledge (eds.), *Environmental Knowing*, Dowden, Hutchinson and Ross, Stroudsburg, PA

Moore, G.T. (1979) Knowing about environmental knowing, *Environment and Behavior*, 11, 33-70.

Moos, A.I. and M.J. Dear (1986) Structuration theory in urban analysis: 1 Theoretical exegesis *Environment and Planning A*, 18, 231-252.

Morris, P. E. and Hampson, P. J. (1983) *Imagery and Consciousness*, Academic Press, New York.

Paivio, A. (1971) *Imagery and Verbal Processes*, Holt, Rinehart and Winston, NY.

Peleg, Z.R. (1982) The representation of time and location in memory for sentences, *Journal of Psycholinguistic Research*, 11, 169-182.

Pipkin, J.S. (1985) Ideology and Geometry, Paper presented at the meetings of the Association of American Geographers, Detroit.

Porteous, J.D. (1985) Smellscape, *Progress in Human Geography*, 9, 356-378.

Poster, M. (1984) *Foucault, Marxism and History*, Polity Press, Cambridge.

Pred, A. (1981) Everyday practice and the discipline of human geography, in A. Pred (ed.) *Space and Time in Geography*, Gleerup, Lund.

Puff, C.R. (ed.) (1979) *Memory Organization and Structure*, Academic Press, New York.

Pylyshyn, Z.W. (1973) What the mind's eye tells the mind's brain: a critique of mental imagery, *Psychological Bulletin*, 80, 1-24.

Rhoades, H.M. (1981) Training spatial ability, pp. 247-256 in E. Klinger (ed.) *Imagery: Volume 2*, Plenum Press, NY.

Richardson, J.T.E. (1980) *Mental Imagery and Human Memory*, Macmillan, London.

Rumelhart. D.E. and D.A. Norman (1985) Representation of knowledge, pp. 15-62 in A.M. Aitkenheard and J.M. Slack (eds.) *Issues in Cognitive Modeling*, Erlbaum, Hillsdale, NJ

Schutz, A. (1971) *Collected Papers, Vols, I and II*, Nijhoff, The Hague.

Scott, A.J. (1986) Industrialization and urbanization: a geographical agenda, *Annals, Association of American Geographers*, 76, 25-37.

Smith, B. (1966) *Memory*, Humanities Press, NY.

Terkel, S. (ed.) (1967) *Division Street America*, Pantheon, NY.

Terkel, S. (ed.) (1970) *Hard Times*, Random House, NY.

Terkel, S. (ed.) (1970) *Working*, Random House, NY.

Terkel, S. (ed.) (1980) *American Dreams: Lost and Found*, Ballantine, NY.

Thorndyke, P. (1981) Distance estimation from cognitive maps, *Cognitive Psychology*, 13, 526-550.

Thrift, N. (1985) Flies and germs: a geography of knowledge, pp. 366-403 in D. Gregory and J. Urry (eds.) *Social Relations and Spatial Structures*, Macmillan, London.

Tulving, E. (1972) Episodic and semantic memory, in E. tulving and W. Donaldson (eds.) *Organization of Memory*, Academic Press, NY.

Urry, J. (1985) Social relations, space and time, in D. Gregory and J. Urry (eds.), *Social Relations and Spatial Structures*, Macmillan, London.

Chapter 5

Issues in Architecture: Perceptions By the Popular and Professional Press

Larkin Dudley and Linda Irvine

What is — and what should be — the relationship between the media, the public, and designers of the built environment are questions which are increasingly asked when architects gather. Although panels of experts and practitioners in architecture have discussed the media-designer relationship, there is little documentation of the press's treatment of architecture and the architectural profession.

This chapter addresses this deficiency by presenting some preliminary findings on the kinds of architectural issues that have been reported in the popular press and the professional press over the past 25 years. For the purposes of this study, The New York Times represents the popular press and the AIA Journal, Architectural Record, Progressive Architecture and Architectural Forum represent the professional press.

During the 25 years under study, there has been considerable debate between journalists and the architectural profession as to the kinds of roles the press should play in reporting, interpreting and criticizing architecture and the built environment — a debate that has changed in kind and intensity since 1960. These changes are due, in part, to the public's growing interest in architecture and design-related issues and to a significant increase in the number of architectural critics writing for major newspapers and magazines. Not only have the questions and issues raised by architects, editors and critics concerning the media-designer relationship been wide-ranging, but there appears to be no consensus on what issues critics should address or what qualifications they need. To better understand this debate, the following paragraphs summarize what has been perceived over the past few decades as the way the press has treated architectural issues.

During the 1960s, the press was often criticized for not reporting on the social consequences of architecture. In 1963, George McCue stated at a conference entitled 'The Press and the Building of Cities' that 'the press cover the bare facts but not the social, economic, civic and design implications of urban buildings'. Further, Ferdinand Kuhn in 1968, in a critique of the press, stated that 'real estate news was polluted with unlabeled advertising and newspapers neglected to report on the current urban crisis' (Kuhn, 1968).

In response to these comments, an article in the AIA Journal in 1965 (Gallagher, 1965), entitled 'Why is the Press Sometimes Wary?' explained that communication between the media and the profession needed to be greatly improved. Journalists felt that what they needed from architects was rapport — not renderings.

More recently, at a panel discussion of the AIA Convention in 1984 ('Media To Architects', 1984 and 'Architects', the Critics'and the Public's View of the Media', 1984), the above-mentioned themes emerged again. Problems emphasized were architects' lack of articulation on design, the media's naiveté concerning architecture, and the tendency of the media to seek controversy, rather than understanding.

Concerns about the media/designer relationship were again addressed extensively in the November 1985 issue of *Metropolis* (Filler, 1985). Eight well-known critics from the professional and lay press, along with prominent architects and editors, discussed the nature, rôle, and difficulties of architectural criticism.

Among the observations made by *architects* were:

1. 'That there is no consensus on issues critics should address, nor what qualifications they need.'

2. 'That criticism in trade (professional) magazines is tamer than in general media because trade magazines probably feel that if they are too critical, then they won't be given the next building for publication.'

3. 'That the nonprofessional press is a little bit more detached from the internal gossip of the profession and because they are further away they are able to get a wider overview more easily' (pp.28-41).

Among the observations by *editors* were:

1. 'That there's no consensus regarding issues that critics in professional magazines should address.'

2. 'That the audience differentiates criticism in the trade magazines from that addressed to the general public.'

3. 'That professional criticism tends to be more lenient ... professional magazines can't afford to alienate their sources' (pp.28-41).

Among the observations by *critics* were:

1. 'That architects view criticism primarily as publicity, and become quite resentful if their work is investigated rather than merely promoted.'

2. 'That (the critic's) responsibility is to the reader, not to the architect.'

3. 'That architecture plays a relatively small rôle in the totality of decisions made about the way a city looks. . . it's important to look at the whole of one built environment.'

4. 'That there are several kinds of criticism: description, interpretation, and evaluation.'

5. 'That newspaper reports, interpretive articles, and criticism help shape public opinion. . . to make people think about their environment and to participate more actively.'

6. 'That the only people who don't see the growing sophistication of the American public are newspaper and magazine editors . . . editors have tunnel vision.'

7. 'That a goal (of the critic) is to raise the awareness level of design to help the average person to make some distinction between the good, bad, and indifferent.'

8. 'That it's as wrong to overstate the power of the press as to understate it. It's strong and powerful, but it's not dictatorial, absolute or immediate' (pp.28-41).

These varying and often contradictory opinions from architects, editors and critics about the nature and rôle of architectural criticism serve to reinforce the need to critically examine the professional and popular press and to document what is and has been reported by each. In an effort to more fully understand the press's treatment of architectural issues, the following questions were raised:

• Does the press contain more articles of an opinion or reporting nature?

• What topics receive the most attention in the popular press?

• Are comparable topics addressed in the professional press?

• What kinds of changes can be seen over the past 25 years in the reporting of architectural issues by the popular and professional press?

In order to answer the above questions, the contents of the indices to the popular and professional press were analyzed [1] to determine the types of issues featured and their frequency of appearance. Although the purpose of this analysis is to give a broad overview, the study does follow the tradition of text analysis already well established in architecture and art. [2]

Popular Press

The perceptions and attitudes of the popular press toward architecture and the architectural profession were assessed by reviewing all entries listed in *The New York Times Index* under the subject heading of 'Architecture'. Under this heading, significant news, notices, editorial matter, and special features pertaining to architecture published in *The New York Times* are abstracted.

These abstracts provide an overview, in chronological order, of *The New York Times'* treatment of architectural issues over the past 25 years. Although articles relating to the built environment are also listed under other subject headings, such as 'Housing', 'Building', 'Urban Design', 'Parks and Recreation' etc., articles entered under 'Architecture' gave a more comprehensive coverage of architecture and the architectural profession and so these entries were chosen for analysis.

The abstracts for each year from 1960 to 1984 were reviewed and coded according to the following **content:** a) executed works: buildings or development and historic preservation; b) professions: in general, professional societies, and professional education; c) individuals and firms; and, d) exhibitions, awards and publications. Further, themes were categorized into **professional orientation:** a) practice: executed works, office practice, and materials and methods of construction; and b) theory: style/aesthetics, factors influencing design, and philosophy/values. Finally, **type of article** (opinion or reporting) and **authorship** (Huxtable/Goldberger or others) were determined.

In almost all cases, the categories were treated as mutually exclusive. An article could only be opinion or reporting, not both, and the content of each article was coded in one category only. The only category which was *not* mutually exclusive was 'professional orientation'. In this case, an article could be counted as having a 'practice' and a 'theory' orientation. However, this occurred less than 5 per cent of the time. In a portion of the cases, some of the categories were not applicable. For example, in a case when the

'Professional Orientation' of an article could not be determined, the article was coded according to 'Content' and 'Type' only.

In addition to coding each abstract, the reviewers identified key words and phrases which summarized the primary theoretical and practice-related issues for each year. These issues were later grouped into two categories — the architectural profession and architecture and society — and were reviewed to determine significant trends for each decade — 1960, 1970, 1980.

The total number of articles, excluding awards, exhibits, and book review entries, coded for each five year interval, was as follows: 1960-64: 212; 1965-69: 200; 1970-74: 235; 1975-79: 249; and 1980-84: 180. The percentage of articles for any given category was computed for each year and averaged over a five year interval commencing at 1960.

Two reviewers (the authors) were responsible for coding *The New York Times Index* abstracts. One reviewer coded 1960-1973 and the other 1974-1984. Coder reliability was not formally calculated but is estimated at 80 per cent.

The Professional Press

The perceptions and attitudes of the professional press toward architecture and the architectural profession were assessed by reviewing titles cited in *The Art Index* under the subject headings of 'Architects', 'Architectural . . .', 'Architecture', and 'Architecture and . . .'. *The Art Index* is an index to domestic and foreign publications and gives author and title listings only; articles are not abstracted. Nonetheless, these title listings provide an overview, in chronological order, of the professional press's treatment of architectural issues over the past 25 years. This is as comparable an overview as was provided by reviewing *The New York Times Index*. As noted earlier, only titles from four domestic journals with prominent national reputations were reviewed: *AIA Journal, Architectural Record, Progressive Architecture,* and *Architectural Forum.* [3]

A count was made of all title listings, including articles, letters, editorials, and regular features which appeared under the following main headings of content: architectural profession (as a profession, criticism, education, and research); architectural styles (modern, post-modern, vernacular, conservation/restoration); social/political context (society, state, politics, capitalism, religion, and morals); environment and energy (climate, earthquakes, nature, environment, and energy usage); associated disciplines (architecture and . . . art, language, music, mathematics, geometry, science, philosophy, psychology, human factors, business, engineering, and planning). A further step included reclassifying articles according to professional orientation (practice, client relationships, ethics, legal status, public relations, drawing, and evaluation) and theory (architectural styles, environment and energy, and social/political factors: philosophy, psychology, human factors, society, and state).

Due to the editorial policy of *The Art Index*, listings are not mutually exclusive and, in a few cases, some titles were listed under several headings. No attempt was made to correct this duplication since it was felt that this would not affect the study's broad review of pertinent themes. Also, all entries were counted and given equal weight, i.e. an article and an entry 'Regular Feature' were counted equally and no attempt was made to calculate the number of times in a year that a 'Regular Feature' may have appeared.

To obtain a more detailed examination of issues, each reviewer wrote out the authors and titles listed under 'Architecture as a Profession', 'Architecture and Society', 'Architecture-Philosophy', and 'Architecture-Psychology'. These titles were later grouped into categories mentioned previously and used as a basis to summarize the primary theoretical and practice-related issues for each decade.

The total number of title listings coded for each five year interval was as follows: 1960-64: 237; 1965-69: 235; 1970-74: 354; 1975-79: 448; and 1980-84: 221. The percentage of title listings for each subheading was computed for each year (aggregating all journals) and averaged over a five year interval commencing in 1960. Two reviewers (one graduate and one undergraduate student) were responsible for counting the titles in *The Art Index*. Coder reliability was not formally calculated but is estimated at 90-95 per cent.

Method for Comparative Analyses

Due to differences in the data sources themselves, the data collection procedures for the popular press and the professional press were slightly different. Articles are abstracted in *The New York Times Index* and not categorized except for exhibitions and awards. In contrast, *The Art Index* gives only the title of each article and is categorized by subject by the publisher. Since the emphasis of this study is on identifying broad themes and prominent issues typical to each press, the difference in data collection was tolerated in order to make general comparisons. In respect of the differences, findings from each index are reported separately below and comparisons are made only in cases where categories were similar.

Findings

For *The New York Times Index*, a discussion of the type of articles (opinion or reporting) is presented below, followed by a description of the content of the articles published. After the discussion of the popular press, the contents of the professional press are reviewed. Then, broad comparisons between the popular and professional press are made and, finally, a summary is presented of the major issues reported over the last 25 years.

The Popular Press: Opinion or Reporting

As noted earlier, the issue as to whether or not the press' rôles are, or should be, primarily opinion or reporting is part of the debate among critics, architects, and editors. To gain some insight into this question, articles from *The New York Times* were coded as either opinion or reporting. Table 5.1 shows the percentage of articles classified as opinion. The opinion category was either 35 or 45 per cent for four of the five periods with a peak in the period from 1975 to 1980 of approximately 70 per cent opinion articles. The high percentage in the 1975-80 time span is probably due to an increase in the number of critiques of exhibitions in this one period and to the fact that both A. Huxtable and P. Goldberger were writing simultaneously.

Table 5.1:   Opinion Articles and Articles By Named Authors, Popular Press, 1960-1984

	1960-65 (N = 212) %	1965-70 (N = 200) %	1970-75 (N = 235) %	1975-80 (N = 249) %	1980-84 (N = 180 %
Opinion Articles	35	35	45	70	35
Named Authors	12	22	27	52	35

Also, the data were reviewed to determine who have been the prominent people in architectural criticism and what percentage of opinion articles was by them. As noted in Table 5.1, the number of articles by named authors, P. Goldberger and A. Huxtable, increased from only 12 per cent in the early 1960s to 52 per cent in the late 1970s and tapered to approximately 35 per cent in the early 1980s. Thus, over the last 25 years, there has been an increase in articles by named authors, but, overall, more articles about architecture were published by those who were not identified as architectural critics than those who were.

The Popular Press: Content

As shown in Table 5.2, the findings from the review of the popular press indicate that exhibitions, awards, and publications have consistently retained more coverage than any other content category although the percentage of articles has declined from approximately 70 per cent in 1960-65 to about 50 per cent in 1980-85. The next largest category of articles, executed works, which includes features with a focus on specific buildings and historical preservation, has an average over the years of about 17 per cent. The other two categories, individuals and firms and professions and education, account for a smaller and varying percentage of articles. For individuals and firms, the range is from 5 per cent in 1975-1980 to 18 per cent in

1970-75 while for professions and education the range is from 10 per cent in 1960 to 20 per cent in 1975-80.

Table 5.2:   Content of Articles in the Popular Press

	1960-65 (N = 212) %	1965-70 (N = 200) %	1970-75 (N = 235) %	1975-80 (N = 249) %	1980-85 (N = 180 %
Executed Works Buildings/ Preservation	15	15	20	12	25
Professions/ Education	7	9	7	23	13
Individuals/ Firms	8	11	18	5	12
Exhibitions/ Awards and Publications	70	65	55	60	50
Total	100	100	100	100	100

Although some change in the percentages may be due to editorial shifts in policy, what and how much policy has changed cannot be determined. Thus, speculation about the relationship of the occurrence of other events is offered below as partial explanation for the trends observed.

For the largest category, exhibition and awards, the decline in percentage of space may be indicative of the hiring of an architectural critic in the 1960s. No doubt the critic sought out and promoted a greater variety of stories and feature articles and did not simply report exhibitions and awards.

As for the second largest category — executed works and preservation — an increase in articles about preservation in the 1970s and 1980s certainly reflects an increased activity in this area in the nation as a whole. Additionally, the increase in reporting on unique buildings or developments most likely reflects an assumption that a better educated populace demands more detailed information on the built environment.

For the third category considered, the increase in the late 1970s in reporting on the 'professions and education' could reflect the many legal issues that became cogent at that time. Also increased reporting on university grants is probably responsible for more incidents of universities in the news.

The large number of articles on 'individuals and/or firms', the fourth category, in the 1970-75 period reflects, at least in part, the deaths of Neutra and Kahn and articles on Venturi and other prominent individuals. In contrast, the 1980-85 period shows an increased emphasis on articles on firms, perhaps an indicator of public relations capacities or perhaps a sign that professional practice issues, including the 'who's, who' of architecture, have become in vogue.

The Professional Press: Content

Of the categories reviewed in *The Art Index*, categories corresponding as closely as possible to those reviewed for *The New York Times*, news about the 'profession in general' has been consistently the largest category with a high of 43 per cent in the late 1960s tapering to 20 per cent in the early 1980s, as Table 5.3 illustrates. Further, on the average, practice is the second largest category, as could be expected for professional journals. Information about styles of architecture is the third largest followed by articles having a socio-political orientation, those featuring energy, and those with a reference to an associated discipline.

Some trends are apparent from the data presented in Table 5.3. Titles under the category of profession have diminished somewhat as titles under practice, a more specific focus, have increased. This trend may indicate that broader questions of research, education, and rôle conflicts are to some extent being replaced by questions of legal relations, client relations, and public relations, a speculation

Table 5.3: Content of Professional Journals

	1960-64 (N = 237) %	1965-69 (N = 235) %	1970-74 (N = 354) %	1975-79 (N = 448) %	1980-84 (N = 221) %
Profession[1]	30	43	32	26	20
Styles[2]	21	25	16	13	11
Socio-Political[3]	19	10	24	11	7
Environment/[4] Energy	1	2.5	3	16	25
Associated[5] Disciplines	8	8	7	11	4
Practice[6]	21	12	18	23	32
Total	100	100	100	100	100

1. (profession, criticism, education, research)

2. (modern, postmodern, vernacular, conservation/restoration)

3. (society, state, politics, capitalism, religion, and morals)

4. (climate, earthquakes, nature, environment, and energy usage)

5. (architecture and associated disciplines)

6. (client relations, ethics, legal status, public relations, drawing, and evaluation)

supported by the findings on specific issues reported later in this essay. Note also that titles under environment/energy steadily increased until the late 1970s and in the early 1980s showed a marked

Table 5.4:   Comparison of Aesthetic-Theory to Practice-Profession Themes by Popular-Professional Press, Five Year Intervals

	Popular Press Aesthetics-Theory[1]/ Practice-Profession[2]		Professional Press Aesthetics-Theory[3]/ Practice-Profession[4]	
	Number	Ratio	Number	Ratio
1960-64	43/34	1.3	110/121	0.9
1965-69	43/29	1.5	122/129	0.9
1970-74	56/36	1.6	172/177	1.0
1975-79	73/58	1.3	228/219	1.0
1980-84	96/56	1.7	125/115	1.1

[1]Style-aesthetics, factors influencing design, philosophy-values, preservation issues.
[2]Profession, professional societies, education, materials/methods and office practice.
[3]Style (modern, post modern, vernacular, conservation/restoration) environment/energy and socio-political values (philosophy, human factors, society, state)
[4]Professions (profession, education, criticism, research) and practice (client relations, ethics, legal, public relations, drawing, and evaluation)

increase, a trend to be expected since the professions would be committed to these themes by this time. Correspondingly, titles with a socio-political orientation peaked in the early 1970s at 24 per cent and taper to only 7 per cent in the early 1980s, a trend likely reflecting changes in value emphasis in society.

Comparisons: Popular/Professional Journals

Since different categories were used in the popular and professional press, and the total contents of *The Art Index* were not reviewed, direct comparisons of the percentage of pertinent themes across the two types of media are not appropriate. However, it was possible to make two general comparisons: the proportion of aesthetic/theory themes to those of practice/profession and the proportion of style themes to ones of human factors.

The balance or lack of it between themes of aesthetic/theory and practice/profession is a recurring debate in architectural education and was investigated in this survey to ascertain the relative prominence given theory or practice across the twenty-five year period and across the two media types. As Table 5.4 indicates, the proportion of aesthetic/theory themes to those of practice/profession for the popular and professional press has remained fairly constant from the 1960s through the 1980s. Although there is a slight tendency in both media toward increasingly favoring aesthetic-theory issues, the tendency is not strong. Note also that the professional press, of the two media types, favors slightly practice-professional articles, as indicated by the lower ratio. Again, the overall trend is only slightly different from the popular press. What is most striking is the balance between the two types of articles and the two types of media.

A second issue, which has already received attention in the press, is presented in Table 5.5: the question of emphasis on either style or human factors questions. Jack L. Nasar in a paper presented at EDRA 17 ('The Shaping of Design Values: Case Studies on the Trade Magazine') concluded in a review of trade magazines that when students are exposed to content emphasizing design they emphasize design solutions, but when exposed to human factor solutions, they emphasize solutions accommodating the human element. Thus, the relative proportion of themes of style versus human factor themes was investigated for the popular and professional press.

As Table 5.5 indicates, for the popular press over time, the ratio of style to human factors themes remained approximately the same through the 1960s and 1970s (1.0 to 1.5). However, a major jump in the early 1980s to 3.4 style themes to every human factor theme is evident in the popular press, perhaps reflecting a trend away from a human factors emphasis.

Table 5.5: Comparison of Style to Human Factor Themes by Popular-Professional Press, Five Year Intervals

	Popular Press Style[1]/Human Factors[2]		*Professional Press* Style[3]/Human Factors[4]	
	Number	Ratio	Number	Ratio
1960-64	20/13	1.5	50/45	1.1
1965-69	22/21	1.0	59/24	2.5
1970-74	28/28	1.0	57/85	0.7
1975-79	44/29	1.5	58/49	1.2
1980-84	74/22	3.4	24/16	1.5

[1]Style (architectural styles and preservation issues)
[2]Human factors (human factors, society and philosophy)
[3]Style (modern, postmodern, vernacular, conservation)
[4]Human factors (philosophy, human factors, society, state)

For the professional press, the ratio of style themes to human factors themes is more uneven with less emphasis on human factors in the late 1960s (2.5 style themes to one) and an increase of human factor themes over style themes in the early 1970s (0.7 style to every one human factor). In summary, the public has been exposed to a fairly balanced emphasis on both style and human factors in the popular press in all periods but the early 1980s. However, in the professional press, balance is shown in the early 1960s, late 1970s, and early 1980s, but a decided emphasis on style in the late 1960s and human factors in the early 1970s is apparent.

Issues in the Popular and Professional Press

To gain more depth in the type of content presented in the popular and professional press, issues concerning the profession, including descriptions of the general state of architecture, rôle of the architect, and themes on education were reviewed. Additionally, issues relating to architecture in society, including socio-economic trends and value changes were investigated. Both types of issues are compared below in Table 5.6 and in the text by decade. In addition, some specific design issues are mentioned for the popular press in concluding paragraphs although comparable information was not gathered for the professional press.

Table 5.6:   Selected Issues in the Press by Decade

The Profession

	Popular Press	*Professional Press*
1960s:	Need better aesthetics, standards.	Need for change in the profession.
	Women, blacks as architects.	What type of practice desirable?
	Rôle of architect questioned. Relationships with builders, public officials, business, students featured	What is responsible rôle? Relating to builders, students, business, interior designers, unions. Education: unique preparation needed
1970s:	Past buildings as measure of today's and emphasis on preservation	Concern for quality and plea for beyond monumentalism.
	Question shift from artist to technician.	Professional competency, project management, registration, licensing.
	Dual rôle of contractor/ architect featured.	Rôles of doer and researcher added. Relationships with interior designers, interdisciplinary teams.
	How to separate rôles of architect, environmentalists, planners.	Real world education.

	Women, blacks as architects.	Women, blacks as architects.
Early 1980s:	Debate at Skidmore; commercial design; worry over lack of quality. Continue themes of architect/ builder, women as architects. Critic added to relationships.	Ethics, question of aesthetic control. Continue practice emphasis. Question of unionizing. Rôle of corporate architect featured.

Architecture and Society

	Popular Press	*Professional Press*
1960s:	Urban crisis, assisting special groups, liability for design.	Cities and planning; human factors; economic themes.
1970s:	Continue social concerns themes; energy crisis appears. Economic questions stressed. Increase in legal issues.	Human user theme strong. Urban wanes, energy theme increases. Design for public buildings, specialized institutions strong. Legal and economic issues stronger.
1980s:	Higher emphasis on legal and economic issues.	Economic issues featured. Participation and new family housing mentioned.

Issues in the Profession

The 1960s

In the 1960s as illustrated in Table 5.6, prominent issues in the profession in the **popular press** as represented in *The New York Times Index* included six general articles lamenting current architecture and pleading for better aesthetics whereas five focused specifically on the need for better standards. Resistance to pop architecture, the corporate image of buildings, the future of architecture, and buildings' reflection of ethics also are noteworthy. An awareness of the makeup of the profession is also striking; women architects are mentioned in

1960 and the first Black firm to get a contract in New York City is noted in 1966.

The rôle of the architect is examined also in the popular press in articles concerning the question of rôle generality (profession or specialist; is a greater rôle for architects in society needed); content of the rôle (to include structural engineering or free-wheeling design; whether there is a need to value public service, and the need to re-vamp education).   In terms of architecture's relationship to other groups, specific issues involving four groups are noteworthy of mention: builders (architect and/or builder, not giving gratuities to building departments), public officials (indifference of to architecture); business (gap with architecture and the need of business co-operation); and students (described as seeing architecture as elitist or repressive).

A final professional issue noted in the 1960s is the use of technology. A focus on computers and design is a recurring theme. Other issues involved solar screens, acoustics and need of new techniques and technology.

As in the popular press, the **professional press** reflects a need for change in architecture in over ten titles, changes in both standards and design. However, in some contrast to the popular press, issues in the professional press are oriented more toward the practitioner. Issues involve, for example: where to practice (small town, city, international); type of practice (small, large, comprehensive); and management of practice (project analysis, training technicians, hardware, retirement accounts, and scientific method). Rôle content is seen as varied in the professional press from introspection (looking at self, pondering new rôle, what makes a good architect) to re-sponsibility to what and whom (public, profession, policy for beauty, creating of environment) to mythical ideals (how to be a giant). Some of the same groups to whom to relate that were present in the popular press recur: builders, students, and business. Different emphases include questions of relations with interior design, unions, and the debate over joint ventures. Although not as prevalent in the titles as the above categories, educational themes include unique preparation for unique professions as well as a theme of educating professionals.

The 1970s

In terms of an overall professional theme in the 1970s, the push for preservation in society is reflected in the **popular press** with more articles on that subject than any other. Following that emphasis, the theme of measuring today's buildings by the past also emerges. Some of the issues raised in *The New York Times* in this period about the profession are a continuation of 1960s themes — five articles address Blacks and architecture and four are on the status of women architects as noted in Table 5.6.

The rôle of the architect is again featured with questions raised about the shifting of architect from artist to technician and the changing responsibility of the architect. Reported also is an interesting shift in the profession's applauding of the dual rôle of the contractor/architect in the 1970s when the ethics of this dual rôle was questioned in the 1960s. Further, new group relationships also emerge in the questioning of where the line is drawn between architects, environmentalists, and planning professionals.

Whereas 'change' was a general theme in the **professional press** in the 1960s, titles from the 1970s indicate professional competency, challenge, and other entrepreneurial themes of the society itself in that period. Themes of future goals and the new generation are also part of the professional image while ethics, standards, and industrial architecture also receive much more prominence. More concern with project construction management, client relationships, and registration/licensing than with 1960s themes of where to practice is also apparent in the 1970s titles. Also in the 1970s, an emphasis on minorities and women appears, with seven articles under the professions on women and one on minorities.

As to rôles of the architect, the titles indicate additions of doer, theorist, visionary, and researcher to the architect's repertoire and also imply that the architect debate leading the public and whether an architect is a luxury or necessity. Additional groups to whom the architect of the 1970s is to relate include interior designers, interdisciplinary teams, and social scientists while new ways of organizing include participatory design. Educational issues indicate a shift from the emphasis on the uniqueness of the profession of the 1960s to an emphasis on 'real world' education and internships in the 1970s.

The 1980s

In the 1980s, the **popular press** includes awareness of preservation, questions of classicism and the debate at Skidmore on Post Modernism. Commercial design and worry over lack of quality also appear. Also women as architects and the architects/builders junction are mentioned. One additional group is singled out as part of the mosaic of relationships — the critic. The well-tailored professional is also part of the new image of the architect.

For the **professional press**, a view of the issues in the early 1980s indicates that, for the profession, six issues were concerned with economics, e.g., private commissions, lack of funding, and marketing. The usual emphasis on practice and the interesting question of whether architects should unionize were also noted. Rôle changes are particularly noteworthy in the move from the questioning of what should be the rôle for the architect in the 1970s to that of what the rôle of the corporate architect is in the 1980s.

In fact, two key articles in professional journals, one in 1975 and one in 1985, illustrate that another dimension of the architect's rôle is being addressed in the 1980s. A series of articles in the AIA Journal, September, 1975, features the debate on ethical standards related to advertising and contracting ('New Rôles and New Rules'), the difficulty of architects in combining the rigors of design and marketing demands ('Whatever the Future, Design Must Remain the Fundamental Skill'), and the adjustments different architects make to the demands of creativity versus authority ('Examining the Nature and Values of the Endangered Species Architect'). In contrast, one of the feature articles in 1985 in the *Architectural Record* examines the rôle of the corporate architect (Round Table, Architectural Record, January, 1985). In this article, questions on the changing rôle of the corporate architect include how corporations select architects, how corporate standards are applied, and to what degree management is involved in planning and design. Although the necessity of good design is still featured, the emphasis is on different issues, issues relating to better ways of structuring work, rather than to questions of ethical and rôle conflicts.

Architecture and Society

The 1960s

A second set of issues, the impact of societal questions on architecture, is revealed in the **popular press** themes dominant in the 1960s as shown in Table 5.6. The theme of 'urban crisis and architecture' recurs throughout the latter part of the decade in six separate articles as well as an emphasis on designing for special groups such as the handicapped. The need for a humanscape and a call for humanism also are mentioned. Legal issues of the decade focus on the Garrick theater case and liability of design and include five themes in all.

Societal/human factor themes are prominent in the **professional journals** in the 1960s also. Sixteen titles reflect this emphasis, including two on cities and planning, two on environment, and twelve on human factors and humanism. In contrast to the popular press, six articles in the societal category feature economic questions, themes appearing earlier and more consistently in the professional than popular press as indicated again in Table 5.6.

The 1970s

The **popular press's** articles on society in the 1970s show a continuation of the themes of social concerns (sharing blame for unliveable cities, human social values). However, two themes are added in the 1970s, concern for moral/spiritual life and the energy crisis. One expected emphasis of the 1970s, the stress placed on economic questions, is revealed in articles ranging from a concern with lack of employment to prediction of recovery. Further, the mid-1970s show a marked increase in legal issues, issues pertaining to malpractice, advertising and state licensing.

As for architecture and society in the **professional press**, sixteen titles in the categories reviewed address human user orientations whereas seven are oriented to social responsibility. Urban concerns are mentioned in two titles, environment in two, while energy concerns increase to six titles. More specific concerns of designing for particular institutions — prisons, hospitals, and areas used by the disabled — are mentioned. The theme of public buildings also is strong and is mentioned in five articles. Legal issues of codes of conduct, monopolies and advertising and economic ones of employment and growth policy appear frequently.

The 1980s

In the **popular press**, broader societal issues are somewhat displaced by legal and economic ones. Technological issues become more sophisticated, as evidenced by an article pleading for the need for cases for systematic research to learn from mistakes.

For the **professional press**, broader societal issues revealed that four articles were particularly descriptive of the professional journals' emphasis in the 1980s. The titles include references to a continuing note on participation, new family concepts yielding new housing types, the question of responsiveness to human needs, and a question of retreat into narcissism as well as a continuing emphasis on economics.

A Note on Specific Design Questions in Popular Press

In reviewing articles concerning the profession and society in the popular press, certain design issues also became apparent for the 1960s and 1970s. Although comparable information was not gathered from the professional press, the issues are mentioned briefly below.

In the 1960s in the popular press, specific issues center on the Bauhaus, megastructures, the glass box, concrete intrusion, ceramic tiles, steel as aesthetic, Victorian revival, iron works, and supermannerism. Interestingly enough, features on places are almost equally divided between the USA and foreign countries with New York, as could be expected, the most often featured place.

Specific issues highlighted in the 1970s are the demise of monumentalism, concern over mediocrity, style versus antistyle, critiques by and of Venturi, architecture of fantasy parks, public spaces, underground architecture, and appeals for form, not radicalization nor technology. Again a balance of places covered between the USA and other countries is found.

Summary

The four basic questions noted at the beginning of the chapter have been the guide for this work. In answer to the first (are articles of an opinion or reporting nature in the popular press?), the findings revealed that in four of the five-year periods reporting outweighed opinion by approximately seven to four. Additionally, over the last 25 years the public was exposed to substantially more opinions by persons who were not identified as professional architectural critics than those who were identified as critics.

Information related to the second guiding question, the type and frequency of selected issues in the popular press, indicated that the category of exhibitions, awards, and publications has consistently been the most favored, with articles on executed works being next in coverage. The other two categories, individuals and firms and professions and education, make up smaller percentages.

In addressing the third concern, investigation of the contents of the professional press in the categories comparable to those reviewed in the popular press revealed that news about the 'profession in general' has been consistently the largest category. Following in respective order were the categories of practice, styles of architecture, sociopolitical orientation, those articles featuring energy, and those with a reference to an associated discipline.

Finally, comparison of the trends and changes in the popular and professional press indicates both similarities and differences. As noted earlier, both the popular and professional press show a remarkable balance between aesthetic/theory themes and those of practice/profession. Also, both reflect a fairly balanced emphasis on style themes versus human factor themes with some exceptions. The most notable exception was the early 1980s preference in the popular press for style themes over human factor ones, a condition that could signal a trend in emphasis. Additionally, both reflect in varying degrees changes in societal issues — the urban crisis and human factors focus in the 1960s and early 1970s, the energy concern in the 1970s, and responses to legal and economic changes in the late 1970s and early 1980s. Thus, as expected, both types of media are to some degree driven by societal trends and are to some extent reactive to external stimuli.

However, differences between the two media types do exist. Each indicates an awareness of its own audience with the popular press emphasizing reviews of exhibitions and awards and feature stories on specific buildings and neighborhoods, items that keep the more general reader informed. On the other hand, the titles in the professional press reveal that media's concern for issues professionals face — where to practice, how to manage, how to educate, and how to retain a share of the market. Thus, each type of media is to some extent driven by recognition of its own audience. Each, therefore, is reactive and proactive.

Similarities and differences also exist in the issues raised and the image of the profession portrayed by those issues. Both the popular and professional press stressed in the 1960s the need for change and better standards and both in the 1970s reflected a trend away from monumentalism. Likewise, in the 1980s, a theme shared in common is concern over lack of quality.

Striking also in both media types is the chronicling of the expansion of the architect's rôle. An expansion occurs in what is to be done — not only design, but research, project management, contracting, and corporate liaison — and to whom one relates — business, builders, interior designers, unions, planners, and social scientists. Incongruity of rôles must accompany this expansion of what the architect should be as is evidenced by the continuing questions, particularly in the professional press, on what the rôle entails.

Some differences in the issues highlighted do exist. Timing of appearance of similar or the same issues vary in the two media types. Some long-standing issues in architecture, e.g. historic preservation, appear earlier and more consistently in the professional press than in the popular press, while many issues concerning architecture in society, e.g. women and minorities as architects or the urban crisis, quite often receive attention first in the popular press. In contrast, as could be expected, issues raised in the professional press more strongly and much more often, included emphasis on type and location of practice, the legal and economic state of the profession, and designing for specific populations.

Finally, then, this overview of the content and issues of both *The New York Times Index* and the entries from the four professional journals in *The Art Index* reveal the profession's growth and the strains associated with that growth. As Kaye (1960) predicted in his essay on architecture, concern over routinization and technological changes in building methods did indeed become an issue in the last twenty-five years. Concurrently, an expansion of the architect's rôles into management and public relations also occurred. These two events may signal that one reaction of architects to standardization of some of their work is the seeking of management rôles, rôles where risk-taking and solving uncertain tasks are more pervasive. Such a reaction to standardization in other professions has been observed by Toren (1975). Additionally, of course, the rôle expansion is related to the scope of projects corporations undertake and to the consolidation of many services within architectural offices.

Although the focus of this essay was an overview and the specific nature of criticism was not addressed, some insight was gained into that current and growing debate described earlier among critics, editors, and architects. The review of the issues indicated that critics, a more informed public, social scientists, unions, corporate managers, and planners are now part of the design process and that the need to design as part of the environment, not in isolation, has become a pervasive theme. Thus, the issues of the last twenty-five years indicate a broadening of not only who can be an architect, but of who has claim to criticize the architect. This inclusion, intrusion, and increasing legitimacy of the critics — both professional and amateur — have had, and will continue to have, their place in the building of the environment. Turning inward, then, is only possible for the architect of the 1990s as he or she also turns outward — resulting in perhaps some bewilderment, some exhilaration — as the profession dances to both inner and outer tunes. The pitfalls and pleasures that the dance brings, of course, will be recorded, sometimes to the profession's delight and sometimes to its chagrin, both in the popular and professional press.

Notes

1. We wish to express appreciation to Karen Lee Jamison and Whit Watts for assistance in data collection and for discussion of ideas about the paper. Thanks also to Charles J. Dudley for reading an earlier draft.

2. Text analysis in architecture has included a range of studies and techniques. A review of the literature on text analysis in architecture by Juan Pablo Bonta (1985) reveals that analysis has spanned study of one period or style and treatises on the entire literature of art, architecture, and planning. Included in Bonta's review are the following: Hersey, 1972; Wolfe, 1975; Boudon, 1969; Jencks and Baird, 1969; Holschneider, 1969; Frankl, 1960; Gritti, Jules, 1967; Eco, 1971; Choay, 1965; and Moore and Oliver, 1977. Further, Bonta notes that the work has been prescriptive and descriptive as well as quantitative and structural. Texts analyzed have included both scholarly texts and other forms of communication as well as users' reactions. Also, the study of design has included both real designs and ideal ones.

3. *The Architectural Forum* ceased publication in March, 1974. Entries from 1960 to that date were included.

References

Anon. 'Examining the Nature and Values of the Endangered Species Architect,' (1975) *AIA Journal*, September, 22-25.

Architect's, the Critic's, Public's View of the Media (1984) *Architecture*, June, 15-16.

The Art Index, (1960-1984) New York: H.W. Wilson.

Bonta, Juan Pablo (1985) *Architecture and Its Interpretation: A Study of Expressive Systems in Architecture*, New York: Rizzoli.

Boudon, Phillippe (1969) *Pessac de Le Corbusier*, Paris: Dunod.

Choay, Françoise (1965) *L'urbanisme. Utopies et realités*, Paris: du Seuil.

Eco, Umberto (1971) A Semiotic Approach to Semantics, *Quaderni di Studi Semiotici*, 1, 21-60.

Filler, Martin (1985) Critics on Criticism, *Metropolis*, November, 28-41.

Frankl, Paul (1960) *The Gothic: Literary Sources and Interpretations Through Eight Centuries*, Princeton, N.J.: Princeton University Press.

Gallagher, Neil E. (1965) Why Is The Press Sometimes Wary? *AIA Journal*, September, 41-42.

Gritti, Jules (1967) Les Contenus Culturels du Guide Bleu: monuments et sites ' à voir', *Communications*, 10, 51-64.

Hersey, George L. (1972) *High Victorian Gothic: A Study In Associationism*, Baltimore and London: The John Hopkins University Press.

Holschneider, Johannes (1969) *Schlüsselbegriffe der Architektur und Stadbaukunst. Eine Bedeutungsanalyse*, Quickborn: Schnelle.

Jencks, Charles and George Baird (eds.) (1969) *Meaning In Architecture*, London: Barrie and Rockliff, The Cresset Press.

Kaye, B. (1960) *The Development of the Architectural Profession in Britain*, Barnes Books, London.

Kuhn, Ferdinand. (1968) Blighted Areas of Our Press, *AIA Journal*, October, pp.55-58.

Media To Architects: We Are Not In The Public Relations Business But In The Business of Representing The Public (1984) *F.W. Dodge Construction News*.

Moore, Charles W. and Richard B. Oliver (1977) Magic, Nostalgia and A Hint of Greatness in the Workaday World of the Building Types Study, *Architectural Record*, 118-37.

Nasar, Jack L. (1986) The Shaping of Design Values: Case Studies on the Trade Magazine, paper presented at EDRA 17.

New Roles and New Rules (1975) *AIA Journal*, September, 17-18.

The New York Times Index, (1960-1984) New York: New York Times Co.

Round Table: The Fast-Growing and Fast-Changing Role of the Corporate Architect (1985) *Architectural Record*, January, 35-47.

Toren, Nina (1975) Deprofessionalization and its Sources, *Sociology of Work and Occupations*, 2, 111-123.

Whatever the Future, Design Must Remain The Fundamental Skill (1975) *AIA Journal*, September, 19-21.

Chapter 6

Where Architects Work:
A Change Analysis, 1970-80

Judith R. Blau

The question posed here is: what best accounts for prevailing patterns of architectural activity in urban places in the United States and changes in that activity between 1970 and 1980? Specifically, the extent of architectural activity in 1980 (indicated by the number of architects per capita for the largest 125 U.S. metropolitan places) is explained by conditions in those places in 1970 and changes in conditions between 1970 and 1980, controlling for the numbers of architects per capita in 1970. In addition, comparisons of changes in architectural activity with changes in the distribution of cultural institutions and in artists' labor market patterns permit some inferences about markets for culture, broadly defined.

There have been several efforts to ascertain trends in architectural employment (Gutman and Westergaard, n.d.; Montgomery, 1985; Larson et al., 1983); however, the attempt is made here to put the problem in comparative perspective by contrasting the conditions of growth in architectural activities with those of growth in the numbers of artists per capita and numbers of cultural establishments. Detailed data extracted from the 1970 and 1980 censuses of population and combined with data from other sources makes it possible to test specific hypotheses about the effects of socio-demographic and economic characteristics of metropolitan places on the relative numbers of architects in 1970 and 1980.

Montgomery (1985) describes long-term historical trends for practicing architects using unpublished historical data collected by Gutman and Westergaard (n.d.) as well as the more current population surveys. During the nineteenth century there was a long but uneven rise in the number of architects relative to the population, reaching a peak just after the turn of the century at nearly 4 architects per 10,000 population. After a brief upswing during the 1920s there was a general decline from 1910 to 1960, followed by a tremendous growth in the 1960s with the improving economic conditions of the nation as a whole. In spite of the recession during the 1970s, which had a particularly strong impact on the construction and building industry, the number of architects per capita was nearly 6.5 per 10,000 urban population by 1980, which represents an increase of about 250 per cent between 1960 and 1980. That relative increase is far more than that for either lawyers, engineers, or physicians over the same two decades.

In interpreting these changes, Montgomery and others have tended to emphasize the relative importance of the manufacturing base, construction activity, affluent clients, and the corporate sector. For example, Stanback et al. (1981), noting the continuing growth of architecture in spite of declines in construction, suggest that construction activities, when in a state of decline, paradoxically require an increase of architectural services, implying a need for higher quality design. Drawing on census figures for 1960, 1970, and 1980, Montgomery speculates about the possibility of basic antagonisms between manufacturing-based local economies and high levels of architecture employment. A main point made by Larson et al. (1983) in discussing the implications of their study of AIA firms is that professional architects, like physicians and lawyers, tend to concentrate where a wealthy or 'interesting' clientele can be found, although as their data suggest, this affinity to an interesting or an affluent clientele is best exploited by the most élite design firms and not by rank and file architectural practices.

What is a proper basis of comparison for architects? For its occupational classification scheme, the Bureau of the Census lists architects with artists but for the business establishment classification, the Bureau joins architects and engineers. There are other plausible comparisons of architects as well: with lawyers or physicians, or with other professions whose members provide services to clients. However, Cullen (1983) concludes that architecture is quite unlike the other major professions when examined on criteria traditionally associated with dimensions of professional work, including prestige, complexity of work with people, median education, and licensure requirements. Because of its strong artistic component, architecture does not conform to the patterns of occupations that are based on codified knowledge.

While it is true that many architects work in highly specialized or in very technical areas, my own investigation (Blau, 1984) of over 400 architects indicates a strong identification with work that is artistic or creative. Of those surveyed, 98 percent mentioned creativity as the distinctive feature of the architectural profession when compared with other professions, and when asked what, if anything, they would like to change in their work and responsibilities, 80 percent mentioned they wanted even more opportunities for creative challenges — to have more design assignments, to be able to work autonomously, and, especially, to have a greater rôle in the initial design stage of a project. For these reasons, it is interesting to compare architects with artists to see if the occupational rôles and spheres of work are similar enough that locational patterns and changes in those patterns resemble one another through the decade between 1970 and 1980.

A theoretical here interest centers on social and economic inequalities, precisely for the reason that both architecture and the arts have traditionally depended on small élites for patronage and that, according to Bourdieu (1984), the arts continue to depend on affluent audiences, consumers, and commissioners. Art as 'cultural capital', legitimizes élite position, maintains symbolic boundaries between a small affluent minority and others, and helps members of the middle class to stake claims for positions in higher classes.

Extensive analysis reveals that the social class composition of the city is especially important for explaining the prevalence of artists (J. Blau et al., 1985), the existence of art institutions at one point in time, and changes in them over time (J. Blau, 1986; P. Blau et al.,

1986). Further unpublished analyses reveal the importance of social class in a longitudinal study of artists. What is important about the social class composition of urban places is not, as it turns out, captured by any specific indicator of affluence, or education, or occupation; rather, *inequalities* with respect to all of these are significant. Moreover, as will be described, while social class inequalities have important consequences for both art institutions and the relative numbers of artists, these consequences are quite different for institutions and artists, and the findings for architects reveal greater similarities to those for cultural institutions than to those for artists. To anticipate the conclusions, there is evidence that architectural services have markets that are more like the markets for cultural establishments — such as art museums, theaters, dance companies, and craft fairs — than the markets for the services of footloose artists.

Research Procedures

One part of the analysis reported here[1] is based on comparisons of the (*per capita*) numbers of architects, of nonperforming artists (painters, sculptors, writers, and designers) and of performing artists (dancers, musicians, and actors) in 1970 and 1980; another part of the comparison examines the numbers of cultural institutions for the early 1970s and, when possible, also for the early 1980s. The unit of analysis is the Standard Metropolitan Statistical Area (SMSA), and under consideration are the 125 largest of them in the United States, specifically those that had a population of more than 250,000 in 1970. These 125 SMSAs include approximately two thirds of the U.S. population, and, undoubtedly, an even greater percentage of all U.S. artists, architects, and art institutions.

The main data source for the 1970 independent variables is the one-in-one-hundred public use sample of U.S. Census from which the 15 per cent county-group file was used to extract relevant information for all persons who lived in these SMSAs. The information on individuals was then aggregated at the SMSA level for the purpose of computing summary measures, such as an SMSA's median education or earnings and its age or ethnic composition. The source of the 1980 data is the 100 per cent census summary tape from which county level data were extracted to reconstitute SMSAs with boundaries that correspond to 1970 SMSA geographical boundaries and to compute aggregate measures comparable to those computed for 1970.

The population characteristic that is of greatest theoretical importance is the social class composition of urban places, specifically, the extent to which there is much or little inequality with respect to income, education, and occupational standing. The conventional index of social class that is used in much quantitative research is the socio-economic index (SEI) that was developed by Duncan (1961) and updated with 1970 occupations by Hauser and Featherman (1976). The principle involved in the computation of SEI scores for individuals is that specific occupations are assigned weights based on regression equations that include occupational prestige, the average earnings in an occupation, and the mean education of its members. Thus, SEI captures the three components that we conventionally consider to be indicators of social class — the occupation in which the person works with occupations ranked by education, income, and reputation; these are also the personal resources that underlie many differences in life styles, neighborhoods, housing characteristics, and leisure activities. For the purpose of this analysis, aggregation at the SMSA level was carried out for major occupations to create summary SEI scores for each SMSA.

The mean or median SEI score is a reliable indicator of social class for the metropolitan place. For example, median SEI is positively related to median income ($r = .44$) and to median education ($r = .56$). However, the theoretical interest in the literature on culture focuses not on indicators of central tendency of affluence, education, or of social class, but rather on indicators of their dispersion, which indicates more or less inequality of various sorts in a metropolis.

One main theoretical conceptualization of the relationship of social class and culture emphasizes the importance of class divisions and also of a small élite. For example, Bourdieu (1984) contends that as groups attempt to define their distinctive upper-class positions they do so symbolically, through their tastes for art and music and their display of cultural possessions. As 'cultural capital', art affirms social class position or assists in establishing a foothold in the upper class. In this way, class inequalities help to establish the value of high culture; but high culture, in turn, serves to maintain class inequalities. This argument was anticipated by Veblen (1953) and, indeed, has considerable support in the historical research on patronage of art prior to the mid-19th century (Di Maggio, 1982; Miller, 1966).

Bourdieu's analysis is grounded in observations of the demand for culture, but quite different conclusions are reached when it is the supply of culture that is being considered. It is plausible that much inequality in social classes fragments contemporary markets for the supply of cultural products and that, rather than promoting competition, precludes the emergence of a critical mass that is necessary to maintain cultural activities and institutions, at least on any scale. This argument accepts the premise that traditional culture depended on the reliable support of a small élite, but posits that contemporary patrons are neither reliable enough nor numerous enough to explain the supply of culture on a metropolitan or national level. This is consistent with the views of Raymond Williams (1961), who argues that one aspect of the 'long revolution' is the democratization of culture, and it is also consistent with the scholarship of cultural historians who fix their attention on developments in high culture in the nineteenth and twentieth century (see Hall, 1984; Trachtenberg, 1982).

The measure of inequality of social class used here is the Gini coefficient computed for each SMSA's distribution of the SEI index. The Gini coefficient can be intuitively understood as the average difference between all possible pairs of individuals in the SMSA with respect to their SEI scores.[2] Empirically, *little* inequality in SEI means that the place has a *high* overall score with respect to its mean or its median SEI score. For example, the correlation between the median value on the Duncan SEI and the Duncan SEI Gini is -.79, indicating that a place that has relatively much inequality is also a place with a population that is relatively prosperous, well-educated, with disproportionately many in white collar and professional occupations.

The sources of information on architects and artists are the public use samples for 1970 and 1980 prepared by the U.S. Census from the 5 per cent and 15 per cent county group files. There were minor changes in the definitions of the categories for architects and artists between the dicennial censuses; for example, directors were added to the category of actors, and window dressers were added to the category of designers. To test whether these changes would have systematic effects on the results, all analyses reported here were carried out after removing outliers on absolute difference scores (1980 minus 1970) for both artists and architects. It was concluded that these minor changes in the definitions for architects and artists for 1970 and 1980 have no systematic effects on any of the results.

Results for Artists

Many of the structural conditions of metropolitan places in 1970 were found to have parallel influences on the *per capita* number of performing artists and nonperforming artists (J. Blau et al., 1985). For example, in 1970 both performers tended to live and work in large places and also in places where there were great disparities in income (as measured by the Gini coefficient of family income). This cross-sectional analysis also indicated that inequalities in social class, as measured by the SEI Gini, have contemporaneous positive effects on performers but contemporaneous negative effects on nonperformers. The interpretation for these results is that socioeconomic inequality increases and diversifies class differences in public tastes and thus enlarges the demand for the performing arts, whereas nonperforming artists are not affected by this demand since they are not constrained to live in the same places as their audiences and consumers.[3]

However, the analysis over time demonstrates the increasing importance of social class inequalities for nonperformers, as their residential patterns in 1980 are a positive function of the lagged effect of 1970 SEI inequalities and an increase in SEI inequalities as well.[4] One interpretation for these results is that artists generally are attracted to places where there are substantial numbers of poor and of poor neighborhoods — where they can live — and also where there is a high concentration of capital, wealth, well-educated people, and, in general, opportunities for selling cultural labor or cultural products. A somewhat different interpretation of these findings can be cast along the lines of Bourdieu's (1984) theory, namely, that much inequality in socioeconomic status entails great differences in cultural orientations that in turn help to define and reinforce class boundaries. Thus, a pluralistic class structure, according to this theory, accompanies competing and heightening demands for art. This is what makes an urban place attractive to artists of all kinds.

Results for Cultural Institutions

In contrast with the findings that great social inequalities provide opportunities for artists and characterize urban places that are congenial for artists to live and to work, cultural establishments are found to be more numerous in SMSAs where there was relatively little inequality in 1970 (J. Blau, 1986b; P. Blau et al., 1986). Using the identical measure of SEI inequality, the results demonstrate that even after controlling for all metropolitan conditions that influence the numbers of institutions, little social inequality in 1970 is related to the numbers of museums (Rauschenbusch, 1971/72), theaters (U.S. Bureau of the Census, 1972a) dance companies and ballet companies (*Dance Magazine Annual*, 1974), art galleries (Rauschenbusch, 1971/72), theater premiers (Fowle, 1976), craft fairs (American Craft Council, 1971, 1972, 1973), and popular concerts (*Rolling Stone Magazine*, 1975).[5] This suggests that the supply of culture on a relatively large scale, that is, at the institutional level, is governed by a high and uniform demand exerted by a large middle and upper-middle class rather than by a differentiated demand exerted by a multitude of taste groups, each of whose interest is to establish a distinctive class identity but, more importantly, a distinctively high-brow class identity.

Over a ten-year period, institutions do not increase dramatically in sheer numbers because it takes years to plan and to construct, say, a facility for a museum, or even to organize a theater company. Yet, some change in the numbers of most small institutions did occur and most change can be explained by the initial number of institutions of that type and by the size of the metropolitan place in 1970. Yet the results also show that what plays a rôle in accounting for an increase in the numbers of some particular types of institutions (notably dance companies, and ballet companies) is a decline in the level of socioeconomic inequality (P. Blau et al., 1986).[6] Thus, for most types of cultural institutions a major predictor of their early prevalence is little inequality and a predictor for the growth of some of them is a further decline in inequality.

In sum, the results indicate that inequality promotes the concentration of artists whereas it impairs the development of institutionalized art. These contradictory findings for artists and for art institutions provide the context for the analysis of architectural activity. It is measured, as it is for artists, by self-reports of individuals' occupations in the census. It is assumed that the relative number of architects is a superior indicator of architectural practice in general since architects are closely tied to work organizations, certainly more so than artists are.

Results for Architects, 1970

Besides considering a variety of characteristics of the urban government (such as revenues *per capita*), of the economic base (median firm size, percent of workers in manufacturing), and population characteristics (family income, occupational diversity), direct indications of market demands for architectural services were examined, such as characteristics of the housing stock and construction activities. The results of the empirical analysis failed to confirm many suppositions about the locational patterns of architects. For example, the notion that architects are concentrated in particular regions of the country is misleading. While it is the case that there were fewer architects relative to population size in the East in 1970, regional differences in 1970 are not large enough to be statistically significant, which is consistent with results reported for many cultural indicators (see Horowitz, 1986; Blau, 1986b). Although there is a positive correlation of .18 between architects *per capita* in 1970 and the proportion of the urban labor market engaged in construction in 1970, this relationship disappears once population size is taken into account.

Furthermore, although one might suppose that urban places with much need of renovation and construction would attract architects, there is a trivial correlation between the percent dilapidated housing (U.S. Bureau of the Census, 1971a) and the relative number of architects.

It has often been observed, with some bewilderment, that architectural practice does not respond in obvious ways to market forces or to building and construction activity (for example, Osman, 1975), and this is confirmed in this analysis. There is some modest support, however, for the position that there are basic antagonisms between manufacturing and architecture (Montgomery, 1985). There is a negative correlation of -.26 between the percent of the work force engaged in manufacturing and the indicator of architectural activity, but this relation is spurious once population size is taken into account.

Recognizing that architecture is often tied to large-scale institutions, such as corporations and local and state governments, further analysis was carried out to test whether or not architects' residential patterns in 1970 reflected dependencies on institutions such as these. However, all indicators of the urban presence of such institutions for which data are available, such as the number of firms in the SMSA, median firm size (U.S. Bureau of the Census, 1972b), *per capita* expenditures of urban governments, and governmental revenues (U.S. Bureau of the Census, 1971b) are all unrelated to the 1970 *per capita* measure of architects. (Of course, some of the simple correlations are nontrivial, but once population size is taken into account they become insignificant.)

The most important variable in these exploratory analyses for 1970 is SEI inequality (though it is not quite significant at the .05 level in the regression analysis). The results tentatively suggest that the less the inequality in social class the greater the relative number of architects.[7] While this contradicts the finding for artists, it is not inconsistent with the cross-sectional and longitudinal results for cultural institutions.

Change Analysis for Architects

To examine what accounts for change in the relative numbers of architects, the strategy used here is to regress on the *per capita* number of architects in 1980 the *per capita* number of architects in 1970, the 1970 predictors of 1970 architects *per capita*, and the difference between the level of each 1980 factor and its 1970 counterpart. This equation provides an estimate of how the changes in conditions between 1970 and 1980 and the initial levels of those conditions influence change in the relative numbers of architects between 1970 and 1980. At the same time, it partitions out the stability factor by holding constant the residential patterns of architects in 1970. Before summarizing these results, a brief comment is in order to demonstrate why it is easier to account for the expansion in the number of artists than for the change in either the numbers of architects or the numbers of institutions. The architectural labor supply is far more stable than that of artists as indicated by a correlation of .90 for architects *per capita* in 1970 and in 1980 in contrast with correlations of .48 for performing artists and .67 for nonperforming artists. Institutions exhibit stabilities similar to those for the labor supply of architects, with correlations for the 1970 and 1980 data for museums of .90, for dance companies of .81, and cinemas, .91. In this sense, a comparison of artists and architects is misleading since artists are far more mobile than architects and increase numerically at a rate far greater than do architects. The increase of architects over this ten year interval is far better predicted by locational inertia than by other factors having to do with markets, alternative locational advantages, urban growth, or changes in the population composition.

Still, some places experience an increase in the numbers of architects relative to the population size. These places include Trenton, Chatanooga, Fort Wayne, Rockford, Duluth, Jackson, Beaumont-Port Arthur, and Tacoma. Places with relative declines in the relative numbers of architects between 1970 and 1980 include Tucson, Appleton, Toledo, Greenville, Richmond, and Binghamton. Clearly, these examples do not suggest any regional effect was operating between 1970 and 1980, and the statistical analysis further indicates that region plays no significant rôle in accounting for change over time, contrary to speculation that the Sunbelt cities were extremely successful in attracting architects during that decade.

The results show that places that were very large in population size in 1970 lost a disproportionate share of architects, and independent of this, places that have experienced little increase or declines in their population size since 1970 have had relative gains in their share of architects.[8] In interpreting these results it should be kept in mind that the 'bread and butter' work of the typical architectural firm is housing and relatively small projects for private business establishments (Larson *et al.*, 1983), and since small and medium size metropolitan areas offer superior opportunities for work of this kind it is likely that such areas are attractive to architects. Why architects increase in relative numbers in places that are not growing or declining in size is more difficult to answer, but it appears that this is the result of the continuing attraction of traditional enclaves for design activities, such as places like Boston, Philadelphia, and New York City, that continue to provide a stimulating environment for architects and opportunities for unusual commissions.

Of greater interest, theoretically, is that increases in the relative number of architects is negatively related to the Gini coefficient of socio-economic inequality. That is, architectural activity expands over time in places with increasingly fewer numbers of the population who are either very rich or very poor, and correspondingly with an increasingly large middle class of many persons who are relatively well-off and well-educated. An expanding white-collar professional and service sector is one of the best predictors of the growth of architectural services during the decade, suggesting that the market for architectural services is more similar to the demand for institutionalized culture than for the services of cultural workers.

Discussion

These findings on the supply of cultural institutions and the labor markets of cultural workers offer an opportunity to address a broader question dealing with demand/supply issues relating to cultural products in capitalist societies. Even though the inferences are necessarily speculative and broad, the strong and persisting influence of a factor that measures the degree of class inequalities suggests that it may be the most important factor in explaining the supply of culture and the nature of cultural labor markets. Besides, the concept of socio-economic inequalities or class composition has been central in theories of art and culture.

Both in mass culture theory (Bensman and Rosenberg, 1963; Shils, 1978; Macdonald, 1957; Lowenthal, 1961) and in critical theory (Adorno, 1941; 1985; Horkheimer, 1941), the emphasis has been on the link between a mass or homogeneous class structure and mundane or even banal cultural products. While there are differences in assumptions that underlie mass culture theory and critical theory, the conclusions drawn concerning a homogeneous market and a qualitatively inferior supply are similar. The demand for art and culture is created by members of a vast middle class, and the supply for culture is provided through mass production. This process results in the deterioration of aesthetic standards, and in the proliferation of cultural products that offer spurious, not genuine, gratification. Perhaps this general theory of the increasing homogenization of markets and products is best summarized by Marcuse (1967) who observes that the expansion of mass culture is the sweep of what *is* over what *ought to be*, the sweep of ordinary civilization over culture. While this approach leads to an aesthetic and normative judgement of contemporary culture, it also offers an explanation, namely that the disintegration of class differences spells the decline and homogenization of art and culture.

In contrast, Raymond Williams (1981) contends that an extension of literacy and the relatively widespread affluence that accompanied the development of post-capitalist society resulted in a rich and variegated cultural tradition, in turn implying that little social-class inequality generates a demand for differentiated cultural products. Bourdieu's (1984) position is very different from all of these, as he asserts that both subtle and prominent differences in social class persist and that high culture is still in demand since it provides a meaningful symbol of membership in the upper class, or pretensions to such membership. The empirical results for artists tend to lend support to Bourdieu's theory since they indicate that the best labor markets for artists are in places where there is much inequality in education, income, and occupational attainments. These are places with a variegated class structure, that is, with extremes of rich and poor. Inequalities thus account for geographical concentrations of artists in 1970 and also for increasing concentrations of artists by 1980.

However, artists are only weakly tied to their products; a New York painter can place his or her works in a Los Angeles art gallery and a novelist can, and usually does, communicate with publishers by phone or letter. This suggests that the supply of artists is a poor indicator of the demand for art products.

Architects, compared with artists, are quite closely tied to clients, their products, and to local markets for their services. Therefore, it is not surprising that the empirical results for architects' labor markets are similar to the results for cultural institutions, including theaters, museums, dance companies, and craft fairs. These results are remarkably consistent, as they all tend to indicate that the supply of culture depends on little social class inequality, or, to use the terms of mass culture theory and critical theory, of a homogeneous class structure that is closely defined by a substantial middle class. These conclusions are consistent with the assumptions of mass culturalists and critical theorists concerning the demand side of culture, and they are also consistent with Raymond Williams' position. There is, on the other hand, little empirical support, except for the findings on artists, for Bourdieu's conclusions about the importance of class differentiation or the rôle played by economic and social elites in generating a demand for art.

It is primarily on normative grounds that Williams' position differs from the more pessimistic one taken by critical theorists and the mass culturalists, and it is perhaps only on normative or philosophical grounds that these differences can be resolved. Nevertheless, the evidence from this research supports Williams. If supply over a short period of time is indicative of general trends, it appears that high culture is doing quite well, and so is esoteric high culture. For example, there has been no decline in the number of chamber ensembles that play contemporary, experimental music (American Music

rather dramatically over the ten year period. While perhaps these are not extremely sensitive measures of public taste, they do suggest that there is a sufficient critical mass in American cities to support experimental high culture as well as more traditional forms of high culture. More importantly, this critical mass is defined as a broad based public sector — not a wealthy élite.

Notes

1. This research was supported by the National Science Foundation (grants SES-8319074 and SES-8320420). The data on architects and artists were provided by the Research Division of the National Endowment for the Arts; I am grateful for institutional support to the Sociology Department of The State University of New York at Albany and the Center for the Social Sciences of Columbia University. Gail A. Quets and Reid M. Golden deserve special acknowledgement for coordinating computer analyses carried out at the separate universities.

2. SEI scores were computed for detailed occupations for 1970, but the 1980 100% census only categorizes individuals by the 12 major occupational categories. Therefore, to ensure comparability, detailed occupations for both 1970 and 1980 were assigned SEI scores and weighted by national frequencies to obtain SEI scores for major occupations from which SMSA Gini coefficients were computed. This procedure yielded highly reliable estimates; the correlation between the SEI Gini for detailed occupations and the SEI Gini for major occupational categories for 1970 is .96. More generally, all change analyses are based on variables with identical categories and with SMSAs defined by the same geographical boundaries.

3. The beta weight for SEI inequality for performers is .35; for nonperformers it is -.47. The other variables in the two equations are: income inequality; educational inequality; occupational diversity; log population size; population change 1970-80; per cent manufacturing; region (dummy variable).

versity; log population size; population change 1970-80; percent manufacturing; region (dummy variable).

4. In formal terms the change model is illustrated by the following equation with V and Z defined as exogenous variables:

$$Y_2 = a + bY_1 + bV_1 + bZ_2 + b(V_2 - V_1) + b(Z_2 - Z_1) + U$$

For performers the beta weights for the 1970 SEI Gini coefficient and the 1980 minus 1970 SEI Gini coefficients are, respectively, .13 and .16. For nonperformers these values are .51 and .19. The other variables in the two equations are: 1970 income inequality; 1970 occupational diversity; percent manufacturing; log population size; 1970 level, performers or nonperformers; region (dummy variable); population change, 1970-80; and, 1980 minus 1970 levels on income inequality, occupational diversity, and percent manufacturing.

5. In regression equations the beta weights for SEI inequality are: museums (-.29), theaters (-.13), dance companies (-.23), ballet companies (-.30), art galleries (-.17), theater premiers (-.20), craft fairs (-.24), popular concerts (-.22). These are all significant at the .05 level at least. Although the other variables in the equations are not identical the log of population size is always controlled.

6. The beta weights are significant (.05 level) for the difference between 1980 SEI Gini and 1970 SEI Gini for: dance companies (-.12) and ballet (-.20). Significant negative effects of the lagged SEI Gini are also evident for dance companies, ballet, and craft fairs. For sources see American Craft Council, 1981, 1982, 1983; *Dance Magazine Annual*, 1983.

7. The only variable found to be related to 1970 per capita architects under statistical controls is SEI Gini. For example, in the regression that includes family income Gini, education Gini, occupational diversity, percent manufacturing, region (dummy), population change 1960-70, and log of population size, the beta for SEI Gini -.25, which is significant at the .07 level.

8. See note 6 for the 1970 variables included in the equation. The only significant influences (at the .05 level, with beta's reported in parentheses) are: architects per capita, 1970 (.92); log population size (-.09); population change 1970-80 (-.22); and difference SEI Gini, 1980-1970 (-.12). The adjusted R^2 is .84.

References

Adorno, T.W. (1941) On popular music, *Studies in Philosophy and Social Science*, 9, 17-48.

Adorno, T. W. (1985) *Philosophy of Modern Music*, New York: Continuum.

American Craft Council (1971, 1972, 1973) *Craft Horizon*. Bimonthly calendars.

American Craft Council (1981, 1982, 1983) *American Craft Magazine*. Bimonthly calendars.

American Museum Association (1975, 1985) *Official Directory*, Washington, D.C.: AMA.

American Music Center (1975, 1985) *Contemporary Music Performance Directory*, New York: AMC.

Bensman, J. and B. Rosenberg (1963) Mass media and mass culture, pp. 166-186 in P. Olson (ed.), *America as a Mass Society*, Glencoe: Free Press.

Blau, J. R. (1984) *Architects and Firms*, Cambridge: MIT Press.

Blau, J. R. (1986a) High culture as mass culture, *Society* 23, 65-70.

Blau, J. R. (1986b) Elite arts, the *de Rigeuer* and the less, *Social Forces* 64, 875-905.

Blau, P. M., J. R. Blau, G. Quets and T. Tada (1986) Social structure and developments in the arts, *Sociological Forum* 2.

Bourdieu, P. (1984) *Distinction*, Cambridge: Harvard University Press.

Cullen J. (1983) Structural aspects of the architectural profession, pp. 280-298 in J. R. Blau, M. E. La Gory, J. S. Pipkin (eds.), *Professionals and Urban Form*, Albany: SUNY Press.

Dance Magazine Annual (1974, 1983), New York: Danad.

Di Maggio, P. (1982) Cultural entrepreneurship in nineteenth century Boston, *Media, Culture and Society* 4, 33-50.

Duncan, O. D., (1961) A sociometric index for all occupations, pp. 109-138 in A. J. Reiss (ed.) *Occupations and Social Status*, New York: Free Press.

Fowle, D. W., (ed.) (1976) *Notable Names in the American Theater*, Clifton, New Jersey, James T. White.

Gutman, R. and B. Westergaard (n.d.) Architecture among the professions.

Hall, P. D. (1984) *The Organization of American Culture, 1700-1900*, New York: New York University Press.

Hauser, R. M. and D. L. Featherman (1976) *The Process of Stratification*, New York: Academic Press.

Horkheimer, M. (1941) Art and mass culture, *Studies in Philosophy and Social Science*, 9, 290-304.

Larson, M. S., G. Leon, J. Bollick (1983) The professional supply of design, pp. 251-279 in J. R. Blau, M. E. La Gory, J. S. Pipkin (eds.), *Professionals and Urban Form*, Albany: SUNY Press.

Larson, M. S., G. Leon, J. Bollick (1983) The professional supply of design, pp. 251-279 in J. R. Blau, M. E. LaGory, J. S. Pipkin (eds.), *Professionals and Urban Form*, Albany: SUNY Press.

Lowenthal, L. (1961) *Literature, Popular Culture and Society*, Palo Alto, CA: Pacific Books.

Marcuse, H. (1967) Remarks on a redefinition of culture, pp. 218-235 in G. Holton (ed.), *Science and Culture*, Boston: Beacon Press.

Miller, L. B. (1966) *Patrons and Patriotism*, Chicago: University of Chicago Press.

Montgomery, R. (1985) The rapid recent expansion of American architecture employment. Unpublished paper.

Osman, M. E. (1975) Survey of firms charts decline in employment, *American Institute of Architects Journal* 66: 41-42.

Rauschenbusch, H., ed. (1971/72) *International Directory of Arts, Vols. 1 & 2.* 11th ed. Berlin: Deutsche Zentraldruckere; Ag.

Rolling Stone Magazine (1975, 1983) Calendars of events. San Francisco: Straight Arrow.

Shils, E. (1978) Mass society and its culture, pp. 200-229 in P. Davison, R. Meyersohn, E. Shils (eds.), *Literary Taste, Culture and Mass Consumption, Vol. 1*, Teaneck, N.J.: Somerset House.

Stanbeck, T. M., Jr., P. J. Bease, T. J. Noyelle, R. A. Karasek (1981) *Services: The New Economy*, Totowa, N.J.: Allenheld.

Trachtenberg, A. (1982) *The Incorporation of America*, New York: Hill and Wang.

U.S. Bureau of the Census (1971a) *Census of Housing, Plumbing Facilities and Estimates of Dilapidated Housing.* Washington, D.C.: GPO.

U.S. Bureau of the Census (1971b) *Statistical Abstract of the United States* 1970, Washington, D.C.: GPO.

U.S. Bureau of the Census (1972a, 1977) *Census for Selected Service Industries*, SIC 7922 pt., Washington, D.C.: GPO.

U.S. Bureau of the Census (1972b) *County Business Patterns 1970.* Washington, D.C.: GPO.

Veblen, J. (1953) [1899] *The Theory of the Leisure Class*, New York: Mentor.

Williams, R. (1961) *The Long Revolution.* New York: Columbia University Press.

Chapter 7

Myth and Paradox in the Building Enterprise

Francis T. Ventre

Scholars in the humanities consider the physical environment—both the built environment, as in buildings, and the induced environment, as in landscapes—to be the bearer or reification of myth and symbol whose meanings are imparted by association. Myth-making is an ancient tradition, and the study of myth has been revivified in recent years by mythologists and by 'structuralist' students of human behavior and social institutions. But myth brings more to the physical environment than just a bountiful source for iconography. Myths also serve instrumental purposes for, in addition to lending resonance to discourse and enriching our vision and aesthetic sensibilities, myths enable the rational mind to apprehend in a single thought two or more seemingly contradictory states of being. Myths mediate paradox.

While myth is a perfectly suitable subject of architectural and environmental design endeavors, mythification of natural phenomena or historical events works invidiously when it clouds a true perception, giving rise to what Langdon Winner (1984) archly labeled 'mythinformation'. The effects of insidious mythification of the process of building design and construction itself induces false perception and its consequent, faulty action. And these false perceptions may especially threaten two things:

147

- the formulation and execution of the public policies that define the social, economic, and cultural environment in which the building design and construction professions are ultimately practiced;

- the education of those professionals.

A vivid example of the former is the inequity and inefficiency of regulation, the realm of public policy most directly affecting building design, construction, and use. Examples of the latter are offered at the close of this essay.

What are the prevailing myths obscuring the building enterprise from the critical view of its own participants? What are the paradoxical qualities of the building enterprise whose mutual coexistence can be rationalized only by preserving them as mysteries and beyond the reach of intelligence, in Dewey's sense of the term, and its consequent, informed action? This essay will counterpose perceptions of building design and construction that, although mutually inconsistent, are widely shared in the building community itself and particularly in its academic wing. Table 7.1 condenses some of them and reveals that these differences are not over obscure terminology, exotic specialties, or arcane knowledge. Rather, misperception and, therefore, misunderstanding, abounds over such fundamental data as the size of the building enterprise considered in both macro- and micro-economic terms; the geographical—geopolitical, really—scale at which it operates; the state of its technology; and its heritage as an art and as a science. These are not slight matters.

Size

Like the well known 'face-urn-face' stimulus of visual psychophysics, the very size of the building industry seems to change even while being examined. As Julian Lange and D. Quinn Mills (1979) have pointed out, construction (two-thirds of which is building construction), when viewed as an industry and compared with, say, fabricated metals, is one of the largest in the economy. But given construction's geographic dispersion, the minute specialization of its work force, the utter differentiation of its products, the decentralized mode of its regulation, and the huge size and variety of its economic inputs, building construction perhaps more usefully should be considered as a broad economic sector as is, say, manufacturing. Viewed this way, the construction sector (say Lange and Mills), is one of the smallest in the economy. This, plus its lack of a single, specific geographic locale, may be a reason for its neglect by formulators of economic policy in the United States.

Table 7.1: Facts (some of them counter-intuitive) and paradoxes about the world of building design and construction

---

1a Architectural firm profitability (pretax, prebonus) *averages* 5-7% of net revenue. Average compensation for firm principals is less than half the figure for counterparts in medical and legal firms.
—Financial statistics surveys published intermittently, by *Professional Services Management Journal*

1b But data from same source on further analysis reveals that the *upper 25 per cent* of architectural firms report pretax, prebonus profits of nearly 15% of net revenue, nearly double the *average* profit. And profitability of the top 15% of firms is just over 22%.
—Weld Coxe in July 1985 *Progressive Architecture*

The Bottom Line: Architectural practice *can* pay *if* you are good at it.

2a Architectural practices are smaller, while buildings are getting larger: AIA reports that firms with fewer than 10 employees grew slightly from 74% of firms in 1978 to 77% in 1983. But average gross revenues for smaller firms are not good: revenues for one-person firms declined in constant and in current dollars; firms with two to nine employees (more than three-quarters of all firms) increased revenues 25%, but this failed to keep pace with inflation. Large firm revenues in contrast grew by 88% in the same interval.
—AIA 1983 Firm Survey

(Table 7.1 cont.)

2b But hope springs eternal, despite this chastening news: Dun and Bradstreet reported that among 20 types of small businesses, firms offering engineering/architectural services are the third fastest growing, behind only management/public relations firms and beauty shops.

    — *Inc.* June, 1985

The Bottom Line: Moralizers will note that the top three fastest growing businesses in the American economy of the 1980s are *image-creating* businesses.

3a The building construction industry faces similar disparities between large numbers of small firms and small numbers of large firms that earn most of the revenues. In 1982, among construction companies, subdividers and developers, one third of the businesses earn 90% of the total industry receipts while two-thirds — mostly sole proprietorships — compete for the remaining tenth.

3b While designers and builders are proud of their versatility and educators and researchers aim at universal programs and replicability of research results, we pride ourselves on being generalists. The fact is that three-quarters of all construction contracting firms are special trade contractors — focusing on only one technology: painting, masonry, etc.

    — 1982 Census of the Construction Industries

(Table 7.1 cont)

4a Why do big firms dominate? Because of the size distribution in the nation's inventory of nonresidential buildings, the segment of the building construction market where designers and contractors earn their livelihoods. That inventory is a highly skewed distribution; namely, a small number of very large buildings and a very large number of small ones (see Fig. 7.1). Almost half of this country's nonresidential space is in only five per cent of its nonresidential buildings, those larger than 50,000 gross sq. ft. One third of the nation's nonresidential floor area is in only 2% of its nonresidential buildings, those larger than 100,000 gross sq. ft.

4b Despite what is presented in the trade and professional periodicals, only 7% of these buildings rise more than three floors and 60-65% of workplaces shelter ten or fewer workers.
    — 1981 Department of Energy report on the Nonresidential Building Inventory.

5a Between 1972 and 1982, nationally aggregated payroll growth for design firms outran aggregated growth in design firm receipts, leaving little accumulated profit to attract national vendors of capital equipment.

5b On a per firm basis, over the same 1972-1982 span, payroll growth outran receipts growth, leaving little accumulated profit to invest in capital equipment.
    — 1982 Census of the Service Industries: Engineering, Architecture and Land Surveying.

If any doubt exists on this last point, one need only consider the buffeting that the investment end of the building community — the real estate industry — took in the Reagan Administration's budgetary decisions (e.g. curtailing investment in community facilities and housing) and tax legislation (the generous depreciation allowances of the Economic Recovery Tax Act of 1981 were sharply reduced by the Tax Reform Act of 1984 and then all but eliminated in the Tax Reform Act of 1986). The dissatisfaction of the homebuilders with

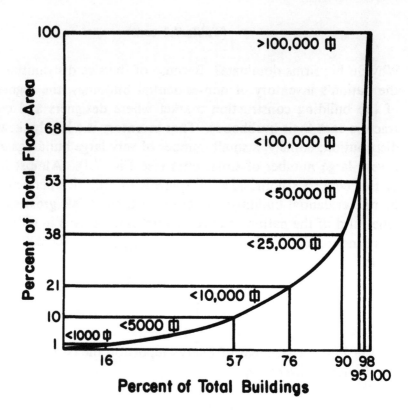

Figure 7.1:   Distribution of nonresidential buildings by size class, 1979.
Data Source: U.S. Department of Energy.

the monetary policies of the Federal Reserve Board is too widely known to bear repeating.

Another measure of the industry's aggregate size is to consider it in proportion to the Gross National Product. Figure 7.2 indicates that the building and construction 'share' of the nation's economic pie has shrunk to less than two-thirds of its 1964 'share'. The reason for this decline: investment in equipment has out-paced investment in buildings for many years (Ventre, 1982), and there is no indication that this relation will shift, at least for the advanced economies of the world. As for the developing and newly industrialized countries, investment in buildings and other constructed facilities, now between 20 and 25 per cent of GNP will similarly decline as the economies of these nations mature (Engineering News-Record, 1986).

Design and Construction: Goods or Services?

The size of the building enterprise is difficult to calibrate for yet
another reason: building is a service to other goods-producing and
service-providing segments of the economy, and its final output —
the spaces and structures that shelter and support human activity —
become inputs to other industries. Zeckhauser and Silverman (1983)
estimate that fully one-quarter of corporate assets in the United
States are in land and buildings. Nevertheless, new buildings and

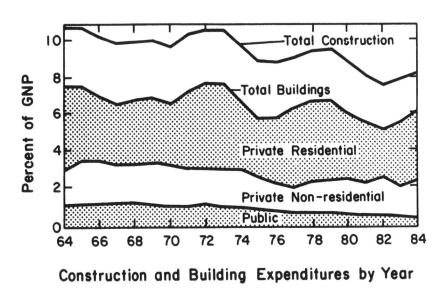

Construction and Building Expenditures by Year

Figure 7.2: Construction and building outlays expressed as a percent of the Gross National Product, by construction type,
1964-1984.
Data Source: U.S. Department of Commerce

site development plans are more often discussed in the arts and culture columns of the newspapers and magazines addressed to leaders
in business and government than on the business pages of those same
periodicals. Ada Louise Huxtable, who (both as a columnist and

as a member of the Board of Editors of the *New York Times*) became an influential critic of architecture and urbanism, wrote incisively on the regulatory and tax policies that guided — she often implied 'misguided' — the design decisions whose results she reviewed. Unfortunately, and despite her being the first journalist to have been awarded a Pulitzer Prize for architectural criticism and the only one to receive a Mac Arthur Foundation 'genius grant', her practices have not been retained by her successors on the *Times*. Nor have they been adopted by other writers on architecture and urbanism, who instead have turned for inspiration to the esoterica of semiology and other conceits of visual and literary aesthetics, leaving the public policies affecting physical development greatly under-examined.

The good or service classification confusion produces other anomalies, particularly statistical ones, that lead to persistent misperceptions. Two examples:

- compared to the goods-producing segment of the economy, the design, construction and construction products industries as a whole fund research and development at very low amounts relative to total industry receipts (National Research Council, 1986). But other analyses — based instead on highly disaggregated 'line of business' data — reveal that construction outperformed all other service-providing industries (except the R and D industry itself) in the fraction of industry receipts devoted to research (Scherer, 1982a; 1982b). Pity the poor policy planners at the National Science Foundation or the White House Office of Science and Technology Policy who are attempting to allocate research funding to enhance U.S. competitiveness (President's Commission, 1985).

- Services exports, exclusive of financial transactions and currency-trading have long been the bright spot in the otherwise dismal U.S. balance of trade picture. And here, design and construction services account for a very large fraction of that positive trade balance in services. Nevertheless, construction goods and services are suffering from import penetration to historically high degrees at present (*Engineering News-Record*, 1986) leading to Congressional concern and resultant inquiry (Office of Technology Assessment, 1986).

Structure

The industry's size might elude some of its own members because building design and construction is numerically dominated by single practitioners, small partnerships, and very small firms. Consider the reports of the quinquennial Economic Censuses of the United States and from recently published industry surveys. The 1982 Census of the Construction Industries (1985) reports half of all construction establishments have no employees at all but are single-person enterprises; 70 per cent of construction establishments perform only a single service, *e.g.*, painting, plumbing, glazing (and two-thirds of those specialty contractors are one-person operations). The design professions are organized in much the same way. Eighty-five per cent of the architectural firms headed by corporate members of the American Institute of Architects — the American architectural establishment — employ four or fewer persons; consulting engineering firms are only slightly larger (Combined Sources, 1984, 1985). But now the 'paradox' emerges: the numerically dominant one-person construction firms earn only 8 per cent of the construction industry's total receipts. Over one-third of all architectural design fees are earned by the 50 largest firms who comprise only 1.5% of all firms (1982 Census of Service Industries, 1985). And the industry concentration is now galloping ahead as a result of record business and banking failures or near-misses. Consider residential construction. In 1985, the 100 largest producers of housing accounted for 27 per cent of total new homes sales up from 22 per cent only four years earlier (AIH/MHD, 1983, 1986). Concentration is even more intense at the very top: the ten largest producers doubled their market share — from less than 6 to over 12 per cent — between 1977 and 1982, while the number of active homebuilders — three-quarters of whom build fewer than 25 units per year — dropped from 100,00 to 75,000 in the same interval (*Business Week*, 1983).

Product

What is the nature of the building inventory American designers and builders create? Consider nonresidential buildings, the market served by the more professionalized building design and construction firms. As Fig. 7.2 illustrates, the distribution is highly skewed: a very large number of small buildings and a small number of very large ones. Fifty-seven per cent of America's nonresidential buildings enclose less than 5,000 sq. ft. (the size of a regulation basketball court), and 95 per cent of them enclose less than 50,000 sq. ft. (the goal line-to-goal line playing area of a football field). Put another way, well over half of America's commercial, institutional, and industrial structures cumulatively shelter only a tenth of the nation's enclosed area, while only 2 per cent account for nearly a third of America's commercial, institutional, and industrial spaces. Where does the market for building design and construction services lie? Is the 5,000 sq. ft. office building even approachable by professional design and general contracting firms other than one-person operations? Conversely, will clients trust a 100,000 sq. ft. office building — now considered incomplete without computerized energy management and security control systems throughout, data highways under the floor, and satellite uplinks on the roof — to the typical four-person, 'generalist' firm? There is little wonder, then, that the very survival of the design and construction professions as we now know them has gained the front and center attention of the professional societies and trade associations in the world's mature economies and the colleges and universities that train entrants to those professions.

Local or cosmopolitan?

The geographical extent of building design and construction markets has always intrigued economists, whose conventional wisdom characterizes the building design and construction industry as anachronistically local in an era of multinational enterprise. But building does have a global reach, a fact that eluded Magaziner and Reich (1983) in their otherwise perceptive analysis of advanced capitalism.

Part of this persistent misperception may be traced to the highly diverse character of the industry: home builders tend to focus on a single metropolitan housing market, and skilled craftsmen would rather leave the industry — often becoming building maintenance workers and suffering drops in income and occupational status — than migrate to follow employment opportunities in construction. But this is manifestly not the case for heavy construction for industry and transportation and for some labor specialties, notably the operating engineers whose trade union 'locals' embrace more than one state.

While American building construction — and, particularly, housing — seems to be moving towards greater output volume by a smaller number of producing units, the Swedish building industry is cutting back in the size of projects undertaken, their duration, and the geographic area across which design and construction services are marketed. Sweden's domestic building industry is reducing its scale to regional operations and may be abandoning the pursuit of a single national market altogether. But, in yet another contradiction, the internationally-oriented segment of the Swedish building industry aggressively promotes overseas sales of research-enhanced products and services (Swedish Council, 1983). The Finnish government had already retargeted its discretionary building research to those products and services for which overseas markets beckoned (Ventre, 1984).

Engineering News-Record annual surveys indicate that overseas sales account for about 15 per cent of design billings (for firms with over $3,000,000 in receipts per year). In one recent year, 29 per cent of construction contract value (for firms with over $33,000,000 in contracts per year) came from overseas sources. So widespread has international design practice become that the Census of the Service Industries (which covers engineering and architectural design firms) asked its first international question in the 1982 enumeration.

Recent international activity notwithstanding, building designs and construction products have long crossed international boundaries, initially as ships' ballast. Thus, Flemish brick is found in the 13th century Tower of London and the marks of Dutch brickmakers can be found in masonry structure along the east coast of Colonial America. But materials also came 'first-class': marble from Carrara's quarries made its way to the Palace of Versailles through Amsterdam's jobbers.

The globalization of design and construction proceeds apace. Consider the energetic acquisition of American firms by foreign rivals. Within the past few years, Phillips of the Netherlands has purchased Westinghouse's lighting business. For a few years, Phillips retained the Westinghouse logo, but no longer could one 'be sure . . . if it's Westinghouse'. The lighting products now bear North American Phillips' own label instead, relegating to oblivion a figure once large in the annals of American engineering, industry and philanthropy: George A. Westinghouse. Certainteed, a manufacturer and distributor of roofing, siding, insulation, and other building products, was acquired in 1976 by Compagnie de Saint-Gobain of France. By the early 1980s Aoki of Japan built — as opposed to passively invested in — three residential townhouse developments within an hour's drive of the White House. The Virginia-based multi-state firm of a recent president of the American Institute of Architects was recently acquired by Suter + Suter, a Swiss firm. Thirty per cent of America's cement-making capacity is in foreign ownership. In 1986, Pilkington Brothers PLC, Britain's largest glass manufacturer, agreed to acquire the glass-making business of Libby-Owens-Ford. And Watergate — the notorious building complex of recent political history — was developed, designed and financed by Italians and is now owned by British interests.

These acquisitions and activities attest that the American domestic market for buildings and building products and services remains large and lucrative and suggests that some of this country's design and construction resources may be under-valued by our own business analysts who remain bedazzled by the glister of 'high tech' industries.

Is Buildable Land a Shrinking Resource?

Thinking about economic geography induces a question about buildable land. The old maxim that 'God doesn't create any more of it' simply is not true. While the land masses of earth are nearly constant in size, technology-informed site-planning practices are producing buildable sites in once-bypassed places. (Don't forget Faust: he struck his bargain with Mephistopheles so he could get on with his land-from-water schemes!) The heroically scaled and ecologically sensitive reclamation of the Dutch polders is perhaps the grandest example, but others abound. My recent favorite is the Strawberry Vale scheme in London designed by Bickerdike, Allen Partners for a narrow 12.5 acre urban site bisected by a small stream (which, in this location, had a history of pollution) and bounded by an industrial area on one side and the North Circular Road, one of the region's busiest thoroughfares on the other. Acoustically-informed site planning and building design have yielded 265 units of moderately priced housing for nearly 1150 persons and space for 269 cars (Figs. 7.3, 7.4 and 7.5). A 169-unit noise barrier block —

Figure 7.3: Aerial view of Strawberry Vale housing development, London, from the west.
Source: Bickerdike, Allen Partners

three stories of apartments surmounted by two-story dwellings the British call 'maisonettes' — wrapped the northwest edge of the site. All living rooms and most bedrooms face inward to the quiet side and the block itself protected the remaining 96 two-story houses, gardens, and terraces. The sheltered portion of the site faces south and the mesoclimate is much improved by the noise and wind protection it gets and the sun's warmth it retains perennially by-passed.

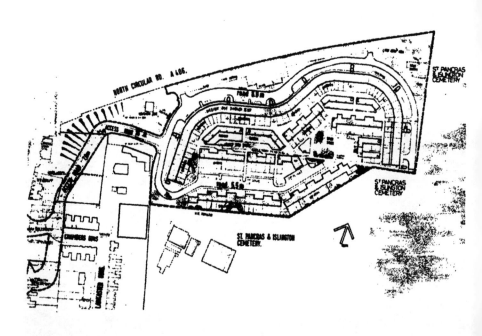

Figure 7.4: Site plan of Strawberry Vale housing development, London.
Source: Bikerdike, Allen Partners

Similar site planning practices seem not to be as fully applied to the American situation, however, though not for lack of opportunity. The 41,000-mile Interstate Highway System devalued countless square miles of urban land because enhanced access was more than offset by accompanying noise intrusion, to cite just one instance.

But there are others. Thirty years of data compiled by the National Association of Home Builders indicate that improved site utilization — and not rationalized construction — is the likely way to produce more housing for the money. As Fig. 7.6 reports, the 'above ground' cost of labor and materials has shrunk in 30 years from two-thirds to less than half the cost of a single-family residence, while the shares going to temporary construction financing (and not the permanent mortgage financing) and the 'below ground' cost of site acquisition and development have doubled. This presents a great opportunity for imaginative and technically informed site-planning.

Technological Innovation in Building Design and Construction

Perhaps the most widespread popular misconception of the building enterprise, about which even building professionals are needlessly apologetic, is in the matter of technology: many believe that the building enterprise is slow to adopt innovative technologies. This error persists because building owners and managers, providing building services to other segments of the economy, are ritually cautious about ultimate market acceptance of innovative technology. After all, if the economic life of a building runs to the traditional 40 years, building owners and managers must assure themselves that evanescent fads will not saddle them with unmarketable or unrentable 'white elephants'. Consequently, most building developers and their designers, except for a relatively small number that serve corporations seeking 'flagship' buildings to further an image, must please conservative clients. Innovative technologies *are* applied, but in order to mollify apprehensive customers they are usually secreted within the walls and in the floor-ceiling assemblies. Residential builders have mastered this shielding technique, sustaining the illusion that residential building technology changes slowly, if at all (Ventre, 1979). But when interindustry rates of technological innovation are compared, the building industry performs at least as well as more conventionally-deployed industries (Ventre, 1980; Scherer, 1982a, b).

Figure 7.5: Interior view of Strawberry Vale housing development, London.
Source: Bickerdike, Allen Partners

So, it is in the nature of the building market to act conservatively. The emotionally-based traditional bias of most homeowners and renters may be understandable, but what about the — rationalized — professional management of businesses and institutions? Doesn't Schumpeter advise that autonomous entrepreneurs are, by definition, venturesome?

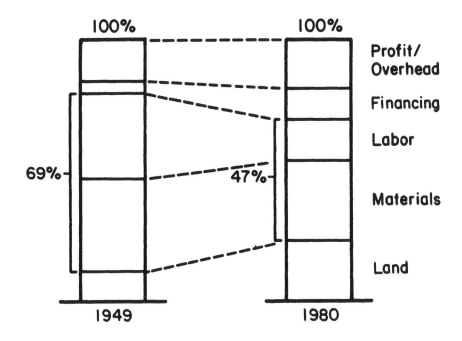

Figure 7.6: Cost components for a new single-family house, 1949 and 1980.
Source: National Association of Home Builders

Ironically, even the innovative industrialist turns toward tradition when facing a building decision, mainly because long-lived buildings are purchased so rarely. It is a truism among market researchers that the 'early adopters' of any innovation — whether of industrial services or consumer products — tend to be the heaviest users of that service or product. Test this against your own experience: don't heavy users of computers tend to be the early buyers of the newer, high-performance model? Isn't the same true for appliances like push-button telephones and for food products: the 10-cup-a-day families are usually the first on their block to try the new coffee makers. But the typical business firm rarely ventures into the market for new buildings or design services. This is true for all except the largest corporations and institutions who, operating across the country, tend to be in the building market continually. But they are a relatively small number of building owners and managers. Even the federal government's General Services Administration/Public Buildings Service — landlord to 880,000 civilian employees in a 230 million square foot inventory — commissions only a vanishingly small fraction of the nation's new office buildings.

The Department of Energy (1981) reported that 70 to 75 per cent of the nation's nonresidential buildings shelter 10 or fewer workers and between 80 and 85 per cent shelter only a single business establishment. About two-thirds of America's commercial, institutional, and industrial (CII) buildings are owned by the organizations that occupy them, and 54 per cent of those units occupy only a single building. Since buildings are so long-lived, a business firm goes to the building market perhaps only once in a generation, a situation that hardly makes for a knowledgeable buyer of building design and construction services. Given these factors, the industry's innovativeness is entirely adequate to the demands its customers make of it.

Of course, technology is only a means to an end, and for most industrial and institutional organizations, one important intermediate end is enhanced productivity. Both government- and industry-issued productivity statistics agree that the building industry itself suffers an ignominiously low rate of productivity growth (Business Roundtable, 1983; Weber and Lippiatt, 1983). Measurement problems, of course, plague all productivity studies, but productivity measurement is vastly more difficult for design and construction services because of the highly differentiated end products that result. Moreover, construction's final product — the completed building — is but an intermediate product, considered as an input factor to the economic activity sheltered in the completed building. Finally, that building will likely be operated by neither the builder nor the occupant but by a third party. This pattern of diffused resource management, an everyday occurrence in buildings, introduces a range of technical issues rarely encountered in other industries and seems to have intimidated the battalions of productivity analysts and the mere squad of building economists.

Would not a truer measure of the productivity of the design and construction enterprise take into account the efficacy with which the completed building serves the objectives of the organization sheltered within it? Most construction productivity statistics, unfortunately, consider the Department of Commerce definition — 'value of construction put in place' — as the output measure for construction activity. Such a measure does not consider the entirely plausible proposition that building users and their agents are willing to pay higher costs per square foot, creating more 'valuable' buildings, if they feel that productivity of the various organizations they manage is enhanced. Building owners believe in the productivity-enhancing possibility of new buildings. *Building Design and Construction's* May 1981 industry survey reported that expected productivity gains were the largest single reason that owners went into the new building market in the first place! But the conventional measures of construction productivity continue to pay meticulous attention to the coliform count and flow rate of the discharged bathwater while neglecting to check the baby's pulse or even to ascertain if it is still in the room.

The matter of product differentiation needs to be considered further because the design and construction enterprise's ability to devise a stream of unique products — intimately fitted responses to minutely specified user requirements — suggests that construction is one of the first 'post-industrial' industries in the American economy. Consider what has occurred in two 'high tech' industries included in nearly everyone's exemplaria of post-industrial industries and compare that to the situation in building design and construction:

- One analyst of the electronics industry, James D. Meindl, while he was director of the Stanford University Electronics Laboratory (whence Silicon Valley sprung forth like Athena from Zeus' forehead) remarked to the author that the only semiconductor manufacturing firms that would survive — and not merely thrive — into the next century would be those capable of quick response to rapidly changing customer requirements. The promise of quick response is why semiconductor manufacturers so rapidly adopted computer-aided design methods even though CAD-produced microprocessor chips contain remarkably fewer features per chip when compared to those produced by human designers.

- Students of the chemical-process industries, including A. S. West of Rohm and Haas and University of Delaware Professor of Chemical Engineering Kenneth Bischoff, observed to the author a similar shift from the production of long runs of generic chemicals sold in bulk as commodities to smaller batches of compounds tailored to specific customer needs, moving from commodity chemicals to specialty chemicals. Genetic engineering is, of course, the limiting case of this highly differentiated, small-batch mode of working: special-purpose organisms are turned out not in tank-car loads but in Mason jar-sized lots.

Both the semiconductor-processing and (especially) the petrochemical industries had previously organized themselves along the lines of nineteenth-century mechanization of serial production. That is a mode of organization that building industry critics have long held up as the ideal mode industrial enterprises in the twentieth century (Myth No. 1), and they have sharply castigated the building industry for its indifference to those precedents (Myth No. 2). But now both electronics and chemicals are turning away from mass production methods and toward more adaptable, customized production heretofore associated with the artisanry of the design professions and the building trades and the autonomy of the sole proprietorships and closely-held firms associated with building contracting (The Paradox).[1]

How much wiser is the building industry, for it has been perfecting the design and production of utterly differentiated one-of-a-kind products, including the necessary distribution system, for about 6,000 years. To the chagrin of the earlier critics — and they are still much with us — the building industry appears to have gone from a 'pre-industrial' (handcraft) to a 'post industrial' mode of organization (differentiated product produced at dispersed sites by workers who still retain a sense of aesthetic gratification in their work) without having gone through the 'industrial' phase at all!

All discussions of technology ultimately dissolve into questions of Art or Science. This is manifestly true for the technologies of building design and construction. Consequently, architectural discourse seems perpetually to equilibrate between the Muses of Art and of Science. (Remember, the Muses inspire both.) And this will be the last paradox we shall consider: design as art *and* science.

Architects re-phrase the science/art split as 'research-design', the two being aspects of the same quest, one instructing the other. This tired and tiring science-art or research-design antagonism, rehearsed whenever architectural educators gather, claims an ancient pedigree: the 'research' argument was put forth by Socrates and brought to us in Plato's *Gorgias*.

Socrates distinguished true art from routine practice because routines — his example was cooking — were devoted exclusively to 'cultivating pleasure' while true art — his example, medicine — 'investigates the nature of the subject it treats'. Routine practices cultivate pleasure

> without once having investigated the nature of pleasure or its cause; and without any pretense whatever and practically no attempt to classify, it preserves by mere experience and routine a memory of what usually happens.

So for Socrates and Plato, it is a reluctance to analyze experience that keeps a practice primitive. Architectural teaching, on the other hand, typically propounds a form of direct intuition rather than analysis, revelation rather than research as the primary source of not only immediate satisfaction with an object but also the generator of the form itself. To be sure, intuition need not be primitive: intuition may be educated, or at minimum, informed with scholarship and trained taste. Indeed, this forms the bulk of architectural education in the present day. That educational objective persists because today's architectural pedagogy was codified in the nineteenth century when Romanticism and the belief in the primacy of intuitive individual action and poetics over praxis swept the European academies. (The founding teachers of every significant American architecture school were trained either in Europe or in the European tradition at that time.)

Whereas twentieth century scientific and engineering education veered earlier towards empiricism, then positivism and, most recently, constructivism as a pedagogical philosophy, architectural education remains with Romantic idealism (Bauhaus-inspired reforms notwithstanding) to the point that now at some of the country's leading schools — and certainly in the intellectual journals that service the field — architecture is discussed largely as conceptual art.

Paradoxically, consideration of architecture as conceptual art may move things closer to the Socratic 'true art' invoking deeper analysis of experience. Kant (1964) defined aesthetic pleasure indeed human judgements of all kinds, as a compound of sensation and thought. In doing so, Kant transformed aesthetic philosophy into its modern framework. Indeed, said Kant, it is only the 'faculty of the understanding' component of aesthetic judgement — knowledge — that is communicable and potentially in accord with a 'universal rule'.

Here exactly is where the pursuit of architectural education through artistic means diverges from that pursuit via scientific means. The tradition of art education and practice is one of the 'private study of personal experience', in Scruton's (1979, p. 84) phrase, versus the

> 'observation of public practice — the practice of attention, command, study and reasoning which distinguishes the realm of imagination and which can be observed as well in the behavior of another as introspectively in ourselves'.

Scientific education and practice, on the other hand, is indubitably public. Indeed, the publicity and transparency of scientific pursuits render them scientific (Ziman, 1968). Evidence of the inversion of the relation between art and architecture is that painters, sculptors and graphic artists are taking a more active role in the design of buildings and environments — Christo's 'Running Fence', the late Robert Smithson's 'Spiral Jetty', and Charles Roses' still-in progress 'Star Axis' and the Jerde Partnership-Sussman/Prejza's 1984 Summer Olympics in Los Angeles being luminous examples — while architectural drawings (drawings, not incidentally, for projects unlikely ever to be realized) are being collected by and shown in museums and fetching fair prices in art galleries.

Paradoxes and contradictions proliferate in the building design and construction enterprise — not for nothing did Robert Venturi (1966) entitle the polemic that intellectually and visually legitimized Postmodernism *Complexity and Contradiction in Architecture* — and this chapter has described some of the significant ones. But those very qualities of paradox and contradiction are continually appealing to some of the liveliest and most creative figures that dot the history of ideas in this century. Ludwig Wittgenstein, who gave the twentieth century some of its characteristic modes of philosophical analysis, designed buildings, too; the house he designed for one of his sisters still stands in Vienna. Nobel laureate Herbert Simon, in the justly praised *The Sciences of the Artificial* (1969), calls out design for singular treatment in the realm of rational action. Indeed, design for him represents the occasion for

> growing communication among intellectual disciplines that takes place around the computer. The ability to communicate across fields— the common ground— comes from the fact that all who use computers in complex ways are using computers to design or to participate in the process of design.

Political theorist Harold Lasswell turned to buildings toward the end of his long and prolific career. (On the bizarre side, architect-turned-Nazi armaments minister Albert Speer complained to his diary how Hitler kept him up late into the night showing him designs for stage sets and cities.) Nathan Glazer, whose writings on the sociology of housing were a *coup de grâce* to the crude environmental determinism of human behavior, recently acknowledged in a personal communication that the deeper social effects of the physical environment remain for him, personally, an intellectual challenge not fully met. And despite the catholicity of his interests and diversity of his achievements in mathematics, structural design, and cartography, R. Buckminster Fuller to the end of his life referred to himself as an architect.

Problems of design and construction are beguiling to very creative minds. But the architectural profession has been economically beset, in recent times, prompting the then-AIA executive vice-president to admit that

> As architects practicing in America in 1983, we are caught in the midst of a paradox. . . . As admiration for our art increases, remuneration for our work decreases. As we acquire respect, we forfeit profits. Or, to borrow a line from Mark Twain, architects are 'now fast rising from affluence to poverty'.

This prospect seems, however, not to deter students of architecture, landscape architecture, environmental planning, and building construction, for enrollments remain strong in the face of sharp declines in the college-age population. Creative minds continue to be challenged by paradox, and those same minds will, no doubt, abolish some and retain and reinterpret others of the myths set forth in this essay. The ultimate paradox of building will no doubt endure. Despite the utter physicality of buildings and other induced environments, they are evocative, too. Truly, as when Churchill argued the urgent reconstruction of the blitz-damaged British Houses of Parliament, 'We shape our buildings, then our buildings shape us.'

Note

1.   The foregoing sections were prepared prior to my reading of Piore and Sabel's (1984) *The Second Industrial Divide*. This book amplifies the features described in this section and draws implications for the economy at large. The building design and construction industries' long-standing use of 'flexible specialization' (Piore and Sabel's term) is acknowledged, and they are virtually alone among contemporary analysts in so doing.

References

The top 100. *Automation in Housing/Manufactured Home Dealer.* (August, 1983, p. 1; August, 1986, p. 30).

The Business Roundtable (1983) Summary report of the Construction Industry Cost Effectiveness Project. New York: Author.

Combined sources. The American Institute of Architects' Annual; the Professional Services Management Association and *Professional Services Management Journal*; Birnberg Associates/*Building Design Construction* each published, respectively, *The AIA Firm Survey, Financial Statistics Survey and PSMJ Executive Management Salary Survey*, and the Financial Performance Survey for Design Firms. This chapter drew on all these sources' 1984 and 1985 Reports.

Foreigners step up U.S. Invasion, (1986) *Engineering News-Record,* November 27, p.12

Homebuilding's new look (1983) *Business Week*, November 7, p.92

Kant, E. (1964). Critique of Judgement, First Division, First Book, Section 14. In Hofstadter, A. and Kuhns, R. (eds). *Philosophies of Art and Beauty.* New York: Modern Library.

Lange, J. and Mills, D. Q. (eds) (1979) *Construction: Balance-Wheel of the economy,* Lexington: Heath.

Plato (1979). *Gorgias.* Tr. Terence Irwin, New York: Oxford University Press.

Magaziner, I. C. and Reich, R. B. (1983) *Minding America's business: the decline and rise of the American economy,* New York: Vintage.

Meeker, D. O. (1983) *F.W. Dodge Construction News,* April 27, p.7

National Research Council, Building Research Board (1986) *Construction Productivity: Proposed Actions by the Federal Government to Promote Increased Efficiency in Construction.* Washington, DC: US Government Printing Office.

Piore, M. J. and Sabel, C. F. (1984) *The Second Industrial Divide: Possibilities for Prosperity*, New York: Basic Books.

President's Commission on Industrial Competitiveness (1985) *Global Competition: the New Reality* vol. 1. Washington, D.C.: U.S. Government Printing Office.

Scherer, F. M. (1982a) Inter-industry technology flows in the United States. *Research Policy*, II.

Scherer, F. M. (1982b) *Using Linked Patent and R & D Data to Measure Interindustry Technology Flows*, Federal Trade Commission, Bureau of Economics Working Paper No. 57.

Scruton, R. (1979) *Aesthetics of Architecture*, London: Methuen.

Simon, H. E. (1969). *The Sciences of the Artificial.* Cambridge, MA: MIT Press.

Swedish Council for Building Research (1983). *The Swedish Building Sector in 1990*, Stockholm.

U.S. Congress, Office of Technology Assessment (1986) *Technology, Trade and the U.S. Residential Construction Industry — Special report* (OTA-TET-315), Washington, D.C.: U.S. Government Printing Office.

U.S. Department of Commerce, Bureau of the Census (1983) *1982 Census of the Construction Industries*, Washington D.C.: U.S. Government Printing Office.

U.S. Department of Commerce, Bureau of the Census (1985) *1982 Census of the Service Industries. Industry series: Engineering,*

Architecture and Surveying (SC82-I-1, Table 6a), Washington, D.C.: U.S. Government Printing Office.

U.S. Department of Energy, Energy Information Administration. (1981) *Nonresidential Buildings Energy Consumption Survey: Building Characteristics* (DOE/EIA-0246), Washington, D.C. U.S. Government Printing Office.

Ventre, F. T. (1982) Building in eclipse; architecture in secession, *Progressive Architecture*, pp. 58-61.

Ventre, F. T. (1984) International trade in design and construction and its implications for standards-oriented research. In V. K. Handa (Ed.). *Proceedings of CIB 84: 4th International Symposium on Organization and Management of Construction*, Waterloo, Ontario, pp.1031-1040

Ventre, F. T. (1979) Innovation in residential construction. *Technology Review*, pp. 50-59.

Ventre, F. T. (1980) On the blackness of kettles: interindustry comparisons in rates of technological innovation. *Policy Sciences*, 11, 309-328.

Venturi, R. (1966). *Complexity and Contradiction in Architecture*, New York: Museum of Modern Art.

Weber, S. F. and Lippiatt, B. C. (1983) *Productivity Measurement for the Construction Industry*, NBS Technical Note 1172, Washington, D.C.: National Bureau of Standards.

Winner, L. (1984) Mythinformation in the High Tech Era, *IEEE Spectrum*, pp. 90-96.

Zeckhauser, S. and Silverman, R. (1983) Rediscover your company's real estate, *Harvard Business Review*, 61, 111-117.

Ziman, J. (1968). *Public Knowledge: an Essay Concerning the Social Dimension of Science*, Cambridge: Cambridge University Press.

Chapter 8

Knowledge-Power and Professional Practice

Shoukry T. Roweis

> the problem of our society is that the longing of the citizenry for orientation and normative patterns invests the expert with an exaggerated authority. Modern society expects him to provide a substitute for past moral and political orientations. Consequently, the concept of 'praxis' which was developed in the last two centuries is an awful deformation of what practice really is. In all the debates of the last century practice was understood as application of science to technical tasks . . . [This] degrades practical reason to technical control.
>
> Hans-Georg Gadamer[1]

There is little doubt that modern professionals exercise considerable power, that this power is somehow related to a function of advice or guidance that they perform, and that they perform it on the basis of verified or at least verifiable knowledge. On all three counts, Gadamer is here expressing what I think are generally acknowledged 'facts' of our time. But beyond this there is much less agreement about the particular historical developments which may account for the emergence of these realities, about the contemporary conditions which support or at least allow the continuation of these realities, or about the consequences and desirability of this state of affairs in the broader order of things.

In relationship to the modern design professions and their influences on the built environment, these issues have for a long time been, and continue to be, investigated and debated (see, for example, Beauregard, 1983; Boyer, 1983; Burgess, Littman and Mayo, 1981;

Burgess, 1983; Dear and Scott, 1981; Elkin, 1974; Foglesong, 1986; Forester, 1982; Gans, 1978; Haar, 1967; Larson, 1983; Roweis, 1983; Silverstein and Jacobson, 1985). In this chapter, I do not intend to join these debates. As the title suggests, I would like to approach a prior task whose accomplishment may enhance the fruitfulness of these debates; namely, to analyze the play of knowledge and power in professional practice. In pursuing this task, I do not argue for certain kinds or 'styles' of practice or against others, nor against professionalism and in favor of something else.   Rather, I seek to address certain questions which, to my knowledge, remain relatively ignored at least in discussions of the design professions.

There is first a set of questions surrounding the all too familiar notion of 'application of knowledge'.   For example: What content do we have in mind when we use this all-embracing and deceptively common notion of 'application of knowledge' to describe the work of professionals?   If 'application' refers to a relationship between to types of objects — one which is applied, and another to which the first is applied — then what is the nature of this relationship?   What are the generative characteristics of these two types of objects?   And what kinds of human interactions are set in motion when profes- sionals apply 'their' knowledge?

A second, and related, set of questions arises with respect to the theme of professional influence.   For example: How does the use of knowledge produce tangible, corporeal, or extra-ideational effects? Does this metamorphosis (of 'ideas' into material results) not involve a kind of action by one agent (the professional) upon the actions of others ('clients', impacted parties, etc)?   Is this not a power effect of knowledge?   How is this effect made possible?   What provides the conditions of its realization?   And what kinds of power relations does it involve?

Together, these two sets of questions point at some mostly ensconced relations and processes which are nonetheless always present in the daily work of professionals. And if our *idée reçue* portrays the figure of the professional as an agent of specialized knowledge with a so- cially useful mission, it is only because it *presupposes* these relations and processes without analyzing them or even naming them.   My aim in this chapter is to attempt such an analysis by approaching some of the questions I posed above. I cannot, at present, provide firm answers to these questions; all I can do now is to indicate some directions in which they may be addressed. There are two other limitations that I impose on the analysis and which deserve a brief mention at this point.

First, the analysis is not adequately specific to the design professions; it does not capture the disinctive features of *design* practices as such. And although I use examples from the design professions to illustrate some of the points, I still consider this lack of specificity a shortcoming that must be overcome in future work. Second, the analysis is restricted to the work of a particular category of professionals which may be described as *public policy professionals*. Elsewhere (Roweis, 1983, p.150) I have defined public policy professionals as those whose substantive fields of competence qualify them to, and whose particular work situations require them to, take part in influencing choices and actions which have non-trivial *public* consequences. An architect advising on a large-scale waterfront redevelopment plan functions as a public policy professional whereas one who is helping a family renovate its home does not. The analysis I conduct here focuses implicitly on the work of public policy professionals. To avoid needless repetition, I shall drop the qualification and use the term professional(s) to mean public policy professional(s).

The perspective I bring to bear on the question of knowledge, power and practice is inspired by the work of Michel Foucault. The prodigious historical studies of this French thinker are germane to the analysis of modern professionalism. His *Madness and Civilization* is a study of modern psychiatry; *The Birth of the Clinic* traces the emergence of modern clinical medicine; *Discipline and Punish* is a history of penal and disciplinary practices since the eighteenth century; and the *History of Sexuality*, a multivolume genealogy of Western ethics starting with an introductory first volume, is an ambitious undertaking that was never completed due to Foucault's untimely death in 1984.

One of the main themes in all these studies, and in his more methodological writings as well, is that of the modern *'disciplines'*: an analytical category which, through a long series of elaborations and modifications, has introduced some crucial insights into the otherwise relatively arid sociological notion of 'profession' (see, for example, Goldstein, 1984; Hiley, 1984). In Foucault, the 'disciplines' refer not only to particular fields of knowledge or to certain occupational groups but also, and simultaneously, to a range of social/cultural practices which, since the eighteenth century, have gradually come to involve characteristically modern forms of power relations. The 'disciplines' therefore remind us:

> that power produces knowledge (and not simply by encouraging it because it serves power or by applying it because it is useful); that there is no power relation without the correlative constitution of a field of knowledge, nor any knowledge that does not presuppose and constitute at the same time power relations (Foucault, 1977, p. 27).

Foucault's views on power, knowledge, and practice are dispersed throughout a copious body of work. Nonetheless, the following proved especially useful in dealing with the issues raised in this chapter: *The Archaeology of Knowledge* (1972), particularly the section on 'Science and Knowledge' and the 'Discourse on Language'; *Discipline and Punish* (1977), particularly parts one and three; and *History of Sexuality* (1980), the chapter on 'Method'. To avoid frequent textual interruptions, I cite this work only when quoting directly. I gladly acknowledge my debt to him but take responsibility for what I say below.

Guidance Power

My purpose here is not to sketch a 'general theory of power' but to isolate some of the distinctive features of *contemporary* power relations, and only insofar as this promises a clearer understanding of the work of professionals. This being the case, 'guidance power' serves as a descriptive point of departure by directing attention to a form of power whose aim is *guidance* and whose main instrument is *knowledge*[2].

What is Guidance Power?

To start with, one must recognize the existence of different *forms* of power relations. Form, in this context, describes a mode of functioning; it refers not to the 'origin', 'source', or 'hidden secret' of a type of power, but to the means, techniques, instruments, or mechanisms through which, or on the basis of which, power functions. In this sense, oppression, for example, designates a specific form of power whose functioning entails the use or at least the threat of violence. In contrast, and to cite another example, the exercise of legitimate authority is another form of power which is rooted in law as its native principle and ultimate instrument.

As a distinctive form, guidance power can be described in terms of a number of characteristics among which the following are perhaps the most immediately relevant to the concerns of this chapter.

- It is a type of relationship between individuals (or between groups) in which power seeks to 'inform' or *guide* the choices, decisions, or actions of those on whom it is exercised. In the history of power, guidance is to modern professionals what salvation was to the medieval priests.

- As implied already, guidance power does not merely *command* but professes to show the proper way. It functions not on the basis of arbitrary or gratuitous exhortations or interdictions but through an incessant and painstaking search for justifiable (or as we say, 'rational') norms. It operates on a division between the normal and the abnormal, the healthy and the deranged, the functional and the dysfunctional, the natural and the aberrant. In this regard, one may say that guidance power adheres, consciously or otherwise, to a principle of *normalization*.

- In this form of power, the agents of guidance are not exempt from their own norms, but willingly submit to them. (For example, it is evident that the Bourgeoisie never exempted its own ranks from the morality it constituted during the eighteenth and nineteenth centuries; as a class, it imposed this morality on itself long before other classes were subjected to its disciplinary effects.)

- As a type of relationship, guidance power is both globalizing and individualizing. The object of guidance is not only the aggregate — a population, a class, a city, etc. — but flexibly differentiated and classified components as well — a family, a minority group, a neighborhood, etc.

- The functioning of guidance power is incessant. In contrast to sovereign power in feudal times — e.g. the extraction of land rent or the collection of tributes — which was exercised fitfully or intermittently, guidance power functions continuously. This is usually a precondition of its effectiveness.

- This effectiveness varies also in proportion to how much the agents of guidance *know* about its subjects. As an aim, guidance cannot be achieved without observing, questioning, examining, recording, classifying, analyzing, and projecting not only what the subjects do — their behavior; their actions — but also what they think, feel, need, perceive, and expect. Guidance power urges its subjects to reveal their innermost 'nature'. It both permits and requires the development of a multitude of elements of knowledge about men and women. I shall return to a discussion of these elements in the next section. For now, and to conclude these observations on guidance power, one may again invoke a historical analogy between the relationship of 'research' to modern professional guidance and that of the confession to medieval ecclesiastical salvation.

On the basis of these observations, it is possible to say that the work of modern professionals (including design professionals) is linked, in many and complex ways, to the functioning of guidance power. The nature of these links will be discussed below. To prepare for this discussion, it is necessary to say a few words on the functioning of guidance power.

How Does Guidance Power Function?

It is perhaps clear, but nonetheless worth stressing, that power is neither a thing to be possessed, nor a mysterious endowment, nor a force in the strict sense. Power, and guidance power is no exception, is exercised not held. In this sense, it exists only when it is put into action (Foucault, 1982, p. 788). For this reason, it is more useful to ask: How does it function? How is it exercised? than to ask: What is it? Where does it come from? Again, the following are meant as tentative propositions regarding how guidance power functions.

- Like other forms of power, guidance functions through more or less structured, more or less durable, relations between individuals (or between groups). But unlike them, guidance power is best conceived as a *relationship between actions*. It does not act directly upon subjects, but rather upon their actions; ' it is a way in which certain actions modify others ' (Foucault, 1982, p.788).

- As a relationship of actions upon the actions of others, guidance presupposes neither consent nor submission. Its exercise may be based on, or give rise to, either (and sometimes a mixture of both), but neither is intrinsic to its character proper. This is one of the features that distinguish it from legally constituted and enforced authority on the one hand and coercive forms of power on the other hand[3]. It also means that guidance power and freedom are not mutually exclusive. On the contrary. 'Power is exercised only over free subjects, and only insofar as they are free' (Foucault, 1982, p. 790). Its functioning, in other words, presupposes subjects facing genuine choices and capable of acting in potentially diverse ways.

- The specificity of this form of power is that it functions within more or less *open fields of possibilities*, and this is the case for both its agents and subjects. And if I chose to call it guidance power, it is partly to underscore the fact that its most essential aim is to structure the possible fields of action of others and to guide and order, in this manner, the resulting outcomes. The essence of guidance power is not domination but rather ordering and normalization.

- Inasmuch as relations of guidance power are neither routine enforcements of pre-existing rules (as with legal authority) nor bloody confrontations (as with violence), their outcomes are always contingent and subject to the play of actions and reactions.

In other words, the functioning of guidance power presupposes, and constantly provokes, reactions, oppositions, resistances, and struggles. And not only by those on whom it is exercised, but also on the part of those who exercise it.

- The fundamental instrument of guidance power is knowledge. Other means — repression, coercion, economic disparities, legally binding sanctions, dogma, tradition, manipulation — are neither essential nor suited to its specific mode of functioning. This is not to say that some of these other means do not come into play in relations of guidance power. It simply means that they are neither necessary nor particularly conducive to its effective exercise. *But knowledge is.* It is an instrument of power but is not always 'on the side of' the agents of guidance. For as much as knowledge can produce, or open paths for, power effects, it can equally expose, neutralize, or even disable such effects.

Before I move on to consider the question of knowledge in some detail, it is important to make explicit a point about power that has so far remained implicit. It has to do with the relationship of power to other types of human relations.

We are used to distinguishing between 'different' types of relations: political, economic, social, and so on. These distinctions may have some value as first approximations but they encourage two misconceptions: that power is exclusive to political relations, and/or that observing the effects of power in other domains — the family, the factory, the consultant's office, etc. — 'proves' that these domains too are 'politicized' or, alternatively, that power is a human psychological drive. These views are not entirely false. They nonetheless obscure the fact that power is not external to other types of relations but is one of their constitutive elements. Power is rooted in the system of social networks and is coextensive with their functioning. It pervades the entirety of the social body, not as a recurrent aberration and not as a hidden drive, but as an ensemble of practices through which a society circumscribes and regulates the interplay of knowledge and action, intentions and outcomes. It is from this vantage point that I shall now consider the nature of professional knowledge.

Professional Knowledge

For the limited purposes of this chapter, I shall set aside a wide range of historical and epistemological issues and restrict myself to two related questions: What elements are included in what we usually think of as a body of professional knowledge? and, What bases of unity, among these elements, allow us to speak of their totality as a *body*?

Elements of Professional Knowledge

As I mentioned earlier in the introduction to this chapter, we generally view a professional as an agent in possession of a specialized *body of knowledge*, mastery of which is a precondition of competent practice. The question here is about the types of elements or components which comprise such a body of knowledge.

Broadly speaking, and abstracting away from all specificities, we can say that professional knowledge may have a wide range of diverse elements or strands such as: a mass of observations and facts about a set of phenomena; various attempts to describe these phenomena and to analyze their correlations; numerous, and frequently rival, hypotheses, in various stages of formalization or testability, about the phenomena; perspicuous examples or archetypes used to illustrate 'ways of thinking' that are ambiguous or inadequately codified; chronicles, narratives, and histories describing how 'these' phenomena evolved and shifted in different places at different times; pedagogical advocacies and teaching models concerned with professional socialization and training; philosophical or pseudo-philosophical credos dealing with the 'essence' or social purposes of the profession; socio-political, ethical, and/or aesthetic doctrines which seek to 'ground' or at least justify choices among rival professional rôle models and/or specific normative positions; biographies and histories of ideas describing the lives and contributions of important past and present figures in the profession and interpreting their visions, advocacies, discoveries, ambitions, and/or frustrations; manuals dealing with and explaining various technical matters; surveys, polls, and other studies, anecdotal or systematic, impressionistic or rigorous, detailing the attitudes, views, beliefs or preferences of various population groups with respect to diverse services, products, or policy issues; bulletins reporting current professional developments and innovations, and commenting on newsworthy activities or episodes; references and case books listing and discussing various legal, administrative, or institutional regulations or provisions of relevance to a field of professional practice; and so on.

This lengthy, yet still incomplete, listing reminds us that the total sum of these elements lacks the tight structure or at least the visible internal links one normally expects of a *body* of knowledge. It thus raises the question of unity or cohesiveness among these seemingly disparate elements.

Unity of Professional Knowledge

At first glance, it appears that nothing much unites these diverse elements. Is it not more like a loose assemblage of facts, correlations, hypotheses, opinions, precepts, and techniques? Are these elements not devoid of systemic connections? Despite appearances, the answer must be in the negative.

For example, let us consider the profession of urban planning. And for brevity let us take just three of the many elements of knowledge considered central to this profession: a corpus of spatial microeconomic analyses of land rent and land use; a group of sociological interpretations of communities and neighborhoods; and, a set of juridico-administrative discussions of planning law, land use regulatory powers and instruments, approval and appeal procedures, and so on.

Now, if one poses the question of unity or cohesiveness of these three elements by looking for common objects of knowledge, shared conceptual structures, tacit compliance with similar epistemological foundations, adherence to particular models of demonstration or rules of justification, or for a core of congruent meanings, the results would most likely show little unity.

From this perspective, one may show, for example, how spatial economics assumes the presence of free land markets and concludes by affirming the rationality of the same; how juridical thought finds such an assumption empirically laughable and such a conclusion normatively objectionable; how legal historians note that land markets were instituted by law and have never been free of its regulations; or how legal philosophy insists that this is how things ought to be if private rights are to be balanced against collective interests. As for community sociology, one would point out, for example, how it blames the anarchy of markets for contributing to the disintegration of communities; or how it criticizes the universalizing tendency of legalistic/bureaucratic thinking for disregarding the diversity of local circumstances and needs. And so on.

Of course any such interpretations are likely to prove contentious (precisely because they join the very debates they seek to interpret). But even if we accept them, I doubt that they 'prove' the absence of cohesiveness among these three elements. They may simply indicate that we are looking for bases of unity in the wrong places. Before I follow this conjecture, let me first note that the kind of interpretations I just considered result from an *epistemic* and/or an *hermeneutic* interrogation of knowledge. In the former, one looks for relationships between elements of knowledge at the level of concepts, propositional structures, truth conditions of the conclusions, principles of justification of normative claims, and so on (see, for example, Bailey, 1975; Lipman and Harris, 1980). In the latter, one questions statements for what they may be hiding or for what they 'really' mean; one resorts to such categories as motives, consciousness, ideology; one looks for relationships between elements of knowledge at the level of their deep meanings or their real intentions (see, for example, Bolan, 1980; Garrott, 1983; Schön, 1984). It is this kind of double approach that I mimicked in dealing with the above example; it is what led us to see little consonance or accord among the three elements of knowledge we considered.

I also think it is necessary to point out that the epistemic and hermeneutic orientations are tied to a prevalent conception of *knowledge as mentation.* For as long as we think of knowledge as something purely noetic; as an 'exercise' that has no materiality and that yields nothing but disembodied ideas; as something that may have effects only in as much as it takes hold or shapes the 'ideas' of individuals, we are bound to view relationships between elements of knowledge as no more and no less than abstract relationships between ideas (be they linguistic, semiotic, conceptual, logical, psychological, or whatever). From this perspective, as we saw, one is willing to affirm the presence of unities among certain elements of knowledge only to the extent the 'ideas' contained therein exhibit adequate mutual relevance, commensurability, and consistency.

There can be no question about the legitimacy and usefulness of these orientations. But by treading endlessly in the double question: Is it valid? and, What does it really mean? an extremely important set of relationships between elements of knowledge is obscured or at least ignored. What I have in mind here is a system of links and connections which emerges between elements of knowledge on the basis of contacts, confluences, or overlaps among the *fields of use* in which these elements are placed. By fields of use I mean *historically constituted* (and hence always specific and shifting) social/cultural practices such as legislation, governance, justice, administration, penal and other correctional treatments, education, medicine, psychiatry, welfare, and so on. These practices organize networks of sites in which complex human relations are consummated, and *always on the basis of certain knowledges*. It is in this sense that practices function as fields of use of knowledge and establish, through their multiple contacts, confluences, and overlaps, effective links between the elements of knowledge used in each.

The links thus established are not necessarily links of consistency or complementarity among ideas. I chose to describe them as *effective links* to underscore the fact that they owe their emergence, existence, and transformations not to some ethereal rules of coherence but to earthly human encounters and practices. I noted earlier how knowledge functions as an instrument of power. Now we can add that knowledge is also an effect of power. Social/cultural practices are fields in which knowledge intermediates the production of power effects; at the same time, they are fields in which power enables and requires the creation, elaboration, and inspection of knowledge. In short, if it is *in* fields of practice that effective links are formed between elements of knowledge, then an analysis of these fields may also provide a key to the intelligibility of these links.

Returning briefly to our urban planning example, we may now try to analyze the relationships between spatial economics, community sociology, and juridico-administrative thought from the perspective of fields of practice and effective links. One must first seek to delineate some of the social/cultural practices in which urban planning practitioners get involved. One may include, for example, the various development or redevelopment review and approval processes; the procedures of 'consultation' or 'participation' through which affected individuals or groups may present their views and/or negotiate their demands; the judicial or quasi-judicial forums in which remedies or injunctions are sought against planning actions with putatively injurious or unjust consequences; and so on. One would also identify some of the parties which usually encounter one another in these practices: developers, financiers, ratepayers, tenants, merchants, consultants, lawyers, civil servants, elected officials, judges, and so on. One would then move on to examine the connections or confluences between these fields: how, for example, what development proponents and planners write, draw, or say during the review process anticipates and takes into account arguments and counter-arguments that are most likely to occur once consultation or citizen participation gets under way; how different parties engaged in either or both of these practices may seek to avert (or provoke) arbitration or litigation; how the knowledge used in the former two practices are therefore influenced by the threat (or promise) of arbitration or litigation; or how the knowledges that circulate in the latter draw directly on those used in the former two; and so on. Finally, one would ask oneself which elements of knowledge circulate in which field(s) of practice; which parties or agents most frequently invoke or reproduce versions of which elements of knowledge and in pursuit of which types of objectives; and which specific roles do these elements of knowledge play, singularly or in combination, in the work of those urban planners who get involved in these social/cultural practices.

One may then begin to see, for example, that something akin to spatial micro-economics is likely to be used by private proponents of development (or redevelopment) in their pursuit of rezonings, higher density allowances, or exemptions from some other land use regulations; that community sociology anticipates or prompts the collective responses of negatively affected groups as they seek to block or alter developments they regard as destabilizing to their areas; that the juridico-administrative perspective on the rights and obligations attached to the use of land is a generalized codification of the stance(s) most likely to be taken by judges or administrative arbitrators in adjudicating these territorial disputes; or that the intelligibility or 'sense' of each of these elements of knowledge, and of the links between them, is not imminent in any one of them but is *furnished in practice* by the specific configurations in which they are made to function: to support or oppose one another, to check the excesses of each other, to mutually define the terms on which they each wish to be understood, etc. Now one may be able to grasp the relationships between spatial economics, community sociology, and the legal-administrative perspective on land use, and judge their cohesiveness or unity as elements of urban planning knowledge.

In general, to approach the question of the links between elements of knowledge by analyzing the interlocking social/cultural practices in which they are used is, therefore, to introduce several important, and I think neglected, dimensions in our knowledge of professional knowledge. Such an analysis accepts that a body of knowledge is a composite of heterogeneous elements and not a monolithic entity. It recognizes the multi-faceted nature of this heterogeneity. For elements belonging to the same body of knowledge may differ not only in terms of their objects, concepts, methods, and/or philosophical presuppositions, but also in their enunciative modes. As we saw, some elements may be theoretical (exhibiting, or at least aspiring to, a propositional structure and complying with criteria of logical consistency and empirical testability) while others may be empirical (documenting covariances among sets of observations). Still others may be speculative (making essentially unverifiable claims), interpretive (attempting to understand, in the German sense of *Verstehen*, the subjective experiences of others), normative (recommending actions, evaluating states of affairs, urging adherence to moral or aesthetic precepts, etc.) subjunctive (envisaging possible or wished for worlds), imperative (proclaiming laws, regulations, decisions), or even literary or fictional.

The degrees of cohesiveness or unity among such elements — which, it must be said in passing, vary considerably from one profession to another, between places, and over time — must not be judged on epistemic and/or hermeneutic grounds alone. For in addition to being systems of ideas or expressions, elements of knowledge also function as relays and conduits between their users and between the fields of practice in which these users interact. Grids of effective links, possessing an intelligibility of their own, are thus constituted among such elements.

A systematic analysis of these links reveals a 'material' or, in any event, a more earthly side of professional knowledge which would otherwise remain obscured or mystified. As well, it provides a basis on which we can now proceed to examine the nature of professional practice.

Professional Practice

What is professional practice? The standard answer is that it is the application of a body of knowledge to certain social needs. But this only shifts the question, for now we must ask what is meant by application. The simplest view on this, and I am afraid the most common and least explicitly justified, is that the application of knowledge is a process in which one uses *generally* valid knowledge to arrive at *specifically* valid conclusions or insights. Following a recipe (i.e., a set of general directions known to produce certain results) or using a general equation (to find the value some unknown would take in a given situation) are instances of this notion of application of knowledge. Innumerable less trivial examples, from virtually any professional field, may be cited. But in general, the validity of this conception of application will be found limited to the domain of theoretical knowledge. Here, by definition, knowledge is structured in the form of generally valid propositions whose conditions of validity (or applicability) are adequately specified. Therefore, in situations where professionals rely on propositional knowledge, and where the relevant conditions of its validity are satisfied, it is quite accurate to describe professional practice as a process of using generally valid knowledge to specific cases subsumable under it.

But professional knowledge involves much more than theoretical knowledge. In particular, and as we saw before, it includes interpretive, normative, subjunctive, and other elements. Now, if we agree that professional knowledge is for naught if it does not provide practitioners with the necessary grounds on which they can make non-arbitrary recommendations and/or evaluations; and if we acknowledge, as we must, that interpretive, normative, and subjunctive premises are necessary in almost all arguments whose conclusions recommend actions and/or evaluate states of affairs (Hitchcock, 1983, p. 196), then it follows that these non-theoretical knowledges are indispensable in practice. And since they do not lend themselves to the manner of application we just discussed, we must reconsider our habitual views on what actually takes place in professional practice. But first, two cautionary remarks.

We must reject the notion that theoretical knowledge or science (to use the term loosely) is the *telos* of professional knowledge; that all non-theoretical elements are temporary impurities which get eliminated as a profession matures (see, for example, Klosterman, 1983 p.123). Science does not, and for the reasons I just summarized cannot, provide the model nor prescribe the ideal structure of professional knowledge (Foucault, 1972, p.184). Slogans such as 'professionalism is the application of scientific knowledge to social concerns' may have rhetorical value in defending professional privileges, but they would not do for an analysis of practice. This is because they imply the same conception of application we found wanting.

The second remark concerns the issue of subjectivity. As professionals, we never tire of saying, for example, that objectivity is an abstract ideal; that even if it can be attained in the pursuit of pure research, it cannot in the context of professional practice; that 'values' and 'motives' inevitably influence the 'consciousness' of practitioners and thus introduce various degrees and forms of bias, prejudice, or fraud in their work. Now if this were meant only as a rejection of a cartesian separation of objectivity and subjectivity, it would be foolish to call it into question. But I suspect that this kind of expression is linked to a self-serving fatalism which, among other things, shrugs off the question of what actually takes place in practice and passively endorses the facile notion of application we discussed above on the tacit claim that it would 'work' had it not been for biases and so on.

Quite apart from all this, this fatalism must be rejected because of the confusions it implies; for example, the notion that professional practices are virtually defenseless against the onslaught of partiality, that all but those who bewail this presumed vulnerability are blind to it or ensnared by its effects, or that the mere having of 'values', or 'intentions' significantly enhances the odds of their realization through professional practice.

We must, therefore, recast the question of professional practice by shunning these three related notions: that practice is basically the application of generally valid knowledge to specific cases; that the current limitations on this model are bound to dissipate as professional knowledge matures and becomes more scientific; and that if the daily experiences of practitioners do not bear out this model, it is only because of the frailty of practices in the face of human biases and prejudices. With these preliminaries in mind, I would now like to bring together elements of the two preceding discussions (on guidance power and professional knowledge) in an attempt to propose a way of looking at professional practice.

Let us say, first of all, that practice can neither be analyzed as a material activity (since it may not involve that) nor as a mental activity (since it always involves more than that). Of course some professional practices involve material activities (a landscape architect, for example, may actually participate in building a park), but these do not define the character proper to professional practice. Material activities are central to many occupations which are nonetheless not considered professions. On the other hand, many professional practices do not involve material activities. This is usually the case, for example, in the design professions. Architects need not actually build the buildings they design in order to be considered architects. Urban designers and planners hardly ever undertake actual construction of facilities, infrastructure, or usable space.

But we cannot conceptualize professional practice as a mental activity either. Much more than mentation is involved as we saw before. To *use* knowledge is to insert it in social/cultural practices; it is to make it play a part in structuring the possible fields of action of individuals or groups who interact in these practices. In short, professional practice involves the coupling of knowledge and power. And it is in this sense that the character proper to it escapes analysis if viewed merely as a mental activity.

To say that professional practice involves a certain coupling of knowledge and power does not, of course, answer the question regarding the nature of practice. But it permits some clarifications. In particular, it makes it possible to see why we can no longer think of knowledge and power as external to one another, but must recognize them as mutually constitutive. *Hence, knowledge-power.* Neither can be understood in abstraction from the other. Nor can either be reduced to the other (Dreyfus and Robinow, 1983, p. 114; compare to Burgess, 1983). In turn, this directs us to examine some of the specific characteristics of this coupling knowledge-power in relationship to professional practice.

We may define the space in which knowledge and power meet as *discourse.* Or more accurately, let us use the term discourse to describe the system of relays which hooks knowledge and power in any ensemble of social/cultural practices[4]. In a way, my analysis of the effective links among elements of professional knowledge was an attempt to show how, in practice, constellations are formed by seemingly disparate elements; constellations which we may now call *professional discourses.*

What is distinctive about these constellations, and what may justify introducing this admittedly elusive term 'discourse' to designate their specificity, is that they establish, and are themselves established by, the effective links that are necessary, in a given socio-historical context, for knowledge and power to function as knowledge-power; that is, for knowledge to acquire the objective *possibility* of producing power effects and, at the same time, for power to require the development and use of knowledge. *Professional practice may, therefore, be properly understood as discursive practice*: it deploys knowledge in fields of guidance power and forms, multiplies, and transforms this knowledge in the same fields[5].

Based on these points, I would now like to complete this analysis by outlining a number of general characteristics of professional practice.

- Professional practice involves the production of context-specific discourse: conceived in, and tailored to fit, the *particular* situation at hand. It is not the application of precast 'theory'. It does not use the same thing differently but constitutes a different thing constantly. This is done, of course, within specific, if tacit, limits inherent in all historically structured discourses.

- It may draw upon numerous elements of knowledge and confines itself to none. It respects no formal 'disciplinary' boundaries but moves freely within a fluid, and shifting, discursive constellation; a constellation which is historically constituted through, and used in, a particular set of interlocking fields of social/cultural practices.

- Professional practice adheres to, and anticipates that it shall be judged by, *active criteria of truth*. Its model of justification is not one in which knowledge passively mimics observed reality, but rather one in which discourse seeks to conduce the conditions which vindicate its truth. Professional practice is not aversive to the former. On the contrary, it uses it freely. But it does not reify it or restrict itself to it[6].

- Acting to impose or dictate particular outcomes is not an essential (or inherent) feature of professional practice. The historical significance and specificity of *modern* professionalism, and of the authorization of professionals to practice — be it on the basis of legal structures, administrative arrangements, certification or licensing, prevailing customs, or a combination of these — do not lie in the phenomena of 'expert hegemony' or dominance of a 'technocratic rationality' (compare to Gans, 1978). This is not to deny the reality of either phenomena, but rather to suggest that the effectiveness of contemporary professional practices does not presuppose or require them[7].

The authorization of professionals to practice entails a different mandate that is rarely acknowledged explicitly; namely, to introduce, and hopefully to institute, stable and orderly relations and mechanisms of guidance power in fields of social/cultural practices exhibiting disorderly, volatile, disruptive, or otherwise unproductive human confrontations, conflicts, insubordinations, or antagonisms. In general, one can say that in societies such as our own, the effectiveness of professional practices does not lie in controlling the contents of choices or decisions but rather in bringing into play relations of guidance power. In short, not domination but normalization.

• Correlatively, specialized (or esoteric) professional knowledge is not the only, and not necessarily the most influential, knowledge that functions in practice. For as soon as expert knowledge is used — that is to say made public; made an object of commentary, review, or debate — it becomes part of a discourse. It surrounds itself with numerous other knowledges through the complex and always contingent play of responses and counter-responses, endorsements and objections, interpretations and imputations, promises and threats, that it necessarily unleashes.

Expert knowledge thus ceases to function according to its 'own' rules of construction and norms of validity[8]; the other knowledges it encounters in discourse modify it, impose new requirements on it, transform its significances and implications, and deny it its 'scholarly' autonomy. But at the same time, *they give it the objective possibility of producing real effects in the social world.*

In short, practice converts the specialized knowledge of the professionals into discourse and absorbs its rules into the rules of knowledge-power. Hence, the knowledge professionals generate in practice — the knowledge that functions and reaches its term by producing power effects — is not isomorphic with the knowledge professionals acquire in formal education or through scholarly publications. We must therefore divest ourselves of the naive notion that the latter has, or can have, *direct* impacts on the outcomes of professional practice.

- The two preceding points permit us to return briefly to the issue of value-neutrality in professional practice. If practical discourse is not isomorphic with formal knowledge, then the practical question of value-neutrality should no longer be confused with the epistemological question of the possibility of objective knowledge. And if the former question is analyzed from the perspective of guidance power and the requirements of effective normalization, one will see in the call for value-neutrality something more than an idle wish or an ideological ruse. If practitioners abstain from partiality, it is not because 'their' knowledge is objective or because they are under the spell of some ideology of value-neutrality, but because (and perhaps only to the extent that) this abstention is one of the conditions of continued authorization to function as agents of guidance power.

To oppose to the doctrine of value-neutrality the position that 'all professional practice is political' does not contribute to freeing practice from its involvement with guidance power. On the contrary, the doctrine and its 'critique' are quite compatible in practice. They function in concert to dismember knowledge-power by positing a 'choice' between them. Professional practice is not caught in the alternative: knowledge or power. Inasmuch as it is an agent of guidance power, practice can only be both.

- Professional practice functions as an agent of guidance power by putting into operation a wide range of *discursive tactics*. These vary, of course, from one profession to another, between places, and over time. Because they are tactics, they are fluid and in a constant state of readjustment. Nonetheless, a number of broad themes may be discerned. In the design professions, from which the following examples are chosen, discursive tactics may be based on:

Schemes of classification: according to which groups of subjects (or of interests) are differentiated by oblique reference to objectified classifications of 'things': activities, functions, building types, land use types, neighborhoods, circulation systems, and so on. Such schemes enable professionals to act differently upon the actions of different groups of humans while appearing to act merely on things. Structuring fields of human choices is therefore accomplished through the coordination of things and by ordering the resulting totalities.

Criteria of normalization: which permit the justification of advice on the basis of presumably objective or self-evident principles; hence the constant search for universal and invariant attributes of 'human nature' and the use of medical metaphors as foundations for establishing norms of environmental 'health' (see, for example, O'Neill, 1986).

Claims of crisis: Since the nineteenth century, the design professions have recurrently proclaimed a state of crisis in the built environment. Of course problems always existed and occasionally bordered on crisis proportions. Professionals have not, therefore, invented the problems; they constituted them as objects of intervention. They spoke profusely and endlessly of disintegration, deterioration, decay, and pending chaos. They also incited virtually all social groups to follow suit. They made crisis the threat that requires guidance and guidance the promise of deliverance from crisis.

Justification of comprehensive guidance: Because the built environment is portrayed as a seamless garment or as an organic whole, changes to parts of it are *abstractly* said to affect other parts. This has always been made the basis for urging 'comprehensive planning'. Whether or not coordinated policies are in fact put into effect, the call for comprehensiveness functions as the code word for selectively bypassing democracy and overriding local concerns and resistances in the name of respecting the rationality of the whole.

Manipulation of ambiguities: Estimating the likely consequences of actions is always contentious because social life is ambiguous. In this context, factual, interpretive, predictive, and normative ambiguities become targets of multiple techniques of manipulation and permit the deployment of a variety of discursive tactics.

• The use of discursive tactics is not, in and of itself, an exclusive property of professional practice. Insofar as relations of guidance power involve acting upon the actions of others, discursive tactics are used by agents and subjects of power alike. The asymmetry between them comes into sharper focus when we consider the aims they each pursue. Subjects resist the effects of guidance and normalization whenever these require them to submit to what are offered as the dictates of superior knowledge with all the deformations, impositions, and restrictions this implies. Agents of guidance, on the other hand, pursue the aim of structuring the fields of actions of subjects in the hope of ordering the cumulative outcomes of these actions. The tensions thus constituted at the heart of relations of guidance power give contemporary professional practices what I think is their basic specificity; they are professional precisely to the extent that they seek to forge adequate discursive accords among the multiplicity of interests held by the parties involved. To adapt a criterion offered by David Wiggins (1978) in a related context, one can say that a discursive accord is 'adequate for the situation if and only if circumstances which could restrict or qualify it and defeat its applicability at a given juncture do not in the practical context [of the accord] obtain' (p. 147).

Further Implications

It is difficult to think afresh about familiar things. Professional practice is one of those things, at least for those of us who have more than a casual involvement with it. In the infrequent moments when our sense of familiarity with professional practice wanes, seemingly inescapable themes such as the 'service ideal', 'problem solving', 'means/ends', 'rationality', 'science' and 'neutrality' swiftly help replenish the plenitude of thoughts we already thought about practice.

In this chapter I have tried to escape this 'eternal return' I wanted neither to propose a 'new' theory of practice nor to offer an 'alternative' professional rôle model, but simply to look at practice from the point of view of knowledge and power. The resulting analysis introduced some shifts in our habitual thinking about professional practice. Most of these were pointed out above. But three further implications deserve mention. I would, therefore, like to conclude with a brief discussion of each of these.

There is first an implication with respect to the tasks of 'theory' in relationship to questions of norms and ideals, be they political, moral, social, or aesthetic. For a long time now, and at least in the design professions, we labored in a tradition according to which 'theory' meant not only verifiable propositional knowledge but philosophically inspired *normative* claims as well. In the latter sense, theory is given the task of proposing ways in which abstract philosophical reflections can be 'operationalized' in professional practice. This assumes, of course, that norms and ideals, whether abstract or practicable, are *anterior* to practice; an assumption that is put in doubt by the preceding analysis.

In discussing guidance power, I have tried to show how norms and ideals are not external to professional practice — not 'given' to it as a datum or standard by 'society' let alone by a theory — but are rather constituted, modified, accepted or rejected, and hence made effective *in* practice. Furthermore, discourse that functions in practice, and which includes normative principles as I pointed out, is much more than the formalized knowledge of the professionals. It is not fixed by, and does not function according to the rules of, this knowledge. It comprises many, and usually incompatible, voices, convictions and agendas. Knowledge that professionals bring to practice, and this includes tacit as well as formalized normative stances, does not create its own conditions of effectiveness; these are furnished (or denied) in practice through the play of knowledge-power relations. We should perhaps abandon, or at least reconsider, the notion that theory can effectively influence professional practice by serving as its super-ego.

Related to this is a second implication regarding the issue of ideology in relationship to professional practices. It is clear that I have not invoked ideology as an analytical category. There are two reasons for this. In the first place, ideology, however defined, connotes distortion or falsification of knowledge; something that blocks our ability to recognize situations for what they 'really' are. In a sense, ideology is undeniably a common experience: not because we possess a common standard of truth against which we discern ideological distortions, but precisely because truth is always contentious. Thus, if one introduces the notion of ideology in an analysis whose purpose is to untangle the contentions provoked by relations of knowledge-power, one runs the risk of self-righteous engagement in these very same contentions. Second, and perhaps more important, an analysis conducted in terms of ideology runs yet another risk; namely, of underestimating the complexity of power relations. To the extent one assigns primacy to ideology as an instrument of power, one sees only the negative side of power: the side that mystifies (reality), distorts (communication), or derails (the formation of rational agreement). But as I tried to show, power, and particularly guidance power, is exercised on the basis of much more intricate, tangible and diverse tactics and procedures.

None of this is meant to deny the existence or importance of ideological effects. It is meant to suggest that the point of questioning knowledge that functions, and that is constituted, in professional practices is not as much to force it to confess its dubious foundations and to reveal its hidden deceptions, but to find out how it is made to function, *even in the absence of ideological distortions*, as a basis of practices which are nonetheless saturated with power, constraint, conflicts, and resistances. The familiar question: How does power use ideology? is compelling only to the extent that we harbor the comforting yet elusive hope that banishing ideology would deliver us from the bellicosities of power. It is clearly much less comforting, but perhaps more effective, to ask: How does power function without ideology?

This last question brings me to the third implication which has to do with the remarks I made earlier about the limits of what I called the epistemic and hermeneutic modes of interrogating knowledge. It seems to me that the epistemic approach — in which one questions knowledge by scrutinizing its concepts, propositional structures, truth conditions, and so on — is best suited to situations which require one to assess the *validity* of theoretical or empirical propositions. It helps answer questions of the type: Should I accept this proposition as valid? Clearly, such questions are always present in practice. The hermeneutic approach — by which one seeks to decipher meaning — is most useful whenever one is concerned with the *truthfulness* of expressions. It comes into play when the question is: Does this expression truly disclose the subjectivity of the author (or speaker)[9]? This too is obviously a question that confronts parties involved in professional practice.

But these two types of question do not exhaust the basic knowledge-related concerns that are triggered in practical situations. There are, in addition, concerns about the *strategic or tactical significance* of knowledge. The questions here are diverse and intricate: What response am I likely to get if I used such-and-such an argument? What do they expect us to say/do in response to this proposal? Of what discursive tactic is this statement an element? To what discursive strategy does this tactic belong? What alliances/divisions (among stakeholders) is this recommendation likely to generate? and so on. Now, if we view discourse as a system of relays linking knowledge and power in given situations, then the discursive elements used by those involved, and the sequence in which they are used, can be seen as moves, tactics and strategies in the context of knowledge-power relations. There is, therefore, a need, imposed by the nature of professional practice thus understood, for a third mode of analyzing knowledge; one that interrogates it *strategically*. To be more accurate, I should note that it is not knowledge but discourse that can and should be questioned strategically. In this approach, one treats discursive elements not as ideas but as *events* triggered by, and triggering, specific dynamics in the situation at hand. And, as events, one analyzes them according to the intelligibility of actions and responses, pressures and resistances, strategies and counter-strategies, knowledge-power.

What I sketched here is a terrain that remains virtually unexplored by analysts although I suspect that it is not that unfamiliar to practising professionals. One may say that this terrain starts where game theory stops: where logically deducible 'equilibrium solutions' can no longer be found; where the calm determinacy of theory gives way to the stormy contingencies of practice. Exploring this terrain does not amount to 'going beyond' the epistemic and hermeneutic approaches; it is more like stepping back to prepare the grounds for their *effective* utilization. For it seems to me that one can neither seriously assess the validity of propositions nor understand the meaning of expressions without a *simultaneous* assessment of the strategic significance of the discursive elements to which these propositions and expressions belong.   The epistemic, hermeneutic and strategic orientations to knowledge are not 'alternatives' among which agents and/or subjects of guidance power may pick and choose.   In practice, the effectiveness of each depends on the simultaneous operation of all three.   The notion that professional practice is the application of knowledge is not false.   But it is not helpful either.   For practice, as all of this suggests, is much more than the application of knowledge; it is the strategic constitution, deployment, and transformation of discourse in diverse and ever-shifting fields of power.   Gilles Deleuze (1977, p. 205) may be right in thinking that 'we're in the process of experiencing a new relationship between theory and practice'.

Notes

1.   From Gadamer (1975), p. 312.

2.   Thomas Jefferson is reported to have said: 'I know of no safe depository of the ultimate powers of society but the people themselves; and if we think them not enlightened enough to exercise their control with a wholesome discretion, the remedy is not to take it from them, but to inform their discretion' (quoted in Carter, 1983, pp. 33 and 34).   I find two interesting things about this statement.   First, its reference to informing the discretion of 'the people' foretells what was to become a pervasive form of power: guidance.   Second, I found it quoted approvingly by Donald K. Carter, a practicing architect, in the context of advocating an alternative to the conventional model of the architect as a prima donna or as an élitist taste-maker. Here, Carter *assumes* that involving citizens in the programming, design, and construction of buildings puts an end to the power relations between architects and clients.

3.   J. K. Galbraith (1983) misses this point and asserts, with no explanation or justification, that power, by definition, involves the imposition of the will of an agent and the acquiescence of a subject. This error is due, in part, to his failure to distinguish between different *forms* of power. (see Chapters 1 and 9).

4.   In addition to the definition offered in the text, a few more words on 'discourse'. In the current context, I need a term that has the following characteristics: a) it should not signify bodies of logically consistent theories, but patterned forms of *thought-in-social-use*, b) it should be evaluatively neutral with regard to the scientificness (or lack of it) of the elements of thought it describes, c) it should have a connotation of ongoing 'talk' about objects including both compatible and incompatible enunciations, and d) it should not restrict the reference to the formal aspects of language, speech acts, or communication.

The term 'discourse' comes close to satisfying these requirements. Nonetheless, I would have preferred to avoid it, first because it remains conceptually elusive (as it also is in Foucault's work), and second because it has become part of a trendy lexicon in which use does not always follow necessity.

5.   In an article he wrote in 1931 on 'Social Science and Social Control', John Dewey exhibits his characteristic clarity on this same point:
'. . . it is a complete error to suppose that efforts at social control depend upon the prior existence of a social science. The reverse is the case. The building up of social science, that is, of a body of knowledge in which facts are ascertained in their significant relations, is dependent upon putting social planning into effect' (1939, p. 951). Interestingly, he ends the article by disclaiming infatuation with 'social planning and control'.

6.   Another way of putting this is to say that discourse does not restrict itself to experimental/empiricist conceptions of validity but invokes, and is judged by, forensic/practical criteria of reasonableness as well. In terms of enunciative structure and mode

of justification, professional discourse echoes the model of *practical reason*. See, for example, Isard and Lewis, 1984; Wiggins, 1978; and Wolin, 1972.

of 5;7. I hope it is clear that in saying this, I am *not* expressing a normative view regarding what ought to be, but an analytical view regarding what I think *is* the case. The history of practices in the design professions shows some interesting corroborations of this view. Practices such as slum clearance, master planning, wholesale urban renewal, and large scale transportation *cum* land use projects were undeniably accompanied by various forms of professional impositions. Each and every one of these practices generated sustained oppositions and resistances; they were all eventually discontinued. At the same time, practices involving consultation, community participation, and, more recently, efforts at conflict mediation, have proven more effective. It is also relevant to remember that the rights to participate were neither fought for by the 'people' nor resisted by the design professionals, and that attempts to introduce practices involving advocacy and/or explicit intent to favor the interests of currently disadvantaged groups have not been accepted despite their moral legitimacy.

8. This is one of the main reasons why I urged skepticism regarding epistemic and/or hermeneutic analyses of professional knowledge.

9. The term 'disclosure of subjectivity' is Habermas's (1979, p.68).

References

Bailey, J. (1975) *Social Theory for Planning*, Routledge and Kegan Paul, London.

Beauregard, R. A. (1983) Planners as workers: a marxist perspective, pp. 183-207 in J. R. Blau, M. La Gory, and J. Pipkin (eds.) *Professionals and Urban Form*, SUNY Press, Albany.

Bolan, R. S. (1980) The practitioner as theorist: the phenomenology of the professional episode, *Journal of the American Institute of Planners*, 46, 261-274.

Boyer, M. C. (1983) *Dreaming the Rational City: the Myth of American City Planning*, MIT Press, Cambridge, MA.

Burgess, P. G. (1983) Social role models, values and the profession, pp.15-19 in P. G. Burgess (ed.) *The Role of the Architect in Society*, Department of Architecture, Carnegie-Mellon University, Pittsburgh.

Burgess, P. G., Littman, E., and Mayo, J. (1981) Political knowledge and the architectural studio, *Journal of Architectural Education*, 34, 24-28.

Carter, D. K. (1983) A practitioner responds, pp. 31-35 in P. G. Burgess (ed.) *The Role of the Architect in Society*, Department of Architecture, Carnegie-Mellon University, Pittsburgh.

Dear, M. and Scott, A. (1981) *Urbanization and Planning in Capitalist Society*, Methuen, London.

Deleuze, G. (1977) Intellectuals and power: A conversation between Michel Foucault and Gilles Deleuze, in D. F. Bouchard (ed. and tr.), *Language, Counter-Memory, Practice*, Cornell University Press, Ithaca, NY.

Dewey, J. (1939) *Intelligence and the Modern World*, Modern Library, New York.

Dreyfus, H. L. and Rabinow, P. (1983) *Michel Foucault: Beyond Structuralism and Hermeneutics*, University of Chicago Press, Chicago.

Elkin, S. L. (1974) *Politics of Land Use Planning: the London Experience*, Cambridge University Press, Cambridge.

Foglesong, R. E. (1986) *Planning the Capitalist City: The Colonial Era to the 1920s*, Princeton University Press, Princeton, NJ.

Forester, J. (1982) Planning in the face of power, *Journal of the American Planning Association*, 48, 67-80.

Foucault, M. (1967) *Madness and Civilization: A History of Insanity in the Age of Reason*, tr. R. Howard, Tavistock, London.

Foucault, M. (1972) *The Archaeology of Knowledge*, tr. A. M. Sheridan Smith, Pantheon, New York.

Foucault, M. (1973) *The Birth of the Clinic: an Archaeology of Medical Perception*, tr. A. M. Sheridan Smith, Tavistock, London.

Foucault, M. (1977) *Discipline and Punish: The Birth of the Prison*, tr. A. M. Sheridan Smith, Pantheon, New York.

Foucault, M. (1980) *The History of Sexuality: Volume 1: an introduction*, tr. R. Hurley, Vintage, New York.

Foucault, M. (1982) The subject and power, *Critical Inquiry*, 8, 777-795.

Gadamer, H-G. (1975) Hermeneutics and social science, *Cultural Hermeneutics*, 2, 307-316.

Galbraith, J. K. (1983) *The Anatomy of Power*, Houghton Mifflin, Boston.

Gans, H. J. (1978) Towards a human architecture: a sociologist's view of the profession, *Journal of Architectural Education*, 31, 26-31.

Garrot, J. G. (1983) Interpreting value systems milieus, pp. 21-29 in
P. G. Burgess (ed.) *The Role of the Architect in Society*, Department of Architecture, Carnegie-Mellon University, Pittsburgh.

Goldstein, J. (1984) Foucault among the sociologists: the 'disciplines'
and the history of the professions, *History and Theory*, 23,
170-192.

Haar, C. M. (1967) The social control of urban space, pp. 175-229
in L. Wingo Jr (ed.) *Cities and Space*, Johns Hopkins University
Press, Baltimore.

Habermas, J. (1979) *Communication and the Evolution of Society*, tr.
T. McCarthy, Beacon Press, Boston.

Hiley, D. (1984) Foucault and the analysis of power: political engagement without liberal hope or comfort, *Praxis International*,
4, 192-207.

Hitchcock, D. (1983) *Critical Thinking: A Guide to Evaluating Information*, Methuen, Toronto.

Isard, W. and Lewis, B. (1984) James P. Bennett on subjunctive
reasoning, policy analysis, and political argument, *Conflict
Management and Peace Science*, 8, 71-112.

Klosterman, R. E. (1983) Foundations for normative planning, pp.
114-133 in J. R. Blau, M. La Gory and J. Pipkin (eds.) *Professionals and Urban Form*, SUNY Press, Albany.

Larson, M. S. (1983) Emblem and exception: the historical definition
of the architect's professional role, pp. 49-86 in J. R. Blau, M.
La Gory and J. Pipkin (eds.) *Professionals and Urban Form*,
SUNY Press, Albany.

Lipman, A. and Harris, H. (1980) Environmental psychology: a
sterile research enterprise?, *Built Environment*, 6, 68-74.

O'Neill, J. (1986) The medicalization of social control, *Canadian Review of Sociology and Anthropology*, 23, 350-364.

Roweis, S. (1983) Urban planning as professional mediation of territorial politics, *Environment and Planning D: Society and Space*, 1, 139-162.

Schön, D. A. (1984) The architectural studio as an exemplar of education for reflection-in-action, *Journal of Architectural Education*, 38, 2-9.

Silverstein, M. and Jacobson, M. (1985) Restructuring the hidden program: towards an architecture of social change, pp. 149-164 in W. Preiser (ed.) *Programming the Built Environment*, Van Nostrand Reinhold, New York.

Wiggins, D. (1978) Deliberation and practical reason, pp. 144-152 in J. Raz (ed.) *Practical Reasoning*, Oxford University Press, London.

Wolin, S. (1972) Political theory as a vocation, in M. Fleischer (ed.) *Machiavelli and the Nature of Political Thought*, Atheneum, New York.

Chapter 9

Sources of Influence in Planning Practice and their Implications for Development Negotiations

John Forester

What influence may planners have in the urban land development process? Even when planners have little formal authority, might they nevertheless negotiate effectively with private developers (or mediate developer-neighborhood conflicts) to shape project outcomes? This essay seeks to address these questions.

Why do these issues matter? Susskind and Ozawa recently answered this question with a compelling challenge to local planning staff:

> The mediator-planner encourages contending stakeholders to explore their differences — seeking zones of overlapping interest or possible items to trade, striving to maximize "joint gains" (Raiffa, 1982). As Raiffa points out, most disputes involve multiple issues. Because disputing parties seldom value all issues equally, trade-offs are possible. By emphasizing the possibility of "joint gains" and mutually satisfying arrangements, the mediator-planner enhances the chances of implementing a particular course of action (1984, p. 9).

Susskind and Ozawa posed the realization of joint gains and the achievement of a stable, implemented outcome as a practical challenge *for* planners. This essay seeks to show that planning staff have systematic opportunities to meet this challenge *in* their day-to-day practice.

The argument proceeds as follows: The first section assesses excerpts from a transcript of a planner-developer meeting early in the development process in an Eastern municipality. The questions asked by the developer in this meeting are telling. Suggesting not only various uncertainties that the developer faces, these queries also point to avenues of influence available to local planning staff.

This analysis is then developed to assess the planning staff's discretion in such meetings. Expectedly, planners may have relatively little discretion in regard to some issues, but perhaps less expectedly, planners may have wider discretion in handling many other issues.

The next section considers the potentially misleading focus that planners may adopt with respect to the developer's 'bottom line' of maximizing returns on investment. Considering the transcript studied in the first section, 'maximizing return on investment' can be understood to involve a wide range of subsidiary interests — in reducing risk or assuring timeliness, for example. The discussion of the developer's multiple interests leads, then, to the consideration of planner-developer project review discussions as elements of a larger process of development negotiations.

The final section considers what can be learned by taking project review conversations to be in fact informal development negotiations. Finding a fit between the basic issues explored in the planner-developer transcript and basic dimensions of negotiation processes more generally, the analysis here suggests (1) why planning staff may have *systematic sources* of influence available to them in local development negotiations, and (2) how 'joint net gains' might exist in such negotiations and be — or fail to be — achieved.

What Influence Can Planners Have?

How can the informal influence of planners be observed in practice and studied?[1] The analysis that follows draws from two sources: the literature discussing 'power' in organizational contexts and the more recent literature exploring research approaches such as conversational analysis and interaction analysis (Thompson, 1967; Bednar and Curington, 1983).

A student of organizational behavior, J. D. Thompson argued that the power of a first person over a second may be tied to the second's dependency upon the first. Where dependency and interdependency exist, then, power and influence will be found as well. More generally, Anthony Giddens argues that power should be understood as an attribute of a relationship between people rather than as a possession of anyone. If Thompson and Giddens are right, then the influence of local planners may be studied by examining the practical relations of interdependence between planners and developers in the local development process.

Consider the working conversations between planners and developers at the early stages of 'project review' or 'design review'. In such meetings, developers explore project options with the planning staff to gauge future development possibilities. Developers explore a variety of concerns in these working sessions with the planning staff, who, in turn, may provide the developers with a rich array of information, advice, suggestions, warnings, and interpretations. Had planners no influence here, these meetings would be purely perfunctory or would not take place at all. Quite often though the opposite is true: these meetings matter, as evidenced not only by developers' participation in them but by their results (to be assessed) as well. But how might such planner-developer meetings be investigated?

One way to study these meetings is to take them seriously as working conversations, as occasions not simply of casual interaction and talk, but of communicative interaction in particular (Forester, 1980). The doing in these meetings happens through the saying. The 'talk' here matters. As developer and planner talk, they explore issues, probe one another, test ideas, and seek to influence one another in various ways. To explore the influence that planning staff may have in project review meetings, then, we can ask about the ways in which the developer is (partially) dependent upon what the planner has to say. What does the developer want from these sessions? Why does the developer bother? What does the planner have to give, or withhold? How can we understand the micro-politics, the small scale politics of these project review meetings?

Questions and Answers as Proxies for the Developer's Uncertainty and the Planner's Influence

To address these issues, we draw from a partial transcript of a developer-planner project review meeting that took place on one September 9. The meeting in question lasted approximately forty-five minutes. The developer owned a small one-story building adjoining a two-story structure on the south in a commercial center. Flanking the building on the north is a long driveway connecting a public parking lot in the back of the property to the commercial street which the developer's property faces. Since the parking lot has other entrances and egresses to the back, the developer will explore purchase of this adjoining driveway from the city as part of his 'plans'. At the back of the one story structure is a small parking area on the developer's property. Since that parking area provides more spaces than required by the present structure, the developer hopes to get credit for the 'extra' spaces in order to add a second floor of commercial offices to the building. That those new offices would abut the second-story windows of the adjoining building is a consequence that seems almost to be discovered in the developer-planner conversation.

In this conversation, the developer sought to explore the possibilities of adding a second story to his building — which meant exploring not only regulatory requirements but more, as we shall see. The planner had no formal authority in this meeting to make decisions or rulings, to issue requirements, or to place conditions on development, yet the planner may still have had influence here. To explore how this may have been the case, let us select from the larger transcript the instances in which the developer expresses some dependency upon the planner. We look then not to what the developer *tells* to the planner but to what the developer *asks* and requests from the planner.

Studying the developer's *questions* will provide a first approximation of what the developer wants from the planner and what he may need

Table 9.1: A Developer's Questions and a Planner's
Responses (Meeting 9/9/85)

1.   D: "Let's talk about both Common St. and College St.,
        OK?"

        P: (Having some pictures of College St., asks) 'Which one
        first?'

2   D: "What's the lot now? Less than 5,000?"

        P: (measures) "Yes, about 3,600 sq. ft."

3.   D: "I believe the FAR there is 2.0, yes?"

        P: "No, it's 1.75."

4.   D: "Let's talk in general about the downzoning of College
        that's been in the air, OK?"

        P: "That was a political compromise ... it's been down-
        zoned, but you can get a bonus up to 2.25 if you have an
        extra lot ..."

5,6.   D: "How does that work? (What is possible?)

        P: "It's contingent upon ..." (explains)

7.   D: "What's the idea being the bonus?"

        P: "The gas station site was the root of it. (The people who
        pushed for the downzoning) wanted to make sure it
        wouldn't go; they definitely wanted less density; so the
        Planning Board proposed the downzoning to 2.0, with a
        bonus of 2.5 (under special conditions).

8.   D: "What was the other case (that provoked the down
        zoning)?"

P: "Children's, Inc.; He's (already) built up to two floors."

9.   D: "Has there been a revision to the Code?"

P: "Yes, last April."

10.   D: "So this (parcel) falls under the 1.75, without any bonus because it's under 20,000 sq. ft.?"

P: "Yes ... unless you have a large lot, the parking will be the determinant of density."

11.   P: "We're sometimes called the Development Department by some who think we're too soft, but now we have a new chair of the Board of Appeals ..."

D: "Who's that?"

P: "Bob Nix; he's a stickler ... be very careful about floor area; he's strict about that."

12.   D: "Let me ask you a question, ok?"

P: "sure; it's just that the parking is the real issue here" (he shows the diagram in the zoning ordinance);

13.   D: "so that would stand regardless of the floor, 1:250 (parking space/sq.ft.)?"

P: "yes, the problem is you can't decrease the parking below what you need; if you can get more than 10 spaces, you could then count that toward the second floor ..."

14.   D: "The Town would rather build back than up, no?"

P: "not necessarily; I don't know what to support — the second floor is tricky."

15.   D: "And these (adjacent) windows could be a problem, right?"

P: "Yes; I never thought of that . . . "

16.   D: "What about the exit now? It ties up the traffic?"

P: "But behind it, not on the street; it backs up into the parking lot."

17, 18. D: "So there's no sense closing it, my buying it from the City and picking up another row of parking?"

P: (measures the exit) "Not with just 20 ft. You need more than 30 . . . "

19.   D: "So you just don't see it?"

P: "Not really."

20.   D: "So it's not worth pursuing now?"

P: "I don't think so."

21.   D: "What would be reasonable for a variance there?"

P: (looks at the zoning) "Well, there's a 6 parking space waiver there . . . "

22.   D: "So I could seek to build an extra 3600 sq. ft?"

P: "You get credit for the extra spaces there . . . "

23.   D: "Do you have new parking space dimensions?"

P: "Yes, and up to 25% could be compact, by special permit."

24.   D: "How's the basement come to play?"

P: "If it's used, for customers, or if it's "habitable", it counts, but most are used for storage, and we don't count them."

25.   D: "If we came in with a proposal for office condo's, there'd be less turnover; that'd present less difficulty for the Planning Board . . . longer term occupants, better users . . ."

P: (poker-faced) "I don't know, I'd have to think it through further."

---

more generally in the development process. Table 9.1 presents a sequential string of 25 questions asked by the developer and answered by the planner as the meeting progressed. The developer's questions indicate in part what he hoped to achieve in this meeting.[2] After we examine what the developer did by asking these questions, we shall ask what the planner did in response.

The Developer's Questions

Consider first the developer's questions in Table 9.1. Why are these asked at all? The developer owns the land; why deal with the planner? No law requires that these questions be asked. Indeed, several of them are answered in public documents (the town's zoning bylaws, for example). So why does the developer bother?

One answer to this question is this: the development process is not simple. Unexpected delays can come from many quarters, and in the development game, delays are expensive. When delays increase, developers' returns decrease. Better then to check early with informants who may know the system, key actors involved, interested parties' sentiments, any unique obstacles to developing the site in question, and so on. One such informant is the friendly local planner (or not so friendly, depending in part upon what the last meeting with this developer was like). In more economic terms, information collection is costly, and early meetings with planning staff cost almost nothing compared to the unnecessary delays that such meetings may help to avoid.

The developer's questions in Table 9.1 suggest the uncertainties and ambiguities that developers may routinely face in the local development process. To the extent that developers depend upon planners for answers to such questions, they empower local planners to influence their actions. Anyone who's ever been lost in Boston, for example, understands the power they give to the person whom they ask hesitantly for directions.

Organization theorists argue that when a first person can address a second's uncertainty, the first person may have power over the second (Crozier, 1964). In the planning literature, Guy Benveniste has made this point vividly and centrally in his *Politics of Expertise*: when the decision-makers face uncertainty, they need to listen to advisors, the planners; and the planners thus have a systematic, structurally rooted source of power. In such cases, power is not information or skill; not a possession, power is rooted in the structural fact of uncertainty that confronts decision-makers in a changing and complex world, coupled with decision-makers' dependency on staff for advice to mitigate that uncertainty. Power is a relationship, not a simple possession.

The Developer's Uncertainties

Table 9.2 lists the uncertainties indicated by the developer's questions presented in Table 9.1. What types of uncertainty does this developer face?

First, several of the developer's questions concern *legal-regulatory* issues. How does the site — and the developer's proposal for it — fit existing regulations? Since the local planner's job is in part to implement those regulations, the planner's advice is likely to be a good deal less expensive than the same advice obtained from an attorney (however likely the attorney's consultative rôle at later stages).

Second, the developer has questions to ask about *political* interests. Not queries about electoral parties or formal policies, these are questions about operative informal policies (de facto politics?) and likely sentiments and votes — of the Planning Board or Board of Zoning Appeals, for example. These are questions, too, about the interests of relevant political actors: what have they done before? What are they likely to do, the developer wonders, if I propose A, B, or C? What support or opposition, what assistance or resistance can I anticipate now — depending on what?

Table 9.2: The Developer's Uncertainties

1. Project Review Agenda
2. Site Specific Facts
3. Applicable Regulations
4. Political Background
5. Procedural Strategy: How To
6. Procedural Strategy: What's Possible
7. Regulatory Intent
8. Relevant History, Precedent
9. Regulatory Changes
10. Fit of Case to Regulations
11. Gauging Political Actors
12. Project Review Scope
13. Regulatory Contingencies
14. Politician's Interests
15. Significance of Issues
16. Interpretation of Facts
17. Sensible Strategies
18. Technical Requirement of Strategies
19. Planner's Recommendations
20. Strategic Likelihood of Success
21. Reasonable (Effective) Argument
22. Strategic Options Available
23. Available Technical Advice
24. Regulatory Provisions for Related Space
25. Political Desirability of Given Strategy

Third, the developer has *procedural and strategic* questions. How shall I proceed with this proposal? What seem to be the issues to address first? How can I present the case, shape the design or the arguments supporting it so that I can move quickly and smoothly through the review process?

Fourth, the developer has *factual* questions. What problematic consequences of the currently proposed project can the planner foresee? Can the planner provide advice about aspects of the proposal that will or will not work functionally?

Several striking results appear just from this rough sorting of the developer's questions. Notice that factual and technical issues seem to be one small part of the larger conversation. Notice too that the bulk of the developer's questions focus upon the *institutional* environment in which development takes place.

Organizations and Institutions: The Practical Geography of the Development Process

The institutional environment is constituted in part by rules and regulations which evolve, change, and indeed are implemented in different ways at different times. So the developer's legal-regulatory questions are not the legal scholar's questions but the pragmatist's: what must I do to build on this site? How am I constrained, with what exceptions, for what purposes? The developer asks not about the law for the law's sake but for his own sake. He wishes to know about what he is allowed and not allowed to do not on paper but on his parcel of land. He is asking less about 'the law' and more about 'the application of the law', and so front line planners are check points, sources indicating how existing regulations are likely to be applied, how exceptions might be made, how special appeals may fare, and so on.

The institutional environment is also an explicitly political environment constituted by actors making conflicting claims upon one another. Some people seek to defend property rights; others seek to defend their neighborhoods as they have known them. Some seek better housing and employment conditions, and some seek power, status, or office. To make matters worse, still more complicated, the script keeps changing; the daily and monthly tussle of politics keeps the political strength of coalitions shifting, the composition of official councils and boards changing, the spotlight of political and public attention shifting as well.

So the developer naturally has questions: what am I getting into? Will a recent neighborhood fight spill-over onto my project? Can a recent precedent there help me? Can the planner give me a political reading — from the neighborhood to the Planning Board, the Appeals Board, the Town Council, other agencies? This political analysis might be even more difficult for an outside consultant to do well than it is to do the already tentative market studies that often accompany larger commercial developments.

The institutional environment is also an administrative 'system' — though 'maze', 'jungle', or a less rationalistic metaphor might be more apt. Any one proposal will be seen by many people, cross many desks, be passed along through many hands. But some people will read more slowly than others; some have less organized desks than others; some will want to hang onto this project longer than others. These facts are not incidental; they are fundamental to the timing and smooth processing of official documents. If the Planning Board will want to hear from the Town Engineer, and the Town Engineer 'has questions' about the project, the developer may face delays much later in the game than he wishes. In variations on the same theme, the same is true for consultations that the Planning Board (or other Boards) might wish to make with other local agencies, State agencies, citizen's groups, elected representatives, and so on. How can developers have an accurate working knowledge of the insides of these administrative processes without living there? Unless they've lived and worked in a community for many years, they can't — and so they go to the planners, who are insiders, for administrative advice.

The Planner's Influence

The result that follows from this discussion of the developer's uncertainties is this: if developers' uncertainty is a source of planners' influence, then the planners' *answers* to the specific questions listed in Table 9.1 should indicate the specific *kinds* of influence that planners may have in the local development process. Table 9.3 shows how, for each of the planner's answers (in Table 9.1) the planner may influence the developer in this case.

Table 9.3 lists just what the planner *does* in his responses to the developer. The planner talks, but he acts as he talks. He can be quoted later to the Planning Board, the Mayor, the Town Council members, 'Your planner told me . . . . ' — so watching his words carefully, the planner acts carefully.

Table 9.3: What Influence Does the Planner Have? What Does the Planner Do? The Planner:

1. Sets agendas (e.g. sequence)
2. Documents baseline data (site, size, classification)
3. Cites applicable regulations (e.g., FAR)
4. Constructs political history, background (a compromise)
5. Guides procedurally (It's contingent upon . . .)
6. Opens up development possibilities (discuss the bonus provision) (cf #23)
7. Expresses the intent of regulations/legislation (less density
8. Invokes relevant precedent/experience (children's built up to . . .)
9. Alerts developer to legal changes (revision . . .last April)
10. Fits this case to the ordinance, notes exceptions (yes, but unless . . .)
11. Characterizes political actors (he's a stickler . . .)
12. Delimits scope, focuses attention (parking is the real issue here)
13. Predicts contingencies (if you can . . . you could . . .)
14. Expresses official interests, sentiment (not necessarily . . .)
15. Ratifies (or rejects) problems (yes, the windows could be a problem)
16. Reformulates problems (but the traffic's behind it,

not on...)
17. Encourages (discourages options (no sense closing it...)
18. Specifies technical requirements (you need more than 30 feet)
19. Expresses professional support (don't see it? Not really)
20. Calculates likely success of options (not worth pursuing? Don't think so.)
21. Formulates workable justifications (there's a waiver...)
22. Affirms possible strategy (so I could...? you get credit for...)
23. Provides technical advice (new parking space dimensions? yes...)
24. Explains regulatory provisions (if it's..., it's..., if..., it's...)
25. Indicates viability of arguments (less difficulty...? Don't know...)

Table 9.3 provides a flavor of what actually happens as the planner responds to the developer's uncertainties. Responding to legal-regulatory queries, the planner cites applicable regulations, interprets and expresses their intent, gauges the fit of this specific project to those general regulations, and draws specific prescriptive implications, 'you'll have to take care of the parking ...' Responding to the political queries, the planner constructs a relevant political history, a reading of the political context in which the project should be seen; the planner invokes political precedent, describes the political sentiments of significant actors, and assesses possible opposition to the project. Further, the planner takes a position himself upon the significance of one of the problems facing the developer. In response to the developer's strategic queries, the planner shapes the meeting's agenda, guides the developer through the 'bonus procedure', discourages some options while encouraging others, and then gauges the viability of certain lines of argument in response to the developer's probe. In response to the developer's more descriptive queries, the planner documents baseline data and specifies a technical requirement for the alteration of parking spaces.

What is striking about this rough empirical inventory of the developer's uncertainties and planner's responses is how little of it is technical in character. The developer goes to the planner not only for facts but for regulatory, political, and strategic (even administrative) advice. Put slightly differently, the developer is concerned about protecting his investment from legal challenge, labyrinthine bureaucratic entanglements, political obstructions, and needless administrative delays. Because only a vast amount of broad research would allow a developer to predict such future problems with certainty, checking with the local planner is a reasonably direct and inexpensive way to attempt to anticipate and avoid such potential problems. But the planner, of course, is not just a disinterested party.

Notice now that if the planner concentrated primarily upon the facts of the case (the site, the proposed design, the likely consequences and so on), he would most likely neglect and fail to respond to the developers' real interests — and *vulnerabilities*. Nothing of course says that planners should *share* developers' interests; their duty as public servants is surely to represent broader public interests. Yet planners must be attentive to developers' specific and detailed interests if only to be able effectively to influence the developers' plans as best they can for the broader public good. What planners do here depends in part upon the discretion they have.

Because developers go to planners for a great deal more than technical information, the influence that planners may have at early stages of the review process may likewise be not so much technical but rather legal, political, and administrative as well. To assess these non-technical modes of influence at any length in themselves requires another essay, for several questions must be addressed: how do planners acquire such influence? What must they learn on the job? What must they know? Whom must they know? What skills are required? What strategies and tactics come into play in each of these dimensions so grossly called 'legal', 'political', and 'administrative?' For our present purposes, though, it will be instructive to consider what *discretion* planners can have as they draw upon these various sources of influence.

The Planner's Discretion

The planner here does many things and plays many rôles: at one moment a lawyer giving legal counsel, at another moment a manager suggesting strategies of moving the project along, at another moment a technician providing technical data and solutions. To understand the 'micro-politics' of such work, we should ask, 'What discretion does the planner have?'

To answer this question, consider which of the developer's questions could be sufficiently formalized or routinized to limit the planner's response to 'one right answer' where discretion would play no rôle. Table 9.4 lists 'minimally discretionary issues' and 'maximally discretionary issues' as a way to depict the range of concerns about which the planner's own judgment, interests, and strategies might be more and less influential.

Table 9.4 is actually composed of three columns of issues: those lending themselves to minimal and maximal discretion, and those bridging these extremes. One difference that distinguishes minimally discretionary from maximally discretionary issues is the generality (or, conversely, the site specific character) of the issue. The more generally specifiable the issue, it seems, the more it lends itself to being documented and made routinely available independent of the site in question. Thus technical parking lot dimensions may be codified in general, as may city-wide regulations. But interpretations of how particular board members may act, or encouragement or discouragement of particular options in this case cannot be generally specified or routinized, and so planners have discretion in their treatment of such issues.

Discretion, Ambiguity, and an Economics of Issue Interpretation

Notice that the 'minimally discretionary issues' in Table 9.4 also seem to be the least ambiguous of the whole set. Compare, for example, how many 'right answers' there are to the developer's questions first about the lot size and second, shortly thereafter, about the political history of the downzoning. However many ways there may be to measure the site, there surely are far more ways to construct the relevant political history of the community's zoning

Table 9.4: The Planner's Discretion

	Minimum Discretion	*Maximum Discretion*
1.		Setting Agendas
2.	Documenting Baseline Data	
3.	Citing Applicable Regulations	
4.		Constructing Political History
5.		Providing Procedural Guidance
6.		Opening Up Development Options
7.	Expressing Legislative/Regulatory Intent	
8.		Invoking Relevant Precedent/Experience
9.	Alerting to Regulatory Changes	
10.		Fitting Case to By Laws, Noting Exceptions
11.		Characterizing Political Actors
12.		Delimiting Scope: Focusing on Issues
13.		Predicting Contingencies
14.		Expressing Politician's Interests
15.		Ratifying Problems
16.		Reformulating Problems
17.		Encouraging/Discouraging Options
18.	Specifying Technical Requirements	
19.		Expressing Professional Support
20.		Calculating Likely Success
21.		Reforming Justifications
22.		Affirming Possible Strategies
23.		Providing Technical Advice
24.	Explaining Regulatory Provisions	

25.   Indicating Viability of
                                       Arguments

policies. Similarly, looking further down the table, specifying technical dimensional requirements for parking spaces involves less ambiguity, and thus less discretion on the part of the planner, than does encouraging or discouraging options, expressing professional support, expressing politicians' interests, and so on. As the questions of the developer involve issues of substantial ambiguity, then — issues lending themselves to many rather than few interpretations — planners are likely to have greater discretion in their responses.

This suggests that a central element of the politics of local planning practice is the practical framing of meaning and the actual creation of meaningful arguments. Planners do not only interpret meaning 'in their heads'; for by ratifying problems, focusing on issues, reformulating justifications, encouraging or discouraging options they communicate those interpretations through practical actions, communicative actions, influencing other participants in the planning process. Put differently, if ambiguous issues call for interpretation and thus value judgment, then as planners make practical claims about these issues, they will effectively *allocate value*. This process hints at a deeper economics of interpretation barely developed anywhere (Forester 1983).

The planner's use of discretion depends, of course, upon cultivated practical judgment. How the planner uses his discretion is a function not only of 'the situation', but of the planner's interests as well.

As the planner shapes the agenda of the meeting, he is interested not only in responsiveness to the developer but also in the efficient allocation of staff time. Documenting baseline data, the planner is interested in an accurate record upon which the review may proceed. Citing applicable regulations, expressing regulatory intent, fitting the case to the bylaws, the planner is interested minimally in invoking the existing regulatory framework as a terrain to be recognized and faced; the planner may be less interested in having any particular regulation met than in presenting existing regulations clearly, avoiding later charges from citizens or officials of being complicit in any developer's attempts to evade the law. Opening up development options, predicting contingencies, ratifying and reformulating problems, the planner is interested in creating possibilities for 'good' project outcomes — where 'good' here is likely to mean 'satisfying a range of citizens', officials', and private interests at once'; e.g. balancing developer's return on investment with local concerns about intensity of use, traffic and landscaping, scale and character of the surroundings, and so on. Expressing politicians' interests and constructing a relevant political history, the planner is likely to be interested in leveraging the influence of others: saying in effect, 'look, it's not me that's upset about your exacerbating the traffic problem there; it's the district representative who's going to raise hell about it!'

These considerations of the interests guiding the planner's use of discretion suggest that in project review the planning staff brings to bear not only professional interests in site or project design, but a range of other interests as well: political interests in satisfying powerful actors or groups, administrative interests in the efficient use of staff and agency time, substantive-regulatory interests in seeing that the amenities protected by existing bylaws are indeed protected or enhanced, procedural-regulatory interests in respecting and avoiding turf battles with other agencies, and so on.

These interests, however, are unlikely to be of equal importance to any one planner. To satisfy a powerful constituency, staff time on other projects might suffer. To gain substantive amenities, side conversations with other agencies might be held. But the question at the heart of potential planner-developer negotiations (or planners' mediation of developer-neighborhood conflicts) is this: what are the developer's interests, which in light of the planner's partially conflicting interests, might make possible the trades allowing the 'joint' gains' to which Susskind and Ozawa, and Raiffa refer?

Development Possibilities and the Developer's Interests

If we consider the developer's questions in Table 9.1 once more, can we infer the interests held by the developer? 'Maximizing return on investment' may be a dominant interest, but that should not obscure the significance of other, even derivative concerns which also shape the developer's actions. In the early stages of project review 'maximizing return on investment' can be quite ambiguous: 'maximizing' in the short or long run, with respect to what uncertainties and risk? In what form is the 'return'? What shall the level of investment be, and of what types, and in what sort of project mix?

'Maximizing return on investment' may be the developer's 'bottom line', but focusing solely on that 'bottom line' can be misleading. When a developer is faced with the practical complexities of building any real project, he or she will have to balance a wide range of concerns and interests. The project to be built must ordinarily be attractive, but it must not be extravagantly expensive. It must be approved by regulatory agencies, and perhaps by political actors as well, but it must be timely. It must take advantage of the site in question and the environs, but it must fall within height, bulk, setback, and parking restrictions or qualify for appropriate variances, bonuses, or special permits.

The developer may have many real interests, yet it seems almost nonsensical to ask, 'how many?' and expect a numerical answer. Why? Simply to say that interests are subjective will not do, for they still may be discrete. Although no one may have a clear answer to this question, one way to resolve the difficulty is to recognize that in the project review process itself the planner and developer construct shared, plausible accounts of their own 'real' interests. To say that interests are 'discovered' in the course of the review process — or the planner-developer conversation — implies that a finite set of interests lies waiting to be found. But does anyone know how once and for all to discover such pre-existing interests? Hardly. Different practitioners may be adept at interpreting the concerns of parties, formulating those as 'interests' to be satisfied in part, and then seeking to construct mutually acceptable and desirable trades. The heart of the review process is the work of probing for what the other will come to regard as in their interest — gauging then how easy or how difficult it will be for them to 'give' on particular issues. Notice too that even the language of description is ambiguous here, for the terms 'interests', 'preferences', 'desires', 'concerns' and 'wants' are at once not synonymous and yet overlapping in application. The theoretical baggage that such terms carry can be quite heavy, but here they are used first in their ordinary language senses.

What range of interests are suggested by the developer's questions and concerns listed in Table 9.1? Consider the rough list presented in Table 9.5, which suggests that even as developers have an overall interest in maximized return on investment (this presumably has brought the developer to talk to the planner in the first place), the developer has many more immediate or proximate interests to satisfy first: obtaining public sector cooperation, focusing efficiently on key problems, navigating bureaucratic hurdles, utilizing site resources fully, and so on. These interests are many, and varied, and no doubt they are also of *various import* to the developer — and therein lies a potential source of opportunity for planning staff.

Table 9.5: The Developer's Interests

---

1. Procuring Planner's Attention *vs* Facing Planner's Resistance
2. Having Full Site Information *vs* Having Incomplete Information
3. Knowing the Regulations *vs* Being Blocked/Surprised Later
4. Fitting Previous Political History *vs* Bucking Political History
5. Navigating the Bureaucracy *vs* Getting Entangled in Bureaucracy
6. Realizing Administrative Strategies *vs* Missing Procedural Opportunities
7. Meeting Regulatory Intent *vs* Violating Regulatory Intent
8. Aligning with Precedent *vs* Contradicting Precedent
9. Facing Current Regulations *vs* Losing Time on Old Regulations
10. Meeting Current Regulations *vs* Violating Current Regulations
11. Anticipating Political Response *vs* Being Politically Surprised/Stopped

12. Obtaining Public Sector Cooperation *vs* Meeting
    Resistance
13. Surveying Political Actors *vs* Missing Legal-Regulatory
    Opportunities
14. Satisfying Political Actors *vs* Antagonizing Political
    Actors
15. Focusing Efficiently on Problems *vs* Wasting Time and
    Effort
16. Establishing Shared Interpretations *vs* Risking Later
    Counter Argument/Evidence
17. Investing In Feasible Options *vs* Wasting Time and Effort
18. Satisfying Technical Requirements *vs* Risking Technical
    Failure
19. Marshalling Professional Support *vs* Risking Planner's
    Opposition
20. Clarifying Expected Utility *vs* Ignoring Risk
21. Formulating Compelling Arguments *vs* Losing Rhetorical
    Opportunities
22. Clarifying Building Options *vs* Missing Design
    Opportunities
23. Broadening Technical Input *vs* Being Vulnerable
    Technically
24. Using Site Resources Fully *vs* Failing to Take Advantage
    of Site
25. Marshalling Regulatory Support *vs* Risking Regulatory
    Opposition

Typically, for example, developers may be concerned less with certain design features (such as the placement of driveways or provisions for drainage) than with maintaining professional and political support for their larger package. Knowing this, of course, enables planners to bargain for design improvements; the planning staff may ask for design changes to avoid future problems with traffic, parking, or drainage, for example, and in return the staff may promise support and guidance for the project rather than a stream of questions and further resistance to it. Assessing the developer's interests, then, opens the door to a give and take in the planning process that is much less like passive 'review', watchful 'regulation' or 'rule application' (Kirlin, 1985) and much more like explicit developer-planner negotiation: i.e., development negotiation.

The micro-politics of local planning practice may thus be understood in part as a 'negotiation' process. The developer-planner interaction ought not simply to be reduced to a 'negotiation', yet several lessons may be learned if that conversation is understood to be an element within a negotiation process (Forester, 1987). Consider the implications.

Considering Project Reviews as Development Negotiations: Implications

First, as in all negotiations, both sides have sources of power and influence. The developer has initiative, capital, and land. The planner, without formal power, nevertheless has numerous sources of influence, as Table 9.3 suggests.

Second, the planner-developer conversation excerpted here involved the basic elements of typical negotiations, if significantly in an ad-hoc and quite informal way. In a recent popular account, Fisher and Ury (1983) suggest four strategic approaches for the 'principled negotiator', and it is interesting to compare their recommendations with the range of the developer's questions presented in Table 9.1. Fisher and Ury suggest that negotiators should:

1. separate people-problems from project-problems;

2. focus upon underlying interests at stake rather than already packaged positions;

3. generate a wide array of options to explore; and

4. search for an objective (read: legitimate) standard to be used to help resolve choices.

Consider each briefly.

but about the planner's opinions, feelings, and support as well. Furthermore, of course, the developer asked about the sentiments, interests, and predispositions of others involved 'downstream' in the project review process.

With respect to (2), the developer probed for the planner's concerns, the historical concerns suggested by the previous downzoning initiative, the concerns of the Planning Board, the interests of 'the Town', and so on. Just as Table 9.5 assesses the developer's potential interests, in the actual conversation with the planner the developer is probing for the jurisdiction's interests, whether those be the planner's, the Planning Board's, influential citizens', or interests of others who might make a difference.

With respect to (3), several of the developer's questions directly explore options: how does the bonus work? Can I buy the adjoining driveway from the Town? What about the basement?

Finally, with respect to (4), the developer searches for several possible legitimate bases of decision: past precedent, a 'reasonable variance', and a compelling argument to the Planning Board.

What should be made of this apparent 'fit' between the developer's questions and Fisher and Ury's strategic recommendations for negotiators? Not too much. Told that what he was 'really' doing with the planner was negotiating, the developer might say, 'why yes, and I've been speaking prose all my life too.' Yet the implications are not altogether trivial either. If the planner-developer discussion involves the basic aspects of issues covered in generic negotiations, in a wholly *ad hoc* manner, then future planner-developer interactions might benefit not simply from the recognition that these are negotiations, but from the *systematic strategies* available to negotiators to achieve not just individual gains but 'joint net gains' (Raiffa, 1983). We elaborate this last point below.

Third, if the project review conversation is taken to be a negotiation, it may be appreciated both for its complexity and for its socially constructed character. What to an outsider at first may appear to be a two-party conversation involving one site quickly comes to be seen as a multi-party, multi-issue negotiation which involves a host

be a two-party conversation involving one site quickly comes to be seen as a multi-party, multi-issue negotiation which involves a host of public sector bodies along with the planner and developer, all concerned with a wide range of issues. Far from being a passive reviewer or lone negotiator, the planner plays an active professional role in addition to serving as a rough proxy for the interests of others on the local Planning Board, in official agencies, in elected offices, and so on. The planner appears here as a bit of negotiator and a bit of mediator, and yet neither in traditional terms (Forester, 1987). However difficult the rôle may be to label, the work of negotiation and bargaining is a central part of the process of project review.

Fourth, as suggested above, *when issues are multiple, the prospects for trades between issues arise.* Such trading is crucial for the realization of 'joint net gains' in which both parties may work from 'zero-sum' toward 'non-zero-sum' if not quite 'win-win' outcomes. This possibility can be appreciated as soon as one realizes that parties are likely to weight differing issues differently. Thus when each side 'gives' on an issue about which they feel weakly but the other side feels strongly, both sides are likely to do far better than if trading across issues did not take place (Raiffa, 1982; Susskind and Cruickshank, 1987). Of course such trading may *not* take place in the local planning process, unless the planner and/or the developer work deliberately to explore such trades. *How* a review process may be structured to facilitate such 'joint net gains' is a crucial practical problem needing to be addressed.

Fifth, the fact that planners seem to have significant discretion in their responses to developers suggests that planners may have systematic opportunities for effective bargaining and negotiation in the local development process. Development project reviews will be routinely characterized by discussion of multiple, uncertain, and ambiguous issues. *Because issues are uncertain, planners will have systematic sources of influence. Because issues are ambiguous, planners will have sources of discretion. Because issues are multiple, planners will face opportunities for trading across issues.*

Planners' work throughout the review process is to shape development possibilities, both with respect to physical, aesthetic and functional designs for the site and the political, administrative, and regulatory routes to be taken on the way to achieving any development whatsoever. Shaping not only the developer's sense of possibilities, but the development possibilities for abuttors and neighbors, Town officials and staff and citizens more generally, local planners have deeply if subtly political rôles to play, shaping the 'can's' and 'can'ts' of developers and citizens alike.

Yet to point to the existence of this micropolitics of local planning practice is to open up a host of further questions. How is it that planners might best employ their influence to seek 'joint net gains' in the local development process? How might they use their influence to assure that affected parties are indeed parties to the negotiations affecting them? How might local planners pursue both efficient net gains, and a just development process with enduring outcomes (Susskind, 1984)? The analysis of this essay does not provide the answers here, but it may enable those interested in the day to day work of local planners to explore these continually pressing questions, and to improve public serving project review processes as a result.

Notes

1. This analysis is appropriate only for a limited, but important range of cases — the cases in the middle-range between a) those projects so large that the influence and power of the city council, Mayor, and others dwarfs that of the city planning staff [see e.g., the account of Allan Jacobs regarding the Transamerica project in San Francisco (Jacobs, 1975)], and b) those projects so small that the staff input is incidental. One local planner spoke of 'triage' when he told me in an interview about which projects he thought he could influence (and choose to work on): in effect, he said, 'some are out of my control altogether and I don't waste time on them; others are so small they don't matter much. In between I have a chance of making a difference.' Empirical research could estimate what proportions of various planners' daily work fall into which of these three categories.

References

Bacow, L. and M. Wheeler, *Environmental Dispute Resolution*, New York: Plenum, 1984.

Bednar, D. and W. Curington, 'Interaction Analysis: A Tool for Understanding Negotiations', *Industrial and Labor Relations Review*, 36, 1983, 389-401.

Benveniste, G., *The Politics of Expertise*, San Francisco: Boyd and Fraser, Second Edition, 1977.

Crozier, M., *The Bureaucratic Phenomenon*, Chicago: University of Chicago Press, 1964.

Fisher, R. and W. Ury, *Getting To Yes*, New York: Penguin, 1983.

Forester, J., 'From Equity and Efficiency to the Practical Analysis of Ambiguity in Planning Practice', prepared for the World Congress on Land Policy, Cambridge, MA. 1983.

Forester, J., *Critical Theory and Public Life*, Cambridge, MA: M.I.T. Press, 1985.

Forester, J., 'Planning in the Face of Conflict: Mediated Negotiations in Local Land-Use Permitting Processes', *Journal of the American Planning Association*, forthcoming 1987.

Forester, J. and Fischer, F., *Confronting Values in Policy Analysis: The Politics of Criteria*, Newbury Park, CA: Sage, 1987.

Forester, J., 'Questioning and Organizing Attention as Planning Strategy: Toward a Critical Theory of Planning', *Administration and Society*, 13, 161-205, 1986.

Forester, J., 'Critical Theory and Planning Practice', *Journal of the American Institute of Planners*, Summer 1980.

Forester, J., 'Understanding Planning Practice: An Empirical, Practical, and Normative Account', *Journal of Planning Education and Research*, 1, 59-71, 1982.

Jacobs, A., *Making City Planning Work*, Chicago: ASPO, 1975.

Leavitt, R. and J. Kirlin, *Managing Development Through Public-Private Negotiations*, Washington, D.C.: Urban Land Institute and the American Bar Association, 1985.

Lewicki, R., and J. Litterer, *Negotiation*, Homewood, Illinois: R. Irwin, 1985.

Raiffa, H., *The Art and Science of Negotiation*, Cambridge: Harvard University Press, 1982.

Sullivan, T., *Resolving Development Disputes Through Negotiations*, New York: Plenum, 1984.

Susskind, L. and Cruickshank, J., *Dealing With Differences*, New York: Basic Books, 1987.

Susskind, L. and C. Ozawa, 'Mediated Negotiation in the Public Sector: The Planner as Mediator', *Journal of Planning Education and Research*, 4, 5-15, 1984.

Susskind, L. and D. Madigan, 'New Approaches to Resolving Disputes in the Public Sector', *The Justice System Journal*, 9, 179-203, 1984

Thompson, J. D., *Organizations in Action*, New York: McGraw-Hill, 1967.

Chapter 10

Professional Orientations of French Urban Planners

Gilles Verpraet

French urban planning has long been characterized by the dominant rôle of the central State and its public policies in implementing urban planning. Changes in the past ten years have increased the rôle of local elected representatives as well as that of local associations in defining and negotiating matters of planning. This has led to profound transformations in the professional practice of urban planners. The main aspect of this transformation relates to mediation between the various actors of urban planning.

This chapter sets out to examine the different models concerning urban planning professions in France and to examine their historical evolution. In this context, we will describe more specifically how professional practice articulates mediatory rôles in different ways. We will discuss how participatory action and the search for a consensus among actors leads to the creation of a new framework within which spatial projects (Geddes, 1915; Sutcliffe, 1981) are elaborated.

In France, the urban planning profession emerged during the war-time of 1940-45 when State agencies were placed in charge of studying the reconstruction of damaged cities and towns. These agencies appointed both urban planners as civil servants and independent urban planning architects as consultants to their departments. From 1960-75, these professions were developed in relation to problems of public management of urban growth, the expansion of public transportation, and social housing. This context emphasized the rôle of urban planners in public management concerning such matters as the allocation of public funds, the financing of public services and social redistribution (Eversley, 1972; Pahl, 1977).

Environmental conflicts and the rise of urban environmental protection associations in the late 1970s increased the demands for public participation in the process of urban planning. The way of thinking and the courses of action available to the profession began to be reshaped by the place given to citizens and associations, making their practice tend towards a mediatory rôle, involving negotiation and the bringing together of the different actors in urban planning. Moreover, with the recent trend of decentralization (Bobroft, 1981) mayors have an increased responsibility for urban planning in their commune, the basic unit of political power in France.

Thus has emerged an entirely new context for the action of urban planners, which is dominated by two principal types of relations:

- relations between the central State and the local government, with the problem of social redistribution the fore;

- relations between the Municipality and its citizens, encouraging public participation in matters of planning.

The rôle of the State is shifting over to regulating the relations between the Municipality and housing developers.

French sociologists have analyzed the training and education of urban planners in relation to the formation of middle classes and intermediary professions. The specific rôle of intellectual mediators, it seems, rests in the support of the legitimacy of the republican ideal, and in the way they formulate the interest of the public, taken as being in the general interest (Ion, 1983). Using this criterion, it is possible to differentiate the intermediary professions in terms of the organizers, the experts, and the mediators (Bauer and Cohen, 1982)

We will examine how French urban planners fulfil two of these categories. The rôle of the expert, which focuses on urban analysis and spatial design, is coupled with the rôle of the mediator, concerned with developing social projects, defining urban development strategies and expressing the public interest.

The following facts have been established according to a survey of 200 practising urban planners in France who were questioned about their professional orientations, the way they perceive their professional rôles and how they identify with this profession. Two categories were taken into account in the choice of sampling: type of function and basic education. The population of French urban planners is composed of those having received the following basic education: architecture degree (32%), engineering degree (19%), and Master of social science degree (32%). They are divided into six types of function: State government, Municipal government, Building Director, Independent design consultant, Urban consultant office, and Intermunicipal organization.

How Professional Rôles are Perceived

Survey by questionnaire allows us to determine, to a certain extent, the way in which urban planners perceive their professional 'orientation'. The idea of professional orientation refers to the priorities given in practising their profession, of which we distinguish three dimensions: economic, spatial, and decisional.

Q/ For you, what are the priorities to be given to your professional function?

1. to provide spatial projects in answer to social demand: **50%**

2. to synchronize urbanization with economic development: **22%**

3. to act as a social advisor for decision-makers: **15%**

In the structure of professional perceptions, spatial requirements appear as more important than the newer economic and political orientations. Above and beyond this observation, an analysis of the perceived rôles and conflicts can provide more information concerning the rôles and patterns of mediation in French urban planning.

The *mode* of action represents the *conscious* part of professional intervention in urban affairs. The following hierarchy appears in the participants' answers with survey and advisory activities at the top:

- Urban survey   81%

- Social advising   79%

- Building operation   59%

- Education and research   33%

- Legal conformity control   25%

The hierarchy of institutional procedures brought into play confirms the priority given to the activities of consulting, planning and preliminary surveys:

- Municipal advising   86%

- Planning of an operation
  (financing, organizing)   74%

- Surveys of new districts   70%

- Surveys of old districts
  (rehabilitation)   61%

In the design professions, any project involves arrangements with centers of power and decision-making. We can therefore determine the hierarchy of management objectives and the manner in which they affect the definition of the project. The survey results here are as follows:

- Spatial management   79%

- Organizational management
  (administration)   73%

- Operational management   67%

- Municipal government
  (urban strategy)   60%

- Housing management
  (rental and services)   12%

The Mediatory Rôles of Urban Planners

In analyzing these mediatory rôles, we can imagine a rising scale which would go from public participation, consultation among specialists, advice to local representatives, and project elaboration, to the expression of the public interest. But in so describing the position of urban planners, the manner in which decisions are made must be taken into account. It has already been underlined how State departments organized professional rôles in the past through the appointment of its urban planners. Given the new context, it is important to specify the place occupied by local (Municipal, Departmental, Regional) representatives in urban mediations (Knox and Cullen, 1981).

The initial results of the survey indicate a genuine consciousness among urban planners concerning the importance of the public interest. As many as 85 per cent of the practitioners questioned acknowledge being in charge of the public interest.

Q/ In your opinion, who defines the public interest?

1. The local representatives   67%

2. State administration   47%

3. The government   30%

4. The commissioning of the survey   20%

The practitioners seem quite conscious of the new responsibilities given to Municipalities with the decentralization reforms. The development of contractual procedures in urban planning over the past ten years has encouraged their rôle of coordination among the actors of urban planning. Nevertheless, the mediatory rôles can be classified and analyzed along various dimensions:

- mediation between State requirements and those of the Municipalities (according to 62% of the practitioners);

- the importance of demands expressed by citizens and urban associations (according to 62% of the practitioners),

- mediation between building directors' requirements and the demands of the inhabitants (according to 51% of the practitioners).

These different mediatory types reveal different types of exercises in the mediation of urban affairs. State commissions, aided by their regulatory authority, overshadowed for a long time any possibility of urban planning which would involve consultation and participation. The implication of building directors and contractors in questions of urban quality occurs on a concrete and operational level.

We should determine now how these mediatory rôles are composed according to their function and qualifications. We aim to determine also what factors, including educational resources and changes in public urban policy, explain the make-up of these mediatory rôles.

Qualification Models and Mediatory Patterns

The diversity of urban planners and their models of qualification can be described not only in terms of position (status, branch) but also by reference groups (Merton, 1969) and their various categorizations (types of identification, profiles of qualifications, mediatory patterns).

An initial factor analysis shows how the cleavage between status (independent/civil servant) is strongly reflected in the professional field. Moreover, those who characterize their professional identification by a diploma tend to have a spatial type of orientation, while those who characterize their professional identification by experience tend to have a decision-making orientation. We should also recall that, for the practitioners, the urban planning profession is defined, first of all, by relevant experience in urban planning (76%), by a position with an organization (37%) and rather less by the acquisition of a diploma (19%).

Such relationships between orientations, professional duties and profiles can be described more precisely in using the notion of 'qualification models'. Occupational sociology has established that a qualification model refers to the manner in which the job position is described by the employer and recognized by the employee. It should be remembered that the definition of a position is the result of a consensus between the demands of the employer and those of the employee, based on an evaluation of the qualifications (Tripier, Sussois and Rivard, 1980).

In the French urban planning profession, we are able to distinguish the following qualification models, with their Anglo-American equivalents:

'Urban survey analyst'	'Chargé d'étude'
'Operation consultant'	'Chargé d'opération'
'Development manager'	'Chargé de mission'
'Organization director'	'Directeur de l'organisme'
'Design consultant'	'Urbaniste libéral'

A second factor analysis reveals that only two qualification models, those of development manager and organization director, emphasize decision-making orientations. The remaining models (design consultant, operation consultant and urban survey analyst) are more closely linked with spatial and economic orientations (Table 10.1).

Qualification models

The make-up of the profile constituting a given qualification model allows us to describe how professional orientations are composed. We shall especially attempt to describe how management and mediatory rôles are combined.

Table 10.1: Qualification Models

	Spatial project elaboration	Economic development	Decisionmaking advice	Function	Qualification
Graduate identification	Design consultant		Development Manager	Conception	Professional expert
		Urban Survey Analyst			
Practice identification	Operation consultant		Organization Director	Administration	Executive Organizer

Profiles Related to a Spatial Orientation

The **design consultant** model (25% of the sample) is related to an independent practice and an initial degree in architecture. Priority is given to spatial project elaboration (58%), whereas the decision-making aspect is of minor importance (8%). Their conception of the mediatory rôle emphasizes the relationship between building directors and the inhabitants (V 157: 66% yes; see Table 10.2). Removed from managerial tasks and decisions, their general mode of anticipation is through design. This emphasis placed on spatial expertise is representative of the traditional model of the urban-planning architect.

The **operation consultant** model (12% of the sample) is active in housing management organizations as well as municipalities and urban consultant offices, dealing with operations organization and the advocacy of urban qualities. Priority is given to spatial orientation (47%) and economic orientations (35%). This profile of qualification is related to operational urban planning, especially concerning rehabilitation. In this position, the relation with the inhabitants is based on market surveys.

The **urban survey analyst** model (47% of the sample) is structured around the specific tasks of urban analysis. Preliminary studies concerning sites and provision and program analysis are particularly developed in State departments and their local agencies, as well as in urban consultants' offices. This profile also gives priority to spatial orientations (53%) and economic orientations (20%). Their mediatory rôles concentrate on the relation between State requirements and those of the municipalities (V 135: 65%). The importance given to local representatives in forming the public interest (V 132: 58%) is offset by a distinct recourse to the State in certain instances of decision (V 134: 43%). This profile seems to take little account of building directors' demands (V 137: 47%).

Table 10.2: Mediatory Roles and Patterns of Qualification

Mediatory roles		%	%	%	%	%	%	%
V128 Do you think you are supporting public interest?	Yes:	83	90	95	86	82	80	85
In your opinion, who formulates public interest? V129 the state V130 the government V131 the survey commissioners V132 local representatives		43 34 24 60	41 23 27 77	56 30 17 91	51 31 18 71	33 17 20 56	60 40 20 73	47 30 — 67
V 133 Are local representatives, in your opinion, able to formulate public interest?	yes: no:	70 13	68 13	82 4	76 6	69 11	53 33	71 11
V 134 Is public interest best represented by the state administration? -in general -just in certain cases		15 42	14 27	8 43	12 49	16 40	33 33	17 42
V 135 Do you consider yourself to be the mediator between requirements of the state and those of municipalities?	yes	64	41	69	63	62	66	63
V 136 Do demands placed by inhabitants and associations represent an important element in your professional practice?	yes no	63 30	72 27	82 13	63 30	55 33	60 33	63 31
V 137 Do you believe yourself to be the mediator between demands of inhabitants and those of building management?		49	50	61	37	62	60	52
/ total sample		47	12	13	33	25	8	100

NB: Responses and choices about qualification models may be multiple. Therefore, the total responses columns exceed 100%. Professional orientations are exclusive of priority choice.

Profiles Related to Decision-making Orientations

The **development manager** profile (13%) is a new model which has developed within the framework of the new consulting organizations placed under the responsibility of several municipalities (regional administrations, departmental urban planning agencies, intermunicipal associations). In supporting decision-making orientations, they fulfil their mediatory rôles both with the local representatives (V 133: 82%) and with the inhabitants (V 135: 82%). Their capacity for anticipation is focused more on a strategic perspective than on spatial project perspective. Their talks include defining social and political objectives for the local officials at a middle management level. In this way, strategic concerns are becoming a part of design concerns, thus prefiguring new urban planning practices.

The profiles of development manager and organization director are similar in practice. However, the director maintains a balance between managerial and mediatory rôles, and between State requirements and local demands.

The analysis of qualification models helps make clear the shifts in professional points of reference and in professional as well as mediatory patterns. For the spatial expert model, skills are acquired through the knowledge of urban matters, and the professional identity is based on a diploma (Parsons, 1958).

Mediatory patterns, which focus more on consultation, take into account the various actors in urban planning and support participation in the decision-making process, now complement professional expertise and action. With this interpretation, the spatial orientation remains a priority (50%), but strategies of professionalization must take into account more established mediatory patterns.

Experts and Mediators

In our approach, the term 'mediation' refers to the system of action within which the planners' actions and the use of their individual techniques can develop. This system is made up of the various urban planning institutions but also the relations of dependence and consultation created among the actors of urban planning in the context of an intervention. Within this analytical framework and through the actors' perception, areas of competence can be defined in which the level of expertise is equally valid (Benveniste, 1972). This close dialectic between expert and mediatory rôles leads to various but relatively stable compromises which are represented and described in the qualification models: development manager, urban survey analyst, operation consultant, design consultant, etc.

The concept of mediation can be defined as a system of negotiation within a decision-making process (Forester, 1980; Susskind and Ozawa, 1984). The question is then to specify the content, levels and stages of negotiation. In this study of French planners, the concept of mediation is constructed as a system of intermediary positions, in which relations between the central State and local governments, or between building directors and local representatives, predominate. Negotiation concerning orientations, transactions and the means chosen to deal with the urban plan is developed within this system of action.

Mediatory Patterns

This analysis of the relationships between professional orientations, mediatory rôles and qualification rôles enables us to understand better the different mediatory patterns in French urban planning.

It has already been mentioned how, in the 1940s, the central State constituted its mediatory rôle through its control of the practices involved in reconstructing damaged cities and, during the 1950s, by responding to massive urbanization. Central management of urban planning was organized by professions of the civil service (state-employed urban planners, civil engineers) and their delegations (especially the French Incorporation of Architects) in the years 1943-1968. In this context of State urban policies, spatial project elaboration was part of middle-range planning (10 years for Municipalities, 25 years for larger urban districts). At this time, a specific qualification model, known as 'urban survey analyst' emerged in response to this particular exercise, and still makes up 47% of the profession.

The economic recession and the trend of rehabilitation in run-down areas reinforced property developers' mediation and action in urban planning. New demands of inhabitants are taken into account as part of strategic management, where objectives concerning energy savings, interior quality of housing, and the definition of a new type of public area surrounding constructions all overlap. With this slackening in the State's normative action, urban-planning architects attempted to rethink the way buildings are inserted in the urban landscape in closer relation to housing types and urban morphology.

Decentralization reforms (1983-85) attempt to promote municipal mediation by withdrawing State mediation. The theme of municipal and regional action deals with public participation, resident cohabitation and the symbols which public areas represent. For development managers and operation consultants, the development of an urban project remains part of a strategic formulation. In addition, Municipal requirements support the coordination of urban planning actors at the municipal level (fostering synergism), and improved recognition of the demands in social management concerning public housing projects. This intersection of various local organizations promotes multi-structure financing of urban projects; however, it increases the necessity for mediation and coordination among the various actors in the municipality.

Education in Urban Planning with Reference to Qualification Models

In order to appreciate the rôle of education in the make-up of a professional background, it seems important to distinguish the rôle played by basic education in a given discipline (architecture engineering, social science) and the rôle played by education in urban planning, focused on an aptitude for synthesis. Comprehensive planning procedures, including spatial project elaboration and preparation for mediatory rôles, are learned at this second stage of training.

The results of our inquiry confirm that education in urban planning prepares for the skills of a spatial expert. However, mediatory rôles can be learned as much through this type of education as through professional experience.

Basic Education and Expertise

The professional field of urban planning recruits from a variety of certifications (architect, engineer, master of social science), through which a social hierarchy is formed and perpetuated. We have already seen that urban planners having a diploma in architecture tend to occupy the independent consultant profile (80%) and, to some extent, the urban survey analyst profile (24%). Urban planners having a social science education usually move towards the urban survey analyst profile (31%) and more recently towards the development manager profile (30%).

Alongside an architectural conception of urban planning, focused on spatial design, and engineer-planning based on urban techniques, the contribution of the social sciences, originally based on urban survey and analysis, has expanded to include programming services and designing of lifestyles. This has resulted in a broadening of the 'urban survey analyst' profile.

Education in Urban Matters and Qualification

The main purpose of urban planning schools in France (two years of study after the master's degree) is to develop an aptitude for synthesis, an understanding of urban phenomena (geographical, economic, and sociological) and conducting the elaboration of a spatial project. This is how the many 'urban survey analyst' profiles came about during the period of urban growth (1960-70).

We have seen how, with the graduate practitioner, project elaboration is fixed as a priority (57%) and is tending toward the support of economic development (25%) but is not so nearly prepared for the advising of decision-makers (8%).

Preparing for Mediatory Rôles

Urban planning graduates seem relatively motivated to defend the public interest (81%) and to perform their rôles as mediators between State and municipal requirements (65%). However, these rates of motivation to defend public interest in central/local mediation (71%) are equally as high for non-graduate urban practitioners.

Professional identity with experience increases the priority for orientations based on decision-making. Preparation for mediatory rôles also depends on professional experience, and a position with an urban planning organization, especially public ones (municipal, regional, State administrations).

An urban planning education contributes to acquiring expertise in spatial project elaboration and economic development aid (Faludi, 1978). Preparation for mediatory rôles depends on professional experience and additional courses in political science.

The result is a 3-step education in urban planning:

- basic education giving a qualification in the discipline at the Master's level: laws and standards, sociology, methods of inquiry, etc.

- urban planning education prepares for spatial expertise,

- mediatory rôles are learned through professional experience.

There remains a particular problem for educators in urban planning: how can they better prepare future practitioners for their increasingly mediatory involvement with public participation (Witch, 1984), the new power of Mayors in urban planning, and the new regional administration. Some partial solutions have been proposed by the educators:

- offer more courses in political science and public management,

- develop workshops and training sessions concerning urban strategies,

- reinforce relationships between urban planning schools and local representatives.

Faced with the evolution of professional profiles in urban policy, the growing rôle of local representatives, the restructuring of relations among urban planning actors and the new courses of action open to organizations, the rôle of urban institutes tends to maintain the tradition of comprehensive urban planning and to reinforce the requirement of preliminary surveys; all the while reformulating these bases to some degree in regard to the new models of 'development manager' and 'operation consultant' (Verpraet, 1986). Professional practices and research for a new type of urban composition, similar to 'urban design', are attempting to restructure the relations between program definition and project elaboration.

References

Bauer A. and Cohen D. (1982) Les limites du savoir des cadres, *Sociologie du Travail*, 4.

Benveniste, G. (1972) *The politics of expertise*, Berkeley: Glendary Press.

Bobroff, D., *et al* (1981), *Réhabiliter les quartiers anciens*, Paris: Plan Construction.

Eversley, D. (1972) *The planners in society: The changing rôle of a profession*, London: Faber & Faber.

Faludi, A. S. (1978) *Essays on planning theory and education*, London: Pergamon

Forester, J. (1980) What are the planners up against ? Planning in the face of power, *The Bulletin of the Associate School of Planners*, XVIII, No 2.

Geddes, P. (1915) *Cities in evolution*, London: William Norgate.

Ion, J. (1983) *Sociabilité et lien social: les intellectuels médiateurs*, in *Les couches moyennes salariées*, Ministère de l'Urbanisme et du Logement.

Knox, P. and Cullen, J. (1981) Planners as urban managers: an exploration of the attitudes and image of senior British planners, *Environment and Planning A*, 13, 881-91.

Merton, K. (1969) *Elements of theory and methods*, Paris: Plan.

Pahl, R. H. (1977) Managers, technical experts and the state, p. 491 in M. Harloe, *Captive cities*, Chichester: J. Wiley

Parsons, T. (1958) *Essays in social theory*, Glencoe: Free Press

Susskind, L. and Ozawa C. (1984) Mediated negotiation in the public sector: the planners as mediator, *Bulletin of the Associate School of Planners*, 3.

Sutcliffe, A. (1981) *Towards the planned city 1880-1914*, Oxford: Blackwell.

Tripier P.; J.M. Saussois, A. Rivard (1980) *L'espace de qualification des cadres*, Paris: Cedress.

Verpraet, G. (1986) *Missions, profils et formation de l'Urbanisme*, *Service technique de l'Urbanisme*, Paris: Cedress

Witch, F. (1984) The political world of urban planners, *Bulletin of The Associate School of Planners*, 3.

Chapter 11

Making Places: Urban Design in Britain

Brian Goodey

Urban design is an activity which, though modest in the number of its practitioners, has grown to influence professional activity in both town planning and architecture over the past twelve years. Although its momentum is maintained through graduate courses, conferences, and reports on schemes proposed and effected, its purpose and relationship with the parent professions is only slowly being defined. This chapter examines the relationship between town planning, architecture and urban design in the recent British context and considers issues and the implications which may face urban designers in the future.

The Planning Profession and Urban Design

Although 1960 was a key year in the development of the British planning profession, it would be wrong to suggest — as some have — that in that year it changed from a youthful, design-oriented and enthusiastic force for change to a group successively preoccupied with notional two-dimensional patterns, with the redistribution of unreliable resources, with the launching of a peculiarly muddled social revolution, and, finally, with safeguarding middle-aged positions. Urban, and especially city, design had been unevenly served by the architect-planners who trained before and immediately after the Second World War. The desire of many to realize the Corbusian dream led to what Hall (1968, 8) described as 'the complete destruction of a landscape.' But 1960 was the first year in which the majority of those joining planning did not have an architectural — and therefore a three-dimensional design — background. As to these newcomers, geography provided a wave of quantifiers, largely unconcerned with either environment or action, but ever-willing to engage in regional, sub-regional or network analyses. Later waves of sociologists and economists were even able to steer clear of spatial planning, and by the early 1970s design was scarcely taught in Britain's planning schools.

This might not have mattered if society had turned its back on place as a matter of concern, but amenity society interest and public protest against 'large, sterile, single-land-use areas, separated by large, negative road areas, crossed by windy pedestrian bridges or bleak, graffiti-ridden subways' (Hall, 1979, 384) had grown rapidly. Through the increasingly rapid changes in legislation, the desparate confusion over major public investment decisions (see Hall, 1980) and the eventual public disgrace of comprehensive solutions inspired by the Modern Movement, the one consistent fact of the planner's life was responsibility for development control, and the harnessing of popular interest in this subject.

Each new building, group of buildings or modest alteration to building or land use has been required to pass through both professional and democratic vetting procedures where society expected the planner to draw on established expertise to evaluate social, spatial and aesthetic benefits and impacts.

Ambiguous criteria and local authority inertia began to generate public and professional concern over development control by the mid 1970s. Architectural comment became more bullish, recognizing the paucity of design skills in many planning departments. The planning profession was slow to react, with its academic wing still preoccupied with establishing planning theory within an essentially social scientific context. Our Urban Design programme at Oxford emerged during this period, and it was to an earlier, architect-planner, generation and to those working in man-environment studies, rather than to our academic contemporaries that we looked for support.

It was the evident poverty of design skills used by private housing and retail developers, who had gained political strength in the 1970s, that eventually stimulated the planning profession to action. With a beginning in Essex County Council (1973) 'design guides' which illustrated preferred layouts, façade treatments, and townscape elements for new developments became a significant product of planning departments. Aimed at the developer, the architect, and the community, these documents could provide the basis for the generation of more specific site briefs which were then available as both negotiative and promotional tools.

Tentatively at first, local planning moved from negative development control to embrace positive development promotion. Planners with design and development skills are now increasingly sought by both public and private sectors, especially following the major changes in local planning encouraged by a Conservative government.

The Local Government, Planning and Land Act of 1980 ushered in a series of measures which removed planning decisions from democratically-accountable local agencies to urban Development Corporations in some areas (of which the London Docklands D.C. is probably the best known). It also reduced planning control over a variety of other areas where development was to be promoted. Taken together with central directives which reduced planning control over building extensions and their design and encouraged the release of land for housing development, the Greater London Council's report lamenting *The Erosion of the Planning System* (1985) seemed appropriately titled, especially as the publishers, London's metropolitan planning authority, were disbanded with all other metropolitan authorities in 1986!

Planning in Britain is predominantly a public sector activity, pursued by local authorities, which persisted as the political focus for local policy development until recently. In the past five years, however, authorities have been challenged by, and in turn have challenged, central government. Discussing his inner city initiatives, former Secretary of State for the Environment Michael Heseltine (1983,8) claimed that 'central government now plays a much more positive rôle'. This inner city rôle focuses on security, employment, health

and other services, with the expectation that, by encouraging investment, quality design will be an inevitable by-product. The inner city
urban designer is therefore likely to face very different issues from
those in suburban or rural areas where residential or small town sites
dominate, and where aesthetic control remains a lively issue (see
Meades, 1979; O'Rourke, 1985; Weller, 1986).

In most contexts the planner is being asked to do just what he or she
has always claimed to do well — resolve demands on land and steer
development towards publicly accountable and acceptable solutions.
Central government hardly assists this process (McGlue, 1985, 32):

> What is the government really saying behind its political
> stance? Emphasis is on green belt, conservation, protection
> of good agricultural land and of important features worthy of
> preservation/conservation. Emphasis is also on meeting mar-
> ket demand (strangely it appears only as far as housing is
> concerned) and providing a presumption in favour of devel-
> opment unless there is a very good reason to refuse.

One is as likely to find the planner practising design skills in favor
of a superstore development at a suburban motorway intersection,
as establishing an interpretive and recreation centre in an area of
landscape importance, and it is not impossible for these to involve
the same site. Each planner will be involved in bringing the development to the site, in pointing up implications of planning for the
location, and briefing for aspects of the development's design.

The urban designer within the planning department is increasingly
expected to be able to design; and with such skills enjoys a greater
measure of employment mobility and is likely to receive more positive support from the community at large than are planning colleagues. Successes in design are place-specific and visible, and
achieve publicity through public interest in conservation and in leisure facilities. As Byrne (1986,5) noted in a recent Presidential address to the Royal Town Planning Institute,

The range and scale of this work is very impressive and wide-spread. Conservation and environmental reclamation must be one of the great success stories of modern planning.

But although design looms large in any recent list of public schemes, the schemes themselves — a riverside reclamation here, a church conversion there — leave doubt as to the overall purpose of the profession. What is planning *for*, as distinct from what it is against? The profession is surprisingly quiet with regard to a positive view of Britain's environmental protection and development, and although claiming certain comprehensive management skills (see Holliday, 1986,15) seems unable to juggle more than the latest prefixes — development and promotional planning being the most recent — at any one time.

It is now clear that planning requires a range of designers whose backgrounds should embrace architectural, landscape, and product design as well as an awareness of conservation issues through architectural history or ecology. For example, although design skills are used in many local authorities, the specifically urban techniques used may obscure a new range of design skills which are needed to cope with fundamental changes in the rural landscape as farm pricing policies restructure British agriculture. Already a new generation of green-belt jumping 'villages' and 'new towns', the privatization and greening of inner city spaces, and removal of urban central functions to the periphery are raising design issues which neither urban design education nor practice seem to be considering. Although re-established in many planning departments, design is too often seen as a 'soft' area of work, concerned with conservation, communication and historic environments rather than with the environmental issues which stretch the minds of the best in the profession.

The Architectural Profession and Urban Design

In British culture, architecture is a more confusing profession than planning: there are simply more places on the body to take the pulse. Unlike planning, there is a diversity of evident and assessable products, a tradition of critical literature, and parallel streams of

professional development in other cultures against which to measure
the home product. (American incomer Nathan Silver (1979) found
no difficulty in asking 'Why is British Architecture Lousy?', and an-
swering in terms of American and Italian developments.)

The post-war era has already seen the passage of a generation with
Modern Movement ideals that saw public service in the next office
to — and in creative conflict with — the planner as a positive career
goal. With a decline in public sector employment, the opportunity
to embrace the urban design scale may have largely passed. The
architect is, and always has been, employed mainly in the private
sector and as Powell (1986, 28) has recently concluded, there are
grounds for cautious optimism with regard to the sector. But most
firms will be little concerned with urban design, for neither the scale
nor the context of their products will demand a positive response to
public space.

In terms of style, Eddy (1986, 38) suggests the dominant theme: 'the
underlying ambitions of a society are always expressed in its architecture. At the moment we sense a turning away, a nostalgic
yearning for more ordered and so more comforting times. The past
is always comforting — it is, after all, past.'

It is all too easy to characterize recent changes in British architecture
by stressing the inevitability of the unthinking corporate client, and
parcelling all discussions on style and professional purpose into a
cupboard reserved for creative ephemera and non-paying jobs. Although there remains the deadening preoccupation with nostalgia
(Goodey, 1986a), the fact that various stylistic or philosophical
groupings — Rationalist, Community, Conservationist — have each
generated discussion concerning the urban design scale has been
most positive. An increasing number of nationally-recognized architects has expanded the scale at which they work in order to reconcile the individual commission with the evident needs of
surrounding space.

With various strategies for keeping the user and passer-by in view,
many of the architectural contributors to recent urban design practice debate have shared something of Christopher Alexander's ap-

proach to the enduring 'patterns' evident in the existing city, though few demand the fundamental restructuring of society which his proposals must entail. Richard MacCormac's essays (1983, 1984) reveal a sensitive awareness of both human needs and the development process at the urban design scale. Citing an earlier proposal for Spitalfields market site in London, he notes (1983,59):

> The market study proposed forms of redevelopment which would sustain urbanity, by responding to the scale and system of the surrounding streets. Much of the current urban polemic is concerned with the visual significance of such traditional arrangements: these studies extend the argument into questions of content and appropriateness, to see which activities can go together.

More recently, a group of Oxford colleagues (Bentley, Alcock, Murrain, McGlynn and Smith, 1986) have produced an urban design handbook which synthesizes good practice in urban design in terms of qualities of permeability, variety, legibility, robustness, visual appropriateness, richness and personalization. Such concepts have an honourable history in the work of Alexander, Lynch and Cullen, but the Oxford authors have gone further in providing a practical bridge from analysis, through design principles, to exemplary practice in the current commercial climate. Already this new, or revived, lexicon is finding its way into the professional press, as in Ward's (1986, 41) account of the Terry Farrell Partnership's approach to the problems of the City of London.

The City, scene of the 1985 legal battle over a proposal to erect a Mies van der Rohe block at Mansion House Square, provides continuing evidence of the new, aggressive, rôle which some architects are taking in urban design and planning debates. The City, where a large percentage of Britain's development capital is managed, has become an architectural battleground, a focus for proposal and counter-proposal. This can all take place at high public visibility within the area's dense historical references and with the name of Britain's one popularly recognized architect (and urban designer), Sir Christopher Wren, usefully available.

If urban design is seen as existing in the space between (or at the fulcrum of a see-saw occupied by) architecture and planning, it is quite clear that the past ten years have seen the ascendancy of the former, to the disadvantage of intellectual and professional development in the latter.

The Urban Design 'Profession' and Urban Design

It is hardly correct to classify urban design as a profession, with either the advantages or problems which such a title bestows. As Alcock (1985) found in his analysis of a sample of those trained in, or proclaiming, an urban design practice, few either foresaw or desired the development of a profession with the status of architecture or planning.

In rejecting the idea that a graduate course in the subject is just a conversion opportunity for an architect or planner to obtain recognition in the other's discipline, several courses hint at wider employment opportunities which result from such training. In the event, urban design graduates have filled local authority and private practice posts where an architect-planner or planner-landscape architect was originally specified.

Courses, such as that recently launched at the Polytechnic of Central London (1984:4) promote the subject as integrative and eclectic . . .

> Urban Design can be defined as the design and management of the urban three-dimensional environment larger than the individual building.

> Practitioners of urban design may find themselves required to design, manage, evaluate, manipulate or improve parts of the urban environment — its buildings, the space between them and its systems of movement.

> These activities may be applied to new buildings or to the existing urban fabric, be it of recent or historic construction ... in all cases the urban designer must be able to draw with dis-

crimination upon the design traditions and skills of architecture, landscape architecture and town planning and be critically aware of the social, economic and legislative frameworks for action.

But such a description says little of the substance and skills of urban design. In 1978 the present author (also Barnett, 1978) identified six characteristics of the subject, presuming the three-dimensional urban context:

1. Emphasis on a spatial scale between the normal concerns of architecture and of planning.

2. Concern for place over an extended period of time.

3. A recognition that person-environment relations are an integral element in the design process at this scale.

4. That a number of paying clients and non-paying clients are inevitably involved.

5. That a number of professional skills must be integrated in the design of specific areas.

6. That guidance, as well as design, plays a key rôle in the urban design process.

While far from convinced that even these characteristics are acceptable to all urban designers in practice, it is important to consider a more critical list of current characteristics of the subject as taught and practised.

The *first* is to note that urban design seems only to have been discussed, 'clubbed-around,' and made subject of academic assessment after its initial practical energy was spent. Parkyn (1981) described the 'heroic period which saw the rise of urban design as a worthy and paying occupation for adults' in the 1960s and 1970s. Although 'the critics will bemoan the famous UD studies as being too physically determinate, too eager for visual nicety . . . the vision seemed worthwhile enough to work its way on to the ground. They excited the men in power as no options and priorities study of the 80s could ever do.'

Urban design, in the guise of 'civic design' or 'urbanism' enjoyed earlier popularity in a period largely untouched by the social, economic and functional concerns which crowd in on teaching and practice today. In Britain, at least, there is now skepticism of the 'heroic period' though this is seldom accompanied by any fundamental reconsideration of the subject.

The *second* point follows: there is a dreadful paucity of either urban design theory or of truly practical case-study advice. Such theory as exists has lacked critical review (see Allies, 1986 on Gosling and Maitland, 1985), has been generated with less than adequate awareness of the professionals involved (see Vernez-Moudon, 1984), or has failed to address contemporary circumstance (see Punter 1982, 14).

Maitland (1983) suggests that Christopher Alexander, Leon Krier and the Essex Design Guide offer three current and contrasting theories for urban design, but even if these are discrete theoretical propositions, they have seldom been regarded as such in the development of teaching or practice. To take one example, Krier's propositions for urban reconstruction (Krier and Culot, 1980) do not appear to have been tested in the context of a recent British project; although they would certainly have some relevance to the generation of new private peripheral settlements.

To my *third* point — instead of being advanced with reference to a theory, or theories, urban design training and projects are developed by traditional pragmatism. Graber (1979,1) makes a similar point with regard to American planning practice:

> Our ideas about environmental quality are seldom expressed in closely-reasoned philosophical statements. Instead, in the back of the planner's mind lies an image of 'the good life in the good landscape'. This image is difficult to verbalize, or to visualize in specific detail.

The most frequently chosen method of communicating, and often of realizing, the image seems to be through historical example.

My *fourth* point therefore concerns the selective use of an imagined past for the design of future places. Wright (1985a, and specifically 1985b) has written of 'the national past in contemporary Britain' and urban design critics, such as Hannay (1985) have attempted to deflate the promotional rhetoric which removes contemporary community in London's Docklands in order to reinstate 'the subtle modelling of solids and voids of Thameside warehouses.'

Neo-vernacular imagery generated by the Essex Design Guide, especially in the new town of South Woodham Ferrers (Neale, 1984) has come to represent this retreat to the past in contemporary urban design. The evolution of Essex proposals over the past ten years may be indicative of the poverty of ideas and opportunities. Locally, the original Essex proposal has been modified through experience and has gone some way towards the process of proposing and testing required of a developing theory. But, in reviewing its implications at the outset, Derbyshire (1975,97) noted its prompt but superficial replication by other local authorities, to be followed at a respectable distance by volume house builders:

> The Essex Guide has set the ball rolling by giving official recognition to the townscape approach to housing design. It has broken much new ground and many may see it as the last word, rather than the first of many steps in a new direction.
>
> Authorities who feel the need for their own guides may well be tempted to copy it. Indeed, one or two recent guides have appeared as pale pastiches of Essex . . . one must consider the form of the guidance. Essex has the advantage of a strong vernacular which enables their aesthetic concepts to be communicated by image: other areas may find this more difficult, and a traditional image is not necessarily appropriate.

Although replication has debased the Essex Design Guide approach, it should have served as a reminder that each design and development opportunity is in a unique place and requires professional investment in understanding the implications of specific locations. While few would argue with the suggestion that urban design is about making places, it is difficult to discern the specific elements of training, or stage in the design and development process, where this learning about place is endorsed. With an increasing tendency towards immediate success in public action programmes, and market-oriented development on tight time-schedules, the search for *genius loci* is often forgotten. The pattern book is in danger of emerging as the architect's surrogate for an involvement in place.

It may also be the tight schedules of a commercial world which militate against community involvement in urban design, though Jarvis (1982, 11) suspects that the flight from participatory contact is deeper rooted amongst 'those desk, drawing and committee bound designers who prefer to keep everyday life out of reach and so keep themselves out of place.' My *fifth* point is that the essential participatory and behavioral research base of urban design has been increasingly neglected over the past ten years. The majority of those in both planning and architectural professions have 'tried' participation but have found it a costly and threatening exercise to be pursued only by a minority in the contexts of 'environmental education' or 'community architecture.' Social and behavioural science, now the subject of doctrinaire political denigration in Britain, did little to advance the practical incorporation of formal and informal survey data in the design process. Within urban design the imperative seems to be to design and achieve built form, rather than to understand human relationships with existing form. A comprehensive study of public space, such as Korosec-Serfaty's Malmo report (1982), seems too detailed and lacking the precise design implications which can easily be utilized by student or practitioner. Popular rumor as to 'cosmic failures' began to outweigh the product of investigations by the early 1970s (see Pawley, 1971), with public space always the most difficult of scales in which to mount design-relevant studies of user behavior or needs.

With the *sixth* characteristic we can turn the corner to more positive matters. In urban renewal, there has been a noticeable turn in governmental and professional attention from 'Physical : Redevelopment : Living Standards : Information : Centralism : Government Investment : Economies of Scale' to 'Integrative : Prevention : Mutual Care : Do-it-Yourself : Small Wards : Informal Economy : Manageability' (Lichfield, 1984).

In terms of urban design this latter approach encourages both concern for place and a practical, rather than consultative, relationship with the community, though 'community architecture' seems to have taken over the 'enabling' or 'facilitating' rôle (Atwell, 1986) which urban design tentatively claimed in the late 1970s.

The development of local community Trusts — as for example in London's Hoxton (Gorman, 1986) — which focus business, environmental and resident interests, serve as clients to a range of professionals and are able to generate grants and public or private investment, has been the keystone of what is now recognized as an appropriate urban renewal policy by all political parties. Inevitably, such locally-based organizations soon begin to show community capacity for self-interest, revealed especially in the recent defensive housing developments of Belfast (Singleton, 1984), and therefore raise questions as to whether an effective pattern of community architecture or design does not still leave a task for the specifically 'urban' designer.

The *seventh* point stems from this. Community design in housing has been explored in detail by Ward (1985), long a critical voice on the margins of the British housing debate. His modest influence on urban design has been brought into focus by the recent appearance of a housing study which illustrates how the sub-profession remains open to external influences. Coleman's *Utopia on Trial* (1985) is based on a major, if flawed, study of external spaces around Britain's public housing undertaken by the Design Disadvantagement Project, a geographical research team. This publication and its immediate impact deserve detailed consideration, but suffice to say that the combination of suspect research methods, popular conclusions which endorse media prejudices, and a polemic assault on architecture, planning and housing authorities provides just the right opportunity for those who remain untainted°by Coleman's criticisms — and urban designers will feel able to avoid this taint — to embark on a program of debate, inquiry and remedial action in such public housing areas (see, as indicative, the Urban Design Group's conference proceedings, *Post-War Housing Estates: Humanising the Legacy* (1986)). Coleman's emphasis on the quality of external space, and on locally-based management of priority areas (see also Coleman, 1984) ensures that many urban designers may now see out their careers in the rehabilitation and renewal of post-war public housing.

My *eighth* characteristic of contemporary urban design involves landscape architecture. In most cultures it would not have been possible to journey thus far without disentangling urban design from the more mature and established profession of landscape architecture, but in Britain an implicit divide between 'land-' and 'town-' scapes has been preserved. Until recently there has been little reason to question this uncreative distancing, but over the past few years, fuelled by popular as well as professional interest, the 'city green' movement has developed. 'Greening', restoration and rehabilitation projects and new Trust organizations for achieving them, represent the more local interest in the 'city green' while a series of national garden festivals, in Liverpool (Holden, 1986), in Stoke-on-Trent, and planned for Glasgow — have united the vast popular interest in gardening as a private activity, with greening as a contribution to public space. Urban design interests have not yet made steps to reconsider their relationship with landscape architecture at the professional level, and there is little of the creative dynamism so evident in American landscape education. But local, 'grassroots' projects are gaining considerable media attention, and at the community scale the artificial barrier between land— and town-scape is being removed.

Making Places: Some Conclusions

'Placemakers is a nice term to describe people involved with designing things for people to inhabit.' Thus did Derbyshire (1985, 849) begin a recent global survey of architectural and planning projects to a meeting of the Royal Society of Arts in London. Although he was able to draw on British planning exports to generate a positive picture of continuity and sensitivity in professional place making, just around the corner, in Trafalgar Square, was evidence of a less confident local approach to urban design. In the Square, two major development sites have been under public discussion. One, adjacent to the National Gallery, has been subject of a sequence of competitions and proposals, punctuated by criticism from H.R.H. The

as architect for the National Gallery extension. But given the opportunity of a nationally-known public space, where were the urban design ideas?

> The hyped-up atmosphere of Trafalgar Square, the architect's fear of entering into competition with Nelson's Column on the one hand and local conservationists on the other, has clearly stayed the hand of the British contingent. They tried so hard to be sensitive that they did not hear the brief telling them to build a fine, loud, popular building that would not only finish off a corner of Trafalgar Square, but would also reflect the dazzling light of the collection inside. The trustees wanted courage (Wild and Janusczak, 1986,42).

At the opposite corner of the Square, the winning entry of three hundred for the Grand Buildings site 'largely copies the existing façade', leading an amenity society spokesman to comment (*Building Design,* 1986):

> This does seem a rather negative result. The existing building is not remarkable and I think most people were prepared to see it go to be replaced by an exciting modern solution. I feel this is another example of the cheapening of the content of London, and makes one wonder now what case there is for pulling down the existing building. Surely the competition must have thrown up more exciting and viable propositions.

A belief that a market- and developer-led era would stimulate a qualitative improvement in British public design, as was suggested in the early days of the Conservative government, was never convincing when applied to the urban design scale where public space and private generosity might be involved. The failure of British architects to rise to the new opportunities has been more surprising. Possibly the sensitivity noted above, or the awareness of Modern Movement errors, makes many architects wary of 'making a place' in public view. The limited competition for a cloistered building for Pembroke College at a riverside location in Oxford (Latham, 1986) generated entries which suggest the high quality of design to be achieved in a protected and arcadian context with a single client.

generated entries which suggest the high quality of design to be achieved in a protected and arcadian context with a single client.

The results of Alcock's survey (1985) of urban designers in practice hints that the sub-profession is happiest at slight remove from the real problems: briefing, guiding and negotiating, rather than struggling with concepts or the implementation of successful projects on major sites. What we have been encouraging is the development of the streetwise architect-planner who can hold his or her place, can advise or snipe from the periphery of those professions, but who has, fatally, failed to embrace some of the latent issues which others see as the core of urban design.

This matter is brought into focus when visiting designers in the so-called 'developing' world. The new town layouts, urban restructuring schemes, mass housing developments, and civil engineering projects which are seldom admitted as part of urban design in Britain, are, as Medhurst (1985) has noted, the everyday concerns of professionals elsewhere:

> If you say that these enormous urban conglomerations are not the concern of the urban designers you are reflecting what I have said, that Urban Design is only for the very rich of this world; it is not for the poor. This I do not believe. Certainly Urban Design comes low on a list of priorities when survival is at stake, but if urban designers are concerned only with those areas of concentrated wealth then they will be working themselves into a tiny corner of the world's problems, and as a group they will be irrelevant to the future.

From discussion with incoming students at Oxford, there emerges a fundamental dichotomy between the needs of those from 'developed' and those from 'developing' areas. On the one hand, those from developed urban cultures perceive the need for a sensitive environmental management and design system which ensures that public space and public places are established and maintained as essential elements in the physical form and cultural expression of the urban place. They seek techniques which will be acceptable to local communities and hope to have some influence over the future evolution of architectural design. They are willing to accept that the developer's needs are paramount provided that jobs, and some modest public betterment, result from the scheme. Personal and political values, once both articulated and evident in proposals, are seldom discussed. Students are encouraged to work on discrete central city sites where the community has largely been removed, and where the latest technological functions of society can be wrapped in a veneer of building style and place tradition.

The student from the developing world arrives with a personal, and possibly a governmental, remit to consider essentially 'greenfield' placemaking at a much larger scale. Trained as either an architect or planner, he or she is likely to play a major rôle in the layout and servicing of new urban places. The skills sought here are therefore of a very different order, and although three-dimensional in nature, embrace site planning, service layouts and project financing on a scale, and with constraints, as are seldom encountered in Britain. These students may be less well served by contemporary British urban design which, for home consumption at least, has withdrawn from public discussion at the scale which they need to address. This represents both a crisis in confidence — evident in the design of Milton Keynes, the 'last' new town — and a failure by the sub-profession to assert its capacity for such work over the architect-planner or other established design professional while firms based on landscape architecture and, surprisingly, product design, diversify into urban design scale schemes.

Commentators on other practice areas in society have observed that the heyday of the sub-profession has passed, and that more established groups with public visibility (in Britain endorsed by 'Royal' title) are strengthening their professional hold through diversification at a time of economic constraint. As a sub-profession, urban design has always lacked both the critical mass and the special, though not necessarily beneficial, form of leadership which might have ensured the establishment of a modest professional base. Instead, the Urban Design Group is currently appealing for members, the number of graduate courses is contracting and the trickle of literature in the field is seldom recognized by the major professions.

I would judge, however, that urban design and its adherents will persist as long as no other profession makes clear its commitment to *placemaking* as a key task in environmental design and management. As in the past, we may expect effective techniques generated by urban designers to be adopted by other design professions which will tolerate urban design until more formal practice and training relationships are established between professional institutes. The revival of just such a dual qualification route in architecture and planning is currently being developed.

Pushed to the corner or not, urban design must ensure that certain priority issues are covered through academic development and practice; Britain may be one of the last cultures to join the theoretical debate in the subject (Goodey, 1986a). .A realistic assessment of the new strategies of landscape architecture is overdue, as is a reconsideration of current popular attitudes to town— and landscape design (Goodey, 1986a). In areas such as housing rehabilitation, the urban designer must identify the unique skills which he or she brings to the task.

Most important, we need to establish if there is a rôle for urban design and structuring in those areas of environmental development which have been conveniently avoided — inner city zones, peripheral private housing expansions and motorway-generated sub-regional centers. Unless urban design can respond to an essentially new geography of Britain, it is unlikely to be able to provide any objective advice to those overseas who already have several layers of rather more challenging 'new geography' to hand.

References

Alcock, C. (1985) *Urban Design Is as Urban Design Does: An Investigation into Urban Design Practice*, Unpublished M.A. thesis, Joint Centre for Urban Design, Oxford Polytechnic.

Allies, B. (1986) Review: Gosling & Maitland, *Concepts of Urban Design, Architects' Journal*, 19 Feb., 79.

Barnett, J. (1978) The Practice of Urban Design, pp. 9-14 in A. Ferebee (ed.) *Proceedings of the First National Conference on Urban Design*, R.C. Publications, Washington, D.C.

Bentley, I., Alcock, A., Murrain, P., McGlynn, S. & Smith, G. (1985) *Responsive Environments*, Architectural Press, London.

Building Design (1986) Battle of Trafalgar, *Building Design*, 28 Mar., 2-3.

Byrne, S. (1986) The Changing Perspective, *The Planner*, 72 (3), 3-10.

Coleman, A. (1984) Trouble in Utopia: Design Influences in Blocks of Flats, *The Geographical Journal*, 150 (3), 351-62.

Coleman, A. (1985) *Utopia on Trial: Vision and Reality in Planned Housing*, Hilary Shipman, London.

Derbyshire, A. G. (1975) New Role for Housing Design Guides, *Building*, 20 June, 95-7.

Derbyshire, A. G. (1985) The Making of Cities — What Are We To Do? III Futures, *Journal of the Royal Society of Arts*, Nov., 849-71.

Eddy, D.H. (1986) Language and Solitude, *Royal Institute of British Architects Journal*, Jan., 34-6.

Essex County Council (1973) *A Design Guide for Residential Areas*, Essex County Council, Chelmsford.

Goodey, B. (1978) The Urban Designer as Co-ordinator, *Royal Institute of British Architects Journal*, Feb., 66-7.

Goodey, B. (1985) Urban Design: Context, Style and History in the Post-Modern Era, *Planning History Bulletin*, 7 (3), 46-52.

Goodey, B. (1986a) The Current Condition of Urban Design, in G. Butina (eds.) *Morphology in Design*, Joint Centre for Urban Design, Oxford Polytechnic.

Goodey, B. (1986b), Spotting, Squatting, Sitting or Setting: Some Public Images of Landscape, in D. Lowenthal & E. Penning-Rowsell (eds.), *Meanings and Values in Landscape*, Allen & Unwin, London.

Gorman, F. (1986) Putting the Heart into Hoxton, *Building Design* 14 Feb., 16-17.

Gosling, D. & Maitland, B. (1985) *Concepts of Urban Design*, Academy Press/St. Martin's Press, London.

Graber, L. H. (1979) *Development Control and the Sense of Place*, Paper for Session 'Experiential Perspectives on Place', Association of American Geographers Annual Meeting, 24 April.

Greater London Council (1985) *Erosion of the Planning System*, Greater London Council, London.

Hall, P. (1968) Monumental Folly, *New Society*, 24 Oct., 7-8.

Hall, P. (1979) Whatever Happened to Planning? *New Society*, 17 May, 384-5.

Hall, P. (1980) *Great Planning Disasters*, Weidenfeld & Nicolson, London.

Hannay, P. (1985) Home Truths, *Architects Journal*, 25 Sept., 68-79.

Heseltine, M. (1983) *Reviving the Inner City*, Conservative Political Centre, London.

Holden, R. (1986) Landscape Revisits: Liverpool Garden Festival, *Architects Journal*, 22 Jan., 67-72.

Holliday, J. (1986) The Values of Planning, *The Planner*, 72 (1), 14-16.

Jarvis, B. (1982) Urban Design Values, *Urban Design Quarterly*, Mar., 11.

Korosec-Serfaty, P. (ed.) (1982) *The Main Square: Functions and Daily Uses of Stortorget in Malmo*, ARIS Nova Series 1, Lund.

Krier, L. & Culot, M. (1980) *Contreprojets: Prefaces*, Archives D'Architecture Moderne, Bruxelles.

Latham, I. (1986) Inspired Dreams, *Building Design*, 21 Mar., 16-29.

Lichfield, D. K. (1984) Changing Approaches to Renewal, *Urban Design Quarterly*, Feb., 18-19.

MacCormac, R. (1983) Urban Reform, *Architects' Journal*, 15 Jan., 59-77.

MacCormac, R. (1984) Actions and Experience of Design, *Architects Journal*, 14 & 11 Jan., 43-7.

McGlue, T. (1985) Local Plans and Market Forces, *The Planner*, 71 (12) 32.

Maitland, B.S. (1983) The Future Townscape, pp. 61-81 in R. L. Davies and A. G. Champion (eds.), *The Future of the City Centre*, I.B.G. Special Publication 19, Academic Press, London.

Meades, J. (1979) Aesthetic Control: Strangling Creativity, *Architects Journal*, 19 and 26 Dec., 1315-24.

Medhurst, F. (1985) Urban Design in Perspective, *Urban Design Quarterly*, Dec./Jan./, 4.

Neale, C. (1984) *South Woodham Ferrers — The Essex Design Guide in Practice*, Planning and Development Case Study 3, Surveyors Publications, London.

O'Rourke, T. (1985) Practice: Planning Control 4: the Design Issue, *Architects' Journal*, 8 May, 77-9.

Parkyn, N. (1981) In Happy Magic Marker Land, *Building Design*, Mar, 6.

Pawley, M. (1971) Architects and the Philosopher's Stone, *New Society* 29 April. 718-20.

Polytechnic of Central London (1985) *Master of Arts in Urban Design: Proposal by the Schools of Architecture and Planning, Faculty of Environment*, Polytechnic of Central London, London.

Powell, C. (1986) Have Architects Ever Had it So Good? *Architects' Journal*, 19 Feb., 28-9.

Punter, J. (1982) Review: Kevin Lynch, A Theory of Good City Form, *Urban Design Quarterly*, Nov., 12-14.

Silver, N. (1979) Why is British Architecture Lousy? *The Listener*, 13 Sept.

Singleton, D. (1984) *The Belfast Experience: Housing Renewal in Northern Ireland*, Northern Ireland Housing Executive, Belfast.

Urban Design Group (1986) Post-War Housing Estates: Humanising the Legacy, *Urban Design Quarterly*, March.

Vernez-Moudon, A. (1984) Review of 'Remaking the City' and 'Professionals and Urban Form', *Urban Design Review*, 7, 18-19.

Ward, B. (1986) Stepping Out For the City, *Architects Journal*, 9 April, 50-5.

Ward, C. (1985) *When We Build Again, Let's Have Housing That Works*, Pluto, London.

Weller, J. (1986) Practice Legislation: Lifting the Burden of Planning, *Architects Journal*, 15 Mar., 69-70.

Wild, D. & Janusczak, W. (1986) National Gallery Finalists, *Architects' Journal*, 19 Mar., 39-68.

Wright, P. (1985a) *On Living in an Old Country*, Verso, London.

Wright, P. (1985b) Ideal Homes, *New Socialist*, Oct., 16-21.

Chapter 12

Computer Modelling for Urban Design

John L. Brown

In 1970 the Royal Institute of British Architects attempted to define the function and status of the newly emerging discipline of urban design. They stated that it is an integral part of the process of city and regional planning and is essentially concerned with the three dimensional design and the non-visual character of an area. Its major task is the arrangement, in external space, of the physical objects and human activities which make up the environment. Urban design is not only concerned with the relationship of new development to existing city form, but also to the social, political, and economic demands and resources available (Gosling and Maitland, 1984).

Thus the scale of urban design intervention appears to lie somewhere between the boundaries of urban planning — the organization of the public realm, and architecture — the physical design of the private realm. It has only been recently, however, that the importance of this dualism has been recognized. Prior to this, urban design problems were solved with either the tools and techniques of urban planning or those of architecture. This approach resulted in solutions with either an exaggeratedly low or high significance attributed to built form. As Gosling and Maitland (1984) have observed, both of these positions promote a limited view of urban design as a largely formal activity which can be pursued independently of the problematic context of existing cities.

Therefore, to adequately analyze and synthesize urban design scale problems there needs to be a set of tools and techniques available in addition to those associated with each of the parent disciplines. Perhaps the most basic of these new tools, and one sorely missing from the profession, is a method for modelling, for any particular urban design problem, the interrelationship between physical/spatial form and its associated social, economic, and infrastructure resources.

This paper examines the possibilities for the development of one such tool, a computer based integrated representation model. Utilizing the concept of a Design Information System, the characteristic elements, desirable features, inherent limitations and possible applications of this tool in urban design are explored.

Representing the Problem

A model is a somewhat simplified abstraction of the real world. It represents some of the structure of reality and omits the rest. It is only useful if it includes those elements in which we are interested, and the challenge is to match the structure of the representation with the structure provided by the problem at hand. Most urban planning models are simulation based. That is, they attempt to imitate a real world process either through a mechanical analog or through some mathematical algorithm. This approach to model making has had only limited success in planning. Langendorf (1985) has suggested that it is often perceived that these kinds of decision aids may not be well suited to decision making styles or to the nature of urban planning problems. He further suggests that most of the problems arise from trying to use a structured problem solving tool, such as a computer simulation model which requires problems that are well understood, orderly, and predictable in outcome. to solve problems which are usually unstructured and novel requiring the exercise of judgement, intelligence, and adaptive problem solving behavior.

Fortunately, many of these objections can be overcome with heuristic modelling. Heuristic approaches to analysis and model-building are largely descriptive and phenomenological in nature and therefore are not usually concerned with the detailed nature of underlying processes (Harris 1965). They are generally used as a descriptive device rather than as a forecasting tool and are especially effective in modelling complex systems containing multiple interrelationships.

Heuristic modelling is well suited for the urban design application at hand. However, an effective and efficient use of this technique demands that the description be formatted into a coherent structure. Recognizing that there is no single representation that allows detailed consideration of the diverse concerns found in an urban situation, it is possible to construct the model as a series of representations, each describing a specific aspect of the urban environment. If this is executed in a computer environment it is possible to obtain composite representations that incorporate all of the relations or descriptions found in each of the individual sets. This type of integrated model is known as a Design Information System.

An Urban Design Information System

A Design Information System is a relatively new concept originating from architectural computer aided design. Based on the idea of a totally integrated approach to the description of a building, these systems exist, or are under development, in universities in both North America and abroad. The following discussion is based around the five constitutive issues that Eastman (1982) has identified as being of central importance for the development of a Design Information System:

- Spatial modelling

- Integration of attributes

- Database management

- Design development

- Design coordination

Spatial Modelling

The primary representation in a Design Information System is a geometric model of the subject's physical form. All other descriptive sets are referenced to it, and it forms the base over which most of the other information can be displayed. The basis of this spatial representation is a three-dimensional model of the subject generated with computer based graphic simulation technology used by the architectural profession. These computer systems combine the best of drawings and traditional model building by providing a three-dimensional representation of a physical form that can be viewed from any location but which can be altered as easily as a paper sketch. In addition, there are a number of options available for the manner in which these models can be displayed. These range from wireframe vector displays, to simple solid modelling, to highly sophisticated rendering routines in which shadow casting, color, reflectivity of surfaces, and ambient light can be included.

These three-dimensional computer based models could be used for the visual spatial analysis and evaluation of a subject's physical form. For example, the location, height, profile, and massing of a proposed structure could be evaluated in terms of such issues as its relationship to the skyline and to the street, its shadow paths on adjacent public spaces, and its impact on view corridors. It is also possible to study detailed design interventions in specific areas. For example, a great deal of information could be introduced into the system to facilitate the modelling and subsequent evaluation of such things as landscaping, surface treatment, materials, and street furniture.

In addition, the ease and flexibility with which the eye and object can be located for perspectival viewing allows the designer to create a series of views corresponding to one's movement in space. These can be viewed individually or in series to produce a real time animation sequence. The precedent for this type of analysis can be traced back to the work of Gordon Cullen and his concept of serial vision which is both a recording or analytical notation as well as a creative design tool. Similarly, Donald Appleyard at the University of California, Berkeley, has explored the simulation of the temporal dimension in urban design through the use of large scale models and sophisticated video systems.

Gosling and Maitland (1984) have suggested that although this type of work is an important tool for urban design it is not widely used because of the graphic fluency required by Cullen and the extensive scale models needed by Appleyard. While a computer based visual model still requires a significant time investment during the initial model definition it could overcome some of these problems by relieving the designer from the chore of constructing perspective views or from the extremely large time and energy commitment involved in actually constructing a physical model.

Integration of Attributes

Geometric shape is only one way in which the constitutive components that comprise a subject can be described. Other descriptions, such as zoning or demographics for example, can be added as attributes to the geometric description of each component. By linking these, often numerical, attributes to the geometric model it is possible to graphically display individual representation sets (Fig. 12.1). Thus, a graphic illustration of building occupancy could be overlayed onto the spatial model to facilitate a visual analysis of their interrelationship. More importantly, more than one set of attributes could be displayed simultaneously, as a series of transparent overlays on the spatial base model, creating a composite representation. Thus, for example, the relationships between building occupancy, land value, zoning, and their impact on physical form could be visually analyzed.

Fortunately most, if not all, of the attributes necessary to model a complex urban subject can be found within the records of municipal governments and their planning authorities. For example, inventories of structures and infrastructure, land use surveys, zoning, property assessments, land valuations, capacity analyses, and construction permits are normally available. However, while most municipalities maintain these records in computer databases there is often little or no integration of information between departments. This problem is slowly being overcome with the implementation of Geographic

Reference Systems, which attempt to standardize and integrate the
multifarious records generated by a municipality into a common

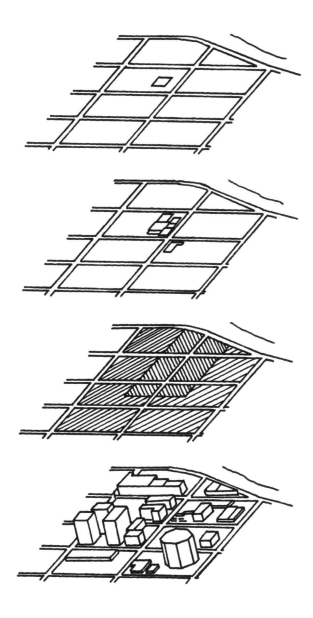

Fig. 12.1:   Urban Design Information System

database from which various applications can be executed (HDR Infrastructure 1986). Within a system such as this, an Urban Design Information System could act as a graphic 'front end' or display controller for the vast amounts of information residing within a municipality's records.

The importance of this capability, to graphically illustrate large amounts of primarily numeric information, should be stressed. Langendorf (1985) states that it is becoming increasingly clear that the computer is a powerful tool, not only in terms of storage, retrieval, and manipulation of information, but also in making it easier to interpret this information through graphic display. A picture can indeed be worth a thousand words and an ability to extract and correlate this kind of information increases its usefulness to the designer as the interrelationships between various records and their relationship to the physical form of the subject can be more readily visualized.

Database Management

A Design Information System stores the attributes associated with a specific model within a fully interrelational database keyed to the spatial model. This allows for sorting and querying functions to be incorporated into the display functions previously mentioned. Therefore the system could search and graphically display only those components within the subject that met certain specified criteria. For example, the system could be asked to graphically highlight only those areas within the subject that have a specific occupancy, a certain land value, and a given floor area ratio.

In addition, the database structure could automatically manage the consistency between the various graphic projections produced from the system. As the three dimensional model and its attributes are contained within one set of data, all updates, revisions, and testing of the subject could be automatically reflected in all of the graphic displays. This is in sharp contrast to conventional representations in which any change requires the updating of each individual sheet of drawings.

Design Development

Up to this point, the discussion has centered around the information gathering and synthesizing characteristics of an Urban Design Information System. However, to be truly valuable in a problem solving situation, the model must also be useful during the design process. That is, it should be possible to extract from the system any particular set of attributes, work with them, and then return the altered attributes to the system to test the appropriateness of that particular design solution. The database characteristics of the system make it well suited for that purpose. With a Design Information System it is possible to extract either all of the attributes for a given component, such as all of the data associated with a particular building, or one set of attributes for all of the components, such as the occupancy data for all of the structures. This information could then be utilized in an existing simulation program to forecast a specific design scenario and then returned to the system where the altered attributes could be examined in the context of the rest of the model.

This approach is also possible with physical design problems. The geometric attributes for either one component or the entire model could be extracted and utilized in a conventional computer aided design system. Various options could be developed and placed within the system model to evaluate their effectiveness, not only in relation to adjacent buildings, but in terms of their impact on the other attribute sets included in the model. Danahy (1984) has identified this evaluation process as being one of the most important features in computer graphic modelling. It offers the possibility of consistency and control over the generation of imagery for evaluation purposes that is not possible using traditional tools of design.

Design Coordination

A Design Information System offers the opportunity to vastly improve the coordination of information among the major players involved in a complex urban design problem. Changes need no longer be communicated verbally or through a new set of drawings. With each participant working from a common database, changes need only be implemented once to be reflected automatically to all concerned.

Eastman (1982) has described the ideal process that this technology implies. Each participant in the design problem has the ability of accessing any specific information he may need from a time shared computer database and then display it in the manner best suited for this purposes. After developing this information into a series of alternatives or extensions to the database, their appropriateness can be checked by each of the other participants before being added to the common model.

Although this kind of integration is theoretically possible its implications in terms of available hardware and software make it impractical in the short term. However, one need only look at the proliferation of computer terminals and commonly accessed databases in other areas of municipal government to see that its feasibility will dramatically increase in the future.

Implementation

An Urban Design Information System does not yet exist. As previously mentioned, this type of integrated representation model is a newcomer in a relatively young field of research into the use of computer aided graphic simulation in design. Technologically, the hardware and software already exist for the creation of such a system. What remains is the task of integrating the various pieces into a functioning whole. While it is beyond the scope of this discussion to present specific options about how this could be done, it is possible to make some general conclusions regarding the constituent elements of a model of this kind.

Following the general trend in computer applications, it is anticipated that an urban Design Information System will be at least partially microcomputer based. The increasing sophistication of these machines, their decreasing cost, and their increasingly widespread availability, especially within the design professions and municipal government, make it the preferred hardware. With that said, however, the current generation of personal computers are not quite powerful enough to handle a complex model. Therefore, it is anticipated that, for the short term at least, the individual microcomputer workstations would be linked together with a small super minicomputer. This machine could provide the storage necessary for a large database and has the c.p.u. power to efficiently run the more sophisticated graphic rendering routines. Using this system, the designer could query the information system on the minicomputer via his individual micro and download the information of specific interest. Most of the procedures, including the three dimensional computer aided drawing, could be completed on the micro with any conclusions or strategies uploaded to the minicomputer to update the common database.

Given the advanced state of the art in microcomputer based graphic and database software, it is anticipated that commercially available software will be used whenever possible. The advantages of this are that it removes some of the burden of software updating and debugging from the user, and facilitates the incorporation of improvements and advances within these technologies into the information system. In addition, there is a greater chance that the model will be compatible with the software used by other design professionals. Ultimately, this could allow planners, architects, or landscape architects to not only transfer their proposals into the model and evaluate them, but to have access to the mapping and query functions within the system.

The primary requirement for any of these software packages is that their structure be open enough to facilitate their being linked to a larger system of integrated applications. This corresponds to recent trends in software development towards integration and the increasing capacity for new software to exchange files with other types of applications. A similar approach has been taken in municipal geoprocessing with the latest efforts focussed on the development of links between existing databases, programs, and equipment (HDR Infrastructure 1986).

Implications and Limitations

Computer modelling is not new to the planning profession, with urban simulation models having been used for several decades. However, as has been previously mentioned, they have generally not fulfilled the promise of their original intentions because of the structural dissimilarities between the tool and the problem it was created for. The preceding discussion of the desirable characteristics of an Urban Design Information System has kept these considerations in mind. Therefore the system differs from most previous models of the city in several significant areas.

First, the model is heuristic rather than simulation based. Unburdened by the necessity of abstracting the subject into a series of easily simulated components, the information system has the capacity to begin to describe the complexity and interrelationships inherent in any urban problem.

Second, the model is convivial rather than manipulative. Ilich has pointed out that the design professions dealing with the city are often confronted with manipulative tools which arranges people's activities for the convenience of the institutional tool rather than the reverse. The clearest example of this is supplied by Goodman when he suggests that there is a tendency for the overall design to grow from the need of one professional, who doesn't live in the environment, to explain his design in simplistic terms, to groups of bureaucrats, who also don't live in the environment, but control it through access to public funds. Therefore, the need to explain the design becomes the prime motivation for what the design turns out to be (Gosling and Maitland 1984). Thus solutions to urban problems tend to be characteristically simple, ambiguous, and static. This is in sharp contrast to the complexity of the city in which problems are often poorly stated, misunderstood, complexly interrelated, and changing over time.

The descriptive rather than prescriptive nature of the urban design information system is inherently less manipulative than a simulation model. Moreover, the graphic presentation format enhances the legibility of complex issues without compromising the integrity of the situation for the sake of explanation.

In conclusion, a computer based Urban Design Information System similar to that discussed in this paper has the potential to integrate and optimize the responses of the design professions to the problems of the city. By providing a common database in which the complexity and interrelated nature of an urban problem can be described, physical interventions can be formulated and evaluated. It has the potential for reducing the opportunity for the isolated solution, taken out of either its physical, economic, or social context. At a time of budgetary restraint it is necessary to optimize the effect of the limited number of interventions that urban designers can make. An Urban Design Information System facilitates this by not only providing a three dimensional spatial model in which various proposals can be tested, but by presenting it in a format that is more readily understood by laypeople, either public or government.

However, this model is not to be seen as a panacea for all the problems facing the urban design profession. It suffers from the same unavoidable danger of oversimplification that is inherent in any abstraction or model. The system could not, nor should it, attempt to describe the whole range of intangible issues and concerns in the city. In addition, it is always possible for a model to be used incorrectly or for the information presented to be naively interpreted. Thus, like any other model, its effective use is predicated on a knowledge of the intentions of the model and the limits of the information being presented.

In addition, there are risks inherent in using a computer based representation. As Langendorf (1985) has pointed out, although the use of computer based systems may require little expertise in computing by the end user, computer assisted decision making implies a division of labor between the user and the machine. The responsible use of these computer aids assumes knowledgeable users who understand and accept this division of labor and do not abdicate their responsibilities.

Finally, a model such as this is primarily a physical planning tool and as such is only one of a number of valid approaches to urban design. The city has long suffered from oversimplified approaches to design intervention and if we are guilty of relying too heavily on engineering solutions and not enough on physical planning in the recent past, we do not want to be guilty of swinging too far to the other side in the near future. A balanced approach, utilizing physical planning tools where appropriate and engineering tools where they are best suited, seems to be the most effective method for formulating a response to the problems facing our late twentieth century cities.

References

Danahy, J. (1984) Computer Aided Design Graphics and Design Process, Council of Educators in Landscape Architecture, 375-381.

Eastman, C. (1982) The Computer as a Design Medium, pp. 245-266 in O. Akin and E. Weinel (ed.) *Representation and Architecture*, Information Dynamics, Silver Spring, Maryland.

Gosling, D. and Maitland B. (1984) *Concepts of Urban Design*, St. Martin's Press, London.

Harris, B. (1965) New Tools for Planning, *Journal of the American Institute of Planners*, 31, May, 90-95.

HDR Infrastructure (ed.) (1986) Geoprocessing and Data Base Management, *Proceedings of the Municipal Geoprocessing Workshop*, Calgary.

Langendorf, R. (1985) Computers and Decision Making, *American Planning Association Journal*, 51, 422-433.

Chapter 13

The Future of the Metropolis:
its Urban Design, Function and Form

Gary Gappert

Several different concepts have dominated thinking about the future of the metropolis. One concept is that of the 'spread city' whereby the city continues to add rings of suburbanization, notwithstanding natural barriers such as a lakeshore, a seafront or a mountain range. Another concept is that of a 'megalopolis' where expanding urbanization unites different, independent metropolitan areas in a continuing strip or corridor of cities, suburbs and transportation infrastructure. A third and less common concept is that of a 'compact city' where new forms of energy-efficient urban technology create an almost space ship approach to a reconsolidated urban community. But there is also the appropriate technology concept of a compact city which is being built by Paolo Soleri at his Arcosanti in the American Southwest. A fourth and perhaps more practical concept is that of the 'metroplex' , symbolized initially by the consolidation of the metropolitan space between Dallas and Fort Worth. The new urbanization between two or more free-standing cities in particular regions is a more prevalent, and less ambitious, tendency than that of the sprawling megalopolis. Other examples that come readily to mind are those of Baltimore-Washington, Cleveland-Akron-Canton, Chicago-Rockford, Los Angeles-San Diego, the Front Range cities in Colorado, most of Florida, portions of southeastern New England and the northwestern shore of Lake Ontario from Buffalo to Toronto.

In thinking about the future of the metropolis and its urban design, function and form, this paper will basically address the period of future time from 1990 to 2020, a 30-year perspective which is a relatively modest projection of the urban future. Already some cities such as the National City Planning Commission of the District of Columbia are trying to anticipate 2050, or the mid-point of the 21st century. From the standpoint of the next three decades, this paper assumes that there will be two sets of forces impacting upon the metropolis, or upon the emerging set of metroplexes, that will be partially complimentary and partially contradictory or countervailing, beyond now and the year 2020.

The first set of forces will be those of a post-affluent society. Those forces will generally continue to be an influence for urban reconsolidation, reservation and recentralization on a metropolitan scale. The second set of forces will be those of an advanced industrial society. These forces will generally contribute to the spreading out of the metropolitan based economic activities to a global scale. Some will interpret these forces as contributing to further urban decentralization. This interpretation however ignores the possibility of new urban functions in the emerging global economy and society.

Beyond 2020, the prospects for the metropolis are not as clear. There are several reasons for this uncertainty. Beginning in 2011 the first of the baby boom generation reaches the age of 65 and the retirement behavior of this generation through 2030, especially in terms of their locational propensities, is not yet known. It is also not yet clear whether a new 'long wave' of economic development will be in place as the 21st century unfolds, or which urban places will be the winners or losers in that process. Other sources of uncertainty are:

- the future of womens' movements,

- the success of efforts to create more livable winter cities,

- the size and disposition of the urban underclass,

- the status of trans-national terrorism and

- settlement patterns in rural areas.

It might also be anticipated however, that, as we manage the reurbanization of our sprawling metropolitan spaces and learn especially to master the in-fill urban design process, our skills at planning and building the intentional — as opposed to accidental — city will be one of the enduring legacies of the end of this century for the next one. In the rest of this chapter some of the context for this optimism will be presented.

As we approach the year 2000, more and more of our planning time will be spent on prognostications about life in the 21st century. The usefulness of these speculations will be related to how well they help us deal with our sense of uncertainty about the future. In the 1960s the key words were *certainty* and *planning* while in the 1970s they were *uncertainty* and *management*. But in the 1980s the key words appear to be *surprises* and *adaptations*. All planners, especially urban planners, do not like uncertainty and hate surprises. Therefore, the psychological adjustment of urban planners to the uncertain and inchoate realities of the next decade must be an item of special concern.

This chapter attempts to describe a framework of socio-economic development in order to provide at least a tentative framework for understanding the recent past and the immediate future. Cities do not change quickly but evolve into their future from an historical context. My suspicion is that in an advanced industrial society, cities (and urban development) will become effectively urbane.

The Post-Affluent Framework

The framework of a post-affluent society developed in the mid-1970s (Gappert, 1979) was one attempt to create a model which could be used to assess the myriad trends and events associated with the fundamental dislocation of the American economy that was caused by OPEC seizing the international resource initiative, which in turn accelerated the development of a new international economic order.

The assumption of the post-affluent framework is that the economic events of 1971-74 represent a significant turning point and developmental shift in our society. These events — price controls, the oil boycott, the dramatic increase in energy costs — triggered the start of a post-affluent transition. This transition was preceded by the beginnings of a post-industrial shift out of traditional manufacturing employment. The significant beginning of this post-industrial shift can be symbolized by the Soviet launching of Sputnik in 1957. The American response to that event led to the National Defense Education Act, and to the acceleration of space and defense programs out of which both new technologies and new sunbelt cities have developed.

The post-industrial framework, however, has lost conceptual vigor as the American economy has evolved towards a further stage of industrial development. The usefulness of the post-affluent framework is also likely to decline if a reconstruction of the American economy is achieved. But we are still in the midst of a transitional phase. The processes of what Schumpeter (1934) once referred to as 'creative destruction' are still rampant. A restructured economy is not yet here.

It is likely that the seven elements of a post-affluent framework will remain relevant for the rest of the 1980s. These elements are:

- the almost overwhelming demographic significance of the Bulge Generation;

- the emergence and recognition of a post-affluent consciousness;

- the recognition if not the acceptance of the transcendental nature of many wants and needs;

- innovative tinkering and substantial reforms in households and workplaces including social-economic counseling and job redesign;

- the gradual development of synergistic lifestyles in an evolving androgynous culture;

- discontent and disruptions with respect to agreement on a 'just' distribution of income among different socio-economic groups;

- patterns of uncertainty and indecision among large-scale organizations including the federal government and Fortune 500 corporations.

Increasingly, the picture of a post-affluent society is not a picture of the future but an expression of the present economic doldrums. It is perhaps timely to (a) accept the post-affluent framework as a useful interpretation of current realities, and (b) generate a more optimistic vision of what economic recovery will generate at some point in the near- or medium-term future. Let us turn to a discussion of a new form of prosperity.

A New Prosperity Paradigm

Recent research from several sources (Knight, 1980; Bradshaw, 1979; Hamrin, 1980) can be used to identify an emerging but elusive picture of the economic future of the United States. This is the idea of an *advanced industrial society*. There is more than a faint hint that we might be experiencing the start of another long wave of economic development. Could the American economy be on the verge of another great surge of prosperity based upon the new information, communications, medical and biological technologies?

Before he died, the controversial futurist Herman Kahn had begun to herald a forthcoming economic boom. Heilbroner and other more seasoned economic observers, while sanguine about the future of capitalism, have begun to identify the massive institutional efforts which will be required to achieve a new, lasting and stable economic prosperity. These efforts are symbolized on the 'right' by the attempt to secure a Balanced Budget Constitutional amendment and on the 'left' by discussions about credit allocations, wage-price control mechanisms and some kind of new Reconstruction Finance Corporation. In the 'center' is the new legislation introduced by Gary Hart and others for an American Defense Education Bill.

The emergence of a new and more dynamic national economic prosperity has been obscured by the normal short-sighted economic debates having to do with (a) quarterly corporate earnings, (b) the annual federal budget, and (c) the monthly behavior of the Dow-Jones Index, interest rates, the rate of inflation and unemployment statistics.

These short-sighted concerns have deflected attention from other significant national economic developments which include:

* the tremendous expansion of the labor force with the coming of age of the baby boom generation and the participation of women of all ages in the labor market;

* the substantial shortfall in technically trained American labor which has been met by a substantial influx of educated immigrants or young student immigrants to technical and engineering educational institutions;

* the expansion of a global manufacturing economic system which will ensure that large numbers of unskilled and semi-skilled manufacturing jobs will be lost to American workers.

In *Post-Affluent America* it was noted that the labor market was expanding at a rate of 68,000 jobs a week. Unfortunately, the labor force was expanding even faster, at a rate of 72,000 workers a week, creating an accumulating shortfall of 4,000 jobs a week. Therefore there has been a steady increase in the unemployment rate. Nevertheless, even in July 1982, when the nation's jobless rate rose to 9.8 per cent, the highest since before World War II, this rise was caused primarily by a growth of 330,000 workers in the civilian labor force because total employment shrank by only 12,000 jobs (net) to slightly under 100,000,000 total employment. It might also be noted that, in mid-1982, total employment in the so-called service industries surpassed for the first time total employment in manufacturing, mining and construction (*New York Times*: July 6, 1982). It is important to acknowledge, however, that much of that service sector activity provides technical support (legal, financial, engineering, etc.) to manufacturing enterprises.

The evidence is not yet conclusive that a new wave of American prosperity will in fact develop or will be strong enough to provide 'a rising tide that will float all boats'. In this particular context I do not care to debate the probability of its occurrence. Instead, I wish to outline the elements of a new socio-economic paradigm which might come to be associated with the emergence of an advanced industrial society if in fact it does develop from the tentative economic recovery of the mid-1980s to a major transformation of socio-economic technostructure and the achievement of a 'new prosperity.'

The Advanced Industrial Alternative

A model of an advanced industrial society can be developed as an alternative framework for the interpretation and projection of emerging trends and realities in American society.

As shown in Fig. 13.1, there are at least three different ways to perceive the socio-economic future. The first perspective, System X, assumes that issues of economic productivity and efficiency will lead to both fiercer competition and greater disappointment unless the vitality of the national economy dramatically improves. In this perspective we can expect more outbreaks of social hostility and underclass turmoil.

The second perspective, System Y, assumes that although the growth rate may decline, the underlying strength of the national economy is undiminished even though individual gains take longer to achieve. In this perspective, individual and household pursuit of purely economic objectives are postponed, deflected or sublimated by activities associated with quality of life concerns. Cities and suburbs both contribute to the growth of self-reliance and a self-directing transformation.

Substantial elements of both System X and System Y exist today as part of a constrained economy. The third perspective, that of System Z, is more elusive and harder to establish. The key assumption of

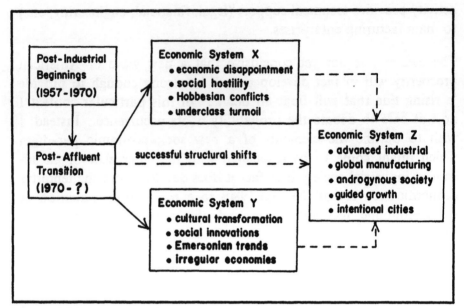

Figure 13.1:   Perspective on Societal Futures

this perspective is that a new kind of technological-industrial progress is possible, indeed probable. It assumes that a second Industrial Revolution is at hand based upon technolgies that are (1) knowledge intensive, (2) resource conserving, and (3) environmentally benign. Several specialists have made contributions to this perspective.

Hamrin, in *Managing Growth in the 1980s*, lays out in a comprehensive fashion the elements of an economy·centered on information activity. He claims that 'the adjective "information" is more precise than 'service' or 'post-industrial' for describing the fundamental dynamic element that will shape the economy and society of the future' A critical element in Hamrin's analysis is that the ultimate limits to growth in an advanced industrial society 'will basically reflect not resource scarcities but a steadily rising preference for noneconomic endeavors and satisfactions' .   Developing what he calls a 'transindustrial world view,' Hamrin also proposes a new paradigm for economic growth in which productivity and technological change are important factors along with capital, labor (human resources) and land (natural resources and energy). The guiding norm or ethic within his model of an advanced industrial society is 'selective growth' as opposed to traditional forms of simple quantitative measures. This suggests that institutions need to make more holistic decisions in the context of long range policy frameworks. Although he is pessimistic about the prospects for an immediate adoption of such a new paradigm, his use of a return-on-resources decision making model for corporations confirms the need to explore different forms of innovative management more appropriate to the changing realities in an advanced industrial society.

Hirschhorn, at the Wharton School in Philadelphia, offers yet another perspective. His reference point is the idea of 'advanced capitalism' as distinct from traditional forms. He claims that 'there is increasing evidence that capitalism is entering a new historical phase of disaccumulation in which the wage labor system is contracting and the accumulation of variable capital is coming slowly to a halt' (1984). Coincident with this, he argues, a new work system, new productive sources and new sources of productivity are emerging which are not consistent with traditional categories of economic classification. The problem which Hirschhorn then goes on to explore concerns the ways in which older social forms and institutional structures may stifle the developmental processes emerging in an advanced form of capitalistic or industrial society.

Hirschhorn attempts to develop a model of the advanced industrial labor process based upon seven related hypotheses. A key issue for him is the distribution of intelligence and information in work systems and the ways in which advanced technologies diffuse and change the management functions. He concludes that:

> It is urgent that research within this framework be developed so that we do not pursue obsolete lines of thought on the one side and are prepared for genuinely new and emergent possibilities, and conflicts, on the other.

Knight, analyzing employment expansion in several older metropolitan regions including Cleveland, has also developed a perspective on industrial transition and transformation. Knight's model is based upon the assumption that the large industrial corporations have reached a stage where their 'technology transfer' functions have expanded their multinational status in a global *economy* which has grown by a factor of 3 in the last decade, while world *trade* has increased by a factor of 7. This has both generated new streams of real income into older regions and the export of traditional production jobs to other states and nations.

Two constructs are essential to Knight's analysis. The first focuses on the 'changing nature of industrial knowledge' to include such elements as research and development, environmental constraints, international marketing and transfer of technologies, etc. The second is the 'changing nature of social and cultural development' as industrial communities either decline or evolve into a higher stage of development.

Other efforts to formulate the social and economic consequences of a new wave of technological development can be found in Ouchi (1981), Mensch (1982) and Masuda (1980). All suggest a new economic system based upon knowledge intensive technologies.

In the absence of any 'policy' which advocates, or even simply articulates, the nature of a different socio-economic system organized around new technological opportunities, the question is: will such a system emerge anyhow? One answer is: Let's wait and see. Another is: It's happening already. But in either case even the mere possibility of an advanced industrial economy and society offers a more dramatic set of opportunities than the grim sense of decline associated with the post-industrial construct.

If one accepts the realities of the current post-affluent condition, but still appreciates the dynamic qualities of American society, its economic strengths and its technological opportunities, then it becomes possible to concentrate on the identification and elaboration of new rôles and opportunities in the new order of things. But many are not yet either cognizant of, or comfortable with, the new realities and opportunities.

Kevin Phillips has recently written:

> Two decades of political and economic trauma have brought this country to a point of considerable risk. . . . In an era of

upheaval like our own, there is no going back, no real way to recapture the past. . . . to future historians, the early 1980s are almost certain to mark a transition to a new politics, a new economics, and a new philosophy of governance (1982, p. 8).

But the transition is not yet concluded and perhaps the transformation has not yet begun. Therefore it is still difficult to forecast the exact nature of our social economic development between now and the 21st century. But Theory Z offers a significant starting point.

The Urban Consequences of a Theory Z Perspective

At one level Theory Z is what Naisbitt refers to as *high tech/high touch*. As he writes:

Whenever new technology is introduced into society, there must be counterbalancing human response, that is, *high touch*, or the technology is rejected.

And Naisbitt goes on to assert that 'we must learn to balance the material wonders of technology with the spiritual demands of human nature'.   He also uses this particular formulation to conclude that the high tech isolation of the so-called electronic cottage will send people back to the office after they try working at home.

Ouchi, in his formulation, has suggested that:

A Theory Z culture has a distinct set of such values, among them long-term employment, trust and close personal relationships. . . . Of all its values, commitment of a Z culture to its people — its workers — is the most important.

Ouchi's development of a Theory Z framework grew out of his work with a number of corporations, based primarily in California (a System Z state?) where Japanese management practices had been adapted to the American context. The resulting synthesis was dubbed 'Type Z' in an intentional reference to the Theory X and Theory Y management styles which were originally characterized by Douglas McGregor in his seminal study *The Human Side of Enterprise*.

McGregor argued that much which is important about a manager can be understood by knowing that manager's underlying assumptions about human nature and society. McGregor felt that these assumptions were primarily of two kinds, which he labelled 'Theory X' and 'Theory Y' assumptions. A Theory X manager assumes that people are fundamentally lazy and need to be strongly supervised. A Theory Y manager assumes that people are fundamentally hardworking, responsible, and need only to be supported and encouraged.

With the advent of the so-called knowledge worker, the simple Theory X and Theory Y distinctions are no longer adequate and a new Theory Z is also motivated by the need to understand 'how the structure of society and the management of organization can be coordinated'. There is a perception that the growing dichotomy between one's workstyle and one's lifestyle creates too much stress and social disfunction (alcoholism, drug misuse, spouse abuse, workplace vandalism, white collar crime, etc.).

Theory Z, a Z culture, System Z, are all emerging because of a growing perception that a more humanistic integration of new forms of workplace needs with new levels of personal and psychological fulfillment will be required in the 21st century. But, in contrast with the System Y perspective, a Theory Z perspective is more cognizant of economic concerns and global competitive realities.

The Elements of System Z

A system Z perspective which suggests the possibilities, and the prospects, of a new and 'higher' stage of industrial development might include these seven elements:

- a growth in national productivity due in part to the maturing of the baby boom labor force;

- the further utilization and expansion of knowledge-intensive and resource-conserving technologies;

- a reorientation of consumer behavior towards a greater appreciation of quality and self-reliance;

- the acceleration of new forms of workplace organization, with social objectives and compatible recurrent learning requirements;

- the articulation and application of new personality theories which recognize the multidimensional nature of the 'self' in an androgynous society;

- the development of new mechanisms of income redistribution, including unorthodox sources of 'second' income;

- the formulation of new styles of management and new forms of policy development which recognize emerging global realities.

These elements of an advanced industrial society — of a new kind of social economic system — must be elaborated further. They suggest that 'growth' and 'development' could be directed or guided towards some definite social and economic goals at different levels of our society over some period of time. These elements can also be shown to flow out of the elements of the post-affluent transition as shown in Fig. 13.2.

System Z, representing the success of the humanistic efficiency of a Theory Z perspective, is not inconsistent with some of the job enrichment programs initiated in the 1950s and 1960s. But it is not consistent with the 'Greening of America' or some of the other 'laid back' fantasies of the early 1970s. The achievement of a System Z will require economic determination, social energy and political flair, to say nothing of a great deal of organization, innovation and changes.

But the manifestations of social and economic change in the next two decades are not impossible to define and are suggested in Fig. 13.2. For the next decade or so, a young adult (under-40) population will dominate American cities, with growing demands for recurrent education and training. A new national economic expansion, driven by information-intensive technologies and the expansion of global business services, should be underway by the early 1990s. New

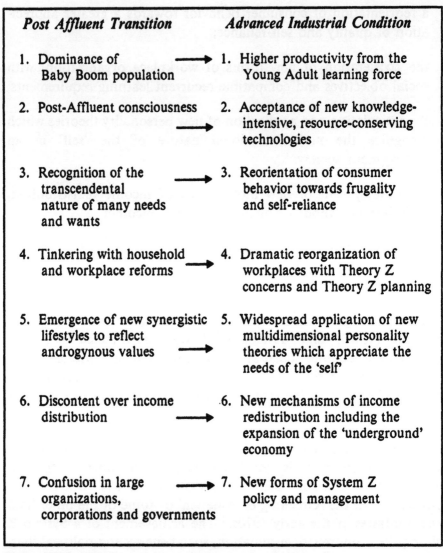

Post Affluent Transition	*Advanced Industrial Condition*
1. Dominance of Baby Boom population ⟶	1. Higher productivity from the Young Adult learning force
2. Post-Affluent consciousness ⟶	2. Acceptance of new knowledge-intensive, resource-conserving technologies
3. Recognition of the transcendental nature of many needs and wants ⟶	3. Reorientation of consumer behavior towards frugality and self-reliance
4. Tinkering with household and workplace reforms ⟶	4. Dramatic reorganization of workplaces with Theory Z concerns and Theory Z planning
5. Emergence of new synergistic lifestyles to reflect androgynous values ⟶	5. Widespread application of new multidimensional personality theories which appreciate the needs of the 'self'
6. Discontent over income distribution ⟶	6. New mechanisms of income redistribution including the expansion of the 'underground' economy
7. Confusion in large organizations, corporations and governments ⟶	7. New forms of System Z policy and management

Figure 13.2: The dynamic emergence of a System Z

biotechnologies will dramatically increase the American capacity to export high tech agriculture products, and new medical technologies will increase the prospects for extending the span of life. The marketplace reorientation to conservation, self-reliance, amenities and quality of life issues will be further along.

Theory Z planning will displace strategic planning as the dominant workplace mode as the midcareer crunch and the midlife crisis of the baby boom population assume epidemic proportions in the early 1990s. At the same time the expanding needs of the 'self' will increase the utilization of new personality theories such as that provided by Ogilvy (1979) in his under-read classic, *Many Dimensional Man*. Furthermore, the neighborhood garage sale, flea market and clothing exchange will become significant components of the recycling and underground economies. Moreover, new political leaders will emerge with new policy innovations as the baby boom population increase their political participation in the elections of the late 1980s and early 1990s. But other changes are also in sight.

Cities will be more polynucleated, with the development of more multiple-use megastructures, and medium-density planned housing unit developments. Large tracts of substandard housing are likely to be replaced by new towns-in-towns while older, solid housing stock will continue to experience gentrification. Urban farming, woodlots and fishponds will not be unusual.

Individual housing units will find their design influenced by the conversion of 'family rooms' into work-study centers and by the use of passive solar techniques. The distinction between work and leisure will begin to break down for several kinds of workers. At the same time the growth of 'involuntary leisure' time among the elderly, the young and the semi-skilled will require new social inventions for its constructive utilization. The more efficient and effective use of urban space, both internal and external, private and public, will follow some of the innovative design arrangements of European cities. The post-modernist, neo-romantic school of urban architecture is likely to flourish as the members of several generations of urban citizens become more urbane consumers.

The Post-Modernist Response

Indeed, the post-modernist school of architecture specifically and post-modernism in general reflect interesting manifestations of how North American culture is responding to the post-industrial, post-affluent conditions of our times. The Alcan building in downtown Montreal is a striking Canadian example of this new type of urban design that combines economic frugality with social effectiveness, a sense of play and pleasure.

As John Russel has written (*New York Times*, August 22, 1982), 'What has been kept out of modernism — illustration, story telling, a deliberate incongruity, esthetic bad manners — is often fundamental to postmodernism'.

The architecture of Robert Venturi is probably the most illustrative manifestation of the postmodernist form. His buildings combine the use of new technologies with 'fantasy, wit and vernacular idiom'. Venturi's architecture reflects an interesting blend of both a high-tech style and some postmodernist forms. His Benjamin Franklin museum in Philadelphia is an interesting combination of both a postmodernist respect for the archaeological value of the site and the striking use of a high-tech style. But, most significant, that museum, primarily underground with a park above it, and with an elaborate use of visual and verbal technologies is also an educational 'experience' which is totally compatible with the suggestion of a System Z society and culture. It doesn't reject technology; the museum embraces it and places it in an almost sensual environment, and all in service to the memory of a man who lived in the 18th century!

It is likely that, as the advanced industry society of the 21st century unfolds, postmodernism will flourish and may even lead to a neo-romantic style or a more exaggerated style of advanced romanticism. Environments which are dominated by, and dependent upon, advanced technologies will cry out for a deliberate humanistic quality. And so will our workplaces, our households and certainly our cities. *It may well be that postmodernist architecture, and not high-tech per se, is going to be what emerges that is strikingly different about cities in the 21st century.* But some other issues and questions also need to be addressed. For instance, it might be that the 'electronic townhouse' rather than the electronic cottage represents a better manifestation of the integration of workplace space into the American single-family home.

In an open competition in 1984, the Minneapolis College of Art and Design asked for house designs that would be more appropriate for the contemporary American family with emphasis on three ideas:

• the dramatic number of households not made up of the nuclear family;

• the rising cost of housing;

• the desire or need to work at home.

The instructions called for six attached units with accommodations for a car and a home office or work space in each unit, on a specific site in a middle-space and working-class neighborhood in Minneapolis.

The modified townhouses that won first place were proposed by Troy West, an architect, and Jacqueline Leavih, an urban planner. Behind individual front gardens in their plan is a row of six small, one-story office structures, each of which links through a corridor kitchen to the three-story main part of the house which is behind a second private courtyard garden adjacent to the kitchen corridor. This main house opens into 'a community area that is back street, driveway, carport, basketball court, yard and entry — an active neighborhood area' (*New York Times*, Joseph Giovannini, June 13, 1985). These electronic townhouses combine homelike elements such as nooks, bays, fireplaces and trellises with an appreciation that active adults will have little time for housework and little need for large entertainment spaces.

Other design solutions that focus on the workplace/household problem (or is it an opportunity?) are likely to emerge as many cities or urban regions continue to accommodate 'residential intensification' and other medium density, in-fill solutions to the high energy and travel costs associated with the 'spread city' manifestation.

Another emerging urban design phenomenon that is likely to persist and extend itself in the 21st century is the use of multi-block, multi-building pedestrian walkways that include the street level arcade, the second-story skywalks and the downtown underground mall (such as Place Ville Marie in Montreal). These new enclosures that 'explode' the scale and quality of interior space for pedestrians, consumers and white collar workers present a new centralizing focus in cities that may offset to a certain extent the decentralizing tendency of the electronic townhouse.

The enclosure of large urban spaces under glass and other transparent materials benefits both winter cities and sunbelt cities with an excess of summer swelter. Because of the relatively cheap mass float glass process (developed by Pilkington), true mass production of glass at low cost presents a design potential for the design of new urban 'rooms' that can easily expand urban culture in all-year cities. Future cities can be more urbane if we wish.

Towards the 21st Century

The city of an advanced industrial society — the future metropolis — will be primarily engaged in indirect and partially abstract transactional activities, and may be hungry for collective rites to offset social fluidity, economic transience and electronic isolation. It may also be oriented to both material and non-material standards and satisfactions which are integrated on a community and regional scale. In a Western industrial society, the city has rarely been an acceptable symbol of a collective consumption ethic or of an integrative cultural style which links both pauper and prince. Instead the industrial city has been more of a symbol of the individual struggle for survival, of private success, or of the ethnic competition for control of public resources.

But, if we are beginning to develop into some kind of knowledge-driven economy, what is the rôle of the great urban and metropolitan centers in a Theory Z society? What is our commitment to an urbane civilization which can support networks of social relationships in an atmosphere of pluralistic tolerance, humane subsistence and, dare one say it, technological progress? Let us agree to create and design urban environments in which the human spirit will soar and the quest for renewed wisdom will flourish.

Near the end of the 19th century, as Christine Boyer has recently reminded us in her *Dreaming the Rational City* (1983), an 'instinct for improvement' gave birth to a movement to elevate 'the material dignity of the city'. As she has written, 'Held against the ideal standard of nature, the city's purpose, form and growth were impossible to describe rationally'. But out of that sense of nineteenth century urban chaos grew the first national effort to improve the quality of urban life through the improvement of the built and natural environment. In the late twentieth century, it is more a sense of urban decay and not that of chaos which is likely to motivate new institutional efforts at urban revitalization and improvement.

Although Boyer concludes that 'the formation of a humanistic order to the American city still lies in the future', it is now possible to perceive that our cities may at least be redemned from the reputations they have suffered since the emergence of modernism in the 1920s. The common characteristics of the style of the international, contemporary city (from Houston to Edmonton, Hong Kong and beyond): 'its alienating abstractions, rational efficiency, fragmented and malign configuration, ruptured tradition and memory' (Boyer, 1983, p. 290) — may begin to give way to post-modernistic alternatives which might, block by block, neighborhood by neighborhood, provide for a truly urban and human city form as the next century unfolds. Such a view of the metropolitan future might be less dramatic than that of others but it offers great promise for new efforts to direct the best talents of urban design to the remaking of our urban heritage. What is past shall be prologue.

References

Bell, D. (1973), *The Coming of Post-Industrial Society*, Basic Books, NY.

Blair, J. P. (1982), 'Irregular Economies', in G. Gappert and R. V. Knight (eds.) *Cities and the 21st Century*, Sage Publications, Beverly Hills, ch. 12.

Blair, J. P. and Gappert, G. (1976), 'The Problems and Consequences of a Slow/Now Growth Economy', Joint Economic Committee, Washington, D.C.

Boyer, C., (1983) *Dreaming the Rational City*, MIT Press, Cambridge, Mass.

Bradshaw, E. K. and Blakely, E. (1979), *Rural Communities in Advanced Industrial Society*, Praeger Publishers, NY.

Bradshaw, E. K. (1980), *California As a Post-Industrial Society*, Institute of Governmental Studies, University of California, Berkeley.

Drucker, P. (1980), *Managing in Turbulent Times*, Harper and Row, NY.

Drucker, P., (1982), 'The Shape of Industry to Come', *Industry Week*, Jan. 11.

Ferguson, M. (1980), *The Aquarian Conspiracy, Personal and Social Transformation in the 1980s*, J.P. Tarcher, Los Angeles.

Gappert, G. (1973), 'The Future of Economic Inequality and the Planning of Urban Services', *AIP Journal*, 39.

Gappert, G. (1979), *Post Affluent America*, Franklin Watts, NY.

Gappert, G., and Rose, H. M. (eds.) (1976), *The Social Economy of Cities*, Vol. 9, Urban Affairs Annual Reviews, Sage, Beverly Hills.

Gray, D.D. (1982), 'The Technological Barnyard', *Bulletin*, World Future Society, April.

Hamrin, R. (1980), *Managing Growth in the 1980s*, Praeger, NY.

Hirsch, F. (1978), *Social Limits to Growth*, Harvard University Press, Cambridge.

Hirschhorn, L. (1984) *Beyond Mechanization: Flexibility and the Theory of Post-Industrial Technology*, MIT Press, Cambridge.

Jones, L. Y. (1980), *Greath Expectations, America and the Baby Boom Generation*, Ballantine Books, NY.

Johnson, W.G. (1979), *Muddling Toward Frugality*, Shambhalla, Boulder.

Knight, R.V. (1980), *The Region's Economy: Transition to What?* Cleveland State University.

Linden, S.B. (1971), *The Life of the Self*, Simon & Schuster, NY.

Marien, M. (1973), 'Daniel Bell and the End of Normal Science', *The Futurist*, December.

Masuda, Y. (1981), *The Information Society as Post Industrial Society*, World Future Society, Washington, D.C.

Mensch, G. (1982), *Stalemate in Technology*, Ballinger Publishing Company, Cambridge.

Naisbitt, J. (1983) *Megatrends*, Basic Books, NY.

National Research Council (1982), *Critical Issues for National Urban Policy*, National Academy Press, Washington, D.C.

Niebuhr, H. (1979), *A Renewal Strategy for Higher Education*, Temple University, Philadelphia.

Nevin, J. (1982), slide presentation, Akron Roundtable.

Ogilvie, J. (1979) *Many Dimensional Man*, Harper and Row, NY.

Ouchi, W.G. (1981), *Theory Z*, Avon, New York.

O'Toole, J. (1977) *Work, Learning and the American Future*, Jossey-Bass, San Francisco.

Phillips, K., (1982) *Post Conservative America*, Unpublished manuscript.

Schumpeter, J. (1934) *The Theory of Economic Development*, Harvard University Press, Cambridge.

Schwartz, P., Ogilvie, J. and Hawken, P. (1982), *Seven Tomorrows, Toward a Voluntary History*, Bantam Books, NY.

Toffler, A. (1981), *The Third Wave*, Bantam, NY.

U.S.G.P.O. (1980), *Urban America in the Eighties, Perspectives and Prospects*, Washington, D.C.

Yankelovich, D. (1981), 'A World Turned Upside Down', *Psychology Today*, April.

Young, M. and Willmott, P. (1973), *The Symmetrical Family*, Pantheon, NY.

INDEX

advanced capitalism 1, 4, 6, 297
advanced industrial society 290,
    293, 301
    model of 295
    selective growth in 296
Alexander, Christopher 258
American Federation of Labor 23
American Institute of Architects
    13, 16, 19, 20, 41
Architects, Designers and
    Planners for Social
    Responsibility 30
Architects Guild of America 23
architects
    and urban design 257
    firm size 149, 152
    locational patterns of 135-8,
    140
    professional education 28
    professionalization 12, 14, 30
    rôles 122
    social goals 12
    social responsibility 30
    trade unions 12, 15
    unemployment 16
architectural criticism 100, 102
architectural drawings 29
architectural employment 127
architectural teaching 167
Association of Collegiate Schools
    of Architecture 13
axonometrics 44

building design 158-61
building industry 148, 155, 166
building land 158-61

central-local relations 237
cognitive geometry 65
communism 22
compact city 289
computer modelling 276, 286
critical theory 139

deconstruction 3
Depression 14, 16-17
design geometry 63
design services 153, 155
design, professional autonomy of
    9
designers, interior logic of 54
determinism 8
developers
    interests 226-30
    uncertainty 211-18
development
    negotiations 230-33
    process 218
Dies Committee 20
discourse analysis 78
drawing
    as art 44
    as communication 43
    as dialogue 51-2

contemporary 50
medieval 45-50
rôle of 43-4

economic debate 294
electronics industry 165-6
electronic townhouse 304-5

fascism 22
Federation of Architects,
    Engineers, Chemists and
    Technicians 15-24, 39-40

geometry
    in discourse 81-5
    in knowledge 66-74
    in language 79-81
    of settlement space 62
guidance power 178-82

Habermas, J. 2
Henry Wright Library 19
heuristic models 277, 286
house designs 305
Huxtable, Ada Louise 153

imagery 8
institutional environment 219
International Style 2

knowledge
    and power 177
    application of 176
    cognitive views of 85

labour fragmentation 56
labour process 77
language 65
    and social reality 74-9

mass culture 139

Massachusetts Archive 45, 50-7
media-designer relationships
    99-100
mediators 246-9
megalopolis 289
memory, schema 69
mental maps 65
mental models 69
metropolis, concepts of future 289
metropolis, forces impacting on
    290
Milton Keynes 269
Modern Movement 5, 258

National Gallery 266-7
New York City Housing
    Authority 18

placemaking 266, 270
planners 223-6
    influence of 209-15, 220-22
planning practice 62, 208, 253-7
post-affluent condition 2, 292-3,
    290-2, 298
postmodernism 2-4, 7-8, 169, 303
postmodern planning 4, 6-7
popular press 103-4, 107-10, 121
professional functions 238-40
professional knowledge 183-8
professional orientations 236
professional practice 193-5, 198
professional rôles 238-40
proxemics 65
public housing 18
public-private partnerships 6

qualification models 241-2,
    248-50

residential intensification 305

Sansedoni elevation 45-50, 54,
  56-7
semiotics 75, 79
social class 129-33
social inequality 133-5
sociology of housing 169
space, control of 62
spatial imagery 80-1
spread city 289
structuration theory 64
System X, Y, Z 295-304

Terkel, Studs 65
territoriality 63

time geography 64
Trafalgar Square 266-7

unionization 12-31
urban design 65, 253-70
urban geography 66
urban geometry 62-95
urban imagery 67
urban planners, French 236
  mediatory rôles 241
urban planning 184, 188
  models of 277-8

Venturi, R. 169, 267, 304